THE GNOSTIC FAUSTUS

THE GNOSTIC FAUSTUS

THE SECRET TEACHINGS BEHIND THE CLASSIC TEXT

RAMONA FRADON

Inner Traditions
Rochester, Vermont

Inner Traditions
One Park Street
Rochester, Vermont 05767
www.InnerTraditions.com

Copyright © 2007 by Ramona Fradon

All rights reserved. No part of this book may be reproduced or utilized in any form or by any means, electronic or mechanical, including photocopying, recording, or by any information storage and retrieval system, without permission in writing from the publisher.

Library of Congress Cataloging-in-Publication Data
Fradon, Ramona.
The Gnostic Faustus : the secret teachings behind the classic text / Ramona Fradon.
p. cm.
Includes bibliographical references and index.
ISBN-13: 978-1-59477-204-7 (pbk.)
ISBN-10: 1-59477-204-5 (pbk.)
1. Gnosticism. 2. Faust, d. ca. 1540. 3. Faust, d. ca. 1540—In literature. I. Title.
BT1390.F725 2007
135—dc22
2007030438

Printed and bound in the United States of America by Lake Book Manufacturing

10 9 8 7 6 5 4 3 2 1

Text design and layout by Priscilla Baker
This book was typeset in Garamond, with Copperplate and Gill Sans used as display typefaces

To send correspondence to the author of this book, mail a first-class letter to the author c/o Inner Traditions • Bear & Company, One Park Street, Rochester, VT 05767, and we will forward the communication.

In memory of Miss Elizabeth Clever,
a gifted teacher who saw light
where there seemed to be only darkness

Contents

A NAASSENE PSALM

The soul . . . is worn away in death's slavery,
Now she has mastery and glimpses light:
Now she is plunged in misery and weeps.
Now she is mourned and herself rejoices.
Now she weeps and is finally condemned.
Now she is condemned and finally dies.
And now she even reaches the point where
Hemmed in by evil, she knows no way out.
Misled, she has entered a labyrinth.
Then Jesus said: "Behold Father,
She wanders the earth pursued by evil.
Far from thy breath she is going astray.
She is trying to flee the bitter Chaos,
And does not know how she is to escape.
Send me forth, O Father, therefore, and I,
Bearing the seal shall descend and wander
All Aeons through, all mysteries reveal.
I shall manifest the forms of the gods
And teach the secrets of the holy
Which I call Gnosis."

INTRODUCTION

Setting the Stage

In the sixteenth century Germany began a long and difficult political, religious, and intellectual transformation, sparked by Martin Luther's challenge to the Catholic Church and the spread of knowledge made possible by the new printing press. But even as Germany evolved and took on aspects of a modern state, the people held fast to their old superstitions, not the least of which was belief in the Devil and the terrible power of his magic.

God-fearing Germans, whether Protestant or Catholic, kept a wary eye out for signs of his presence and many thought they detected them in the practices of the mysterious Hermetic magi, men who strove to manipulate nature with magic and the esoteric arts. The magi sought miraculous powers through alchemy, Egyptian mathematics and cabala, the mystical Jewish science of the inner planes, and pursued forbidden knowledge with the help of angels or demons. They aimed to transform matter with the power of their minds and wills, and, in an age of unbounded hubris, some of them even aspired to be gods.

The Germans thought their magic was diabolical, but many of these men were utopian visionaries who hoped to heal the deep divisions of society through a universal spiritual awakening. They associated with the radical Lutherans and the anti-papal Rosicrucians who were forming underground in the late sixteenth century. The confrontation of these movements with the forces of the threatened Church would soon plunge Germany and the continent into wars and religious persecutions that lasted throughout the following century.

Out of the stuff of this fraught and superstitious environment a modern myth was born. Its first manifestation was a crudely written manuscript called *The Vita and Historia of Doctor Johannes Faustus,* a story laden with mysterious symbols and filled with magical events. It appeared anonymously sometime around 1570 and began to circulate surreptitiously in central and southern Germany. A quaintly tragic little sorcerer's tale concocted of German folk material and ancient religious lore, it preached the dogma of the Catholic Church but its content was clearly heretical. Doctor Faustus longed for knowledge forbidden by the Church and, in order to obtain it, made league with the Devil. He indulged in wine and women with the Devil's connivance, acquired miraculous powers, consorted with a phantom goddess, and suffered a horrible end.

Although Faustus's punishment conformed to Catholic expectations, his extraclerical search for enlightenment was frowned on by the Church and the story was considered blasphemous. The scandalous little tale found a ready audience among the German people, however, and it grew in popularity, passing from hand to hand. As time went by it was embellished or adapted into peasant plays and puppet farces that made their way across Europe, wherever Roman rule was being challenged.

Some twenty years after its appearance, a version of the story came to the attention of the English playwright, Christopher Marlowe, and inspired him to write his own *Dr. Faustus.* A rebellious scholar himself who had abandoned church and university, Marlowe lent the tragic theme an intensity and sheen that transformed the crude original work. He amplified the sense of doom that weighed on Faustus's soul and raised his fatal longing to a level that approached the sublime. With this first great adaptation, the European Faust tradition was born.

In the centuries that followed, a steady stream of dramatic, literary, and musical interpretation—crowned by Goethe's towering *Faust*—adapted the theme to the values of succeeding ages and shaped it into a modern myth whose restless, ever-striving hero is thought to typify the soul of Western man.

Ironically, this remarkably germinal little tale, which has come to be known as "the Faust Book," is assumed to have been written lightheartedly and simply for entertainment. Some opinion suggests that a Protestant or Humanist scholar may have written it in an effort to appeal to or profit from an impious interest that was absorbing the German people at the time. For a generation prior to the Faust Book's appearance, popular attention had been focused on the scandalous doings of one Georg Faustus, a soothsayer, necromancer, and physician of sorts from a central German town, who had died in 1550. The mysterious circumstances of his life and death had become a local legend, gathering many a superstitious folk tale as it spread, and it is thought that the Faust Book, posing as the life of this scoundrel and including a number of such tales in its plot, was engineered to amuse a ready audience.

Borrowings from other material have also been detected in the Faust Book. Scholars have long noted its resemblance to the New Testament Synoptic Gospels. These sketchy accounts of a doomed and wandering miracle worker follow the same crooked path as the Faust Book does and share its chronological disarray and lack of cause and effect. The source for Faustus's mistress, Helen, has been traced back to a legendary companion of Simon Magus, a first-century Gnostic. *Gnostic* is a broad term that encompasses a variety of practices and religious beliefs that were common in the few centuries immediately before and after the birth of Christ. Gnostic comes from the Greek word for "knowledge," *gnosis,* and refers to the idea that there is special, hidden knowledge that only the initiated may possess. This knowledge is, ultimately, an individual's direct experience of the God that lies within. Simon Magus, called the "father of the Gnostics," claimed that he was Christ and was vilified by Christian writers. Simon's Helen was a reformed prostitute whose checkered history mirrored the myth of Sophia, the fallen and repentant Gnostic goddess of wisdom. Sophia was known as "the whore" in her fallen state and Faustus's enchanting mistress, Helen, was also a lady of doubtful reputation.[1]

The name Faustus, meaning "favored one" in Latin, was used by

Simon Magus who also gave himself the cognomen "magician,"[2] and it is interesting to note that Georg Faustus called himself the "second Magus" or the "younger Faustus." E. M. Butler matched key features of the Faust Book plot to essential elements of the Magus myth and uncovered another important borrowing. Faustus's story resembles those of outstanding figures of the genre, such as the first-century spiritual master, Apollonius of Tyana, and Jeanne d'Arc, both of whom suffered tragic and seemingly foreordained deaths.

Butler characterizes the Faust Book as an "unsightly ruin"—the myth fallen on evil days—a reflection, perhaps, of the lowered status of magicians under Christian influence.[3] Her suggestion of a theme underlying the surface tale goes no further, and—while much has been made of the alchemical imagery in Goethe's *Faust* (Carl Jung called it "an alchemical drama from beginning to end")[4]—no such significance has been attributed to the Faust Book. It has been regarded, rather, as a quaint, spontaneous fruiting of the European mythological soil whose deepest purpose was to entertain.

A GNOSTIC CREATION MYTH

While it is true that the Faust Book may be dismissed on literary grounds, in another sense it deserves the closest attention. The reader might well be curious about the number of Gnostic and early Christian references in the borrowed material, for, indeed, these items do not appear by accident nor do they accumulate by chance. Far from being randomly or cynically chosen by the unknown author, they betray a carefully wrought and skillfully executed plan and may have served as signals designed to alert initiated readers of the time. They are actually outcroppings of an elaborate metaphorical code that reveals a mystical religious message heretical to the sixteenth-century Church.

The Faust Book is, in fact, a cleverly disguised Gnostic composite creation myth consisting of passages from a collection of Gnostic, Christian Gnostic, and Sethian revelation myths, hymns, polemics, gospels, and Hermetic dialogues. Many of them are from a fourth-century collection of Coptic Gnostic manuscripts that was discovered in Nag Hammadi, Egypt, in 1945.

The myth describes the majestic process of cosmic creation and features the story of Sophia, the Gnostic goddess whose hubris, transgression, and fall from grace created the material realm. Her suffering, repentance, and subsequent return to the world of Light constitute the central Gnostic soteriological, or salvation, drama and serve as a model for a human spiritual initiation that is also encoded in the Faust Book. The latter's message is decidedly heretical, pointing the way to salvation through sacramental sex, ecstatic revelation, and mystical communion with the God that lies within. Such a message would have been anathema to the Church and could only have been disseminated secretly or by the kind of coded subterfuge we find in the Faust Book.

The blasphemous little story has an introduction and forty-four short chapters, each of which is an allegory of a phase or feature of the composite myth. The author of the Faust Book selected highlights from the revelation myths and from the soteriological and polemical tractates and arranged them to form a creation myth replete with theological and moral speculation. As this book will demonstrate, the highlights were converted into analogs, metaphors, or symbolic images, or were paraphrased, reversed, or parodied to create the Faust Book plot. The framework of the myth remained the same but the altered passages produced a different story with a radically different message. While the myth assured salvation through acknowledging the inner God, the Faust Book threatened damnation for consorting with the Devil. Faustus represents the alienated soul who succumbs to temptation and suffers the fate of sinners, while the myth speaks of steadfast souls who follow the righteous path and are saved. These are the choices that confront the divided human being, the fate of whose soul is the central concern of the Faust Book.

The Underlying Texts

The composite myth is composed of highlights from several primary works: the Books of the Savior, commonly known as the Pistis Sophia; the Hymn of the Pearl from the Apocryphal Acts of Thomas; the

Apochryphon of John; the Tripartite Tractate, the Gospel of Truth; and the Creation According to Mani. Additional points of comparison can be found in these other Gnostic and Hermetic texts: On the Origin of the World, Zostrianos, Allogenes, The Testimony of Truth, Gospel of the Egyptians, and the Divine Pymander. All except the Pistis Sophia, the Mani myth, the Hymn of the Pearl, and the Divine Pymander are from the Nag Hammadi collection. Some of the codices in that library, as well as the Mani myth, had been known to modern religious scholars prior to their discovery, but only through the summaries or critical writings of Christian heresy hunters.

While the Hermetic Divine Pymander was a staple of Renaissance studies, the Pistis Sophia has been known to Western scholars only since the middle of the nineteenth century and there has been little reason to believe that it or any of the other treatises were available in original versions in sixteenth-century Europe. However, their encoded presence in the Faust Book suggests that these remains of the ancient heresy were, indeed, familiar to certain scholars at that time and, moreover, were circulating secretly in several Christian countries under cover of the popular little folk book.

The Hymn of the Pearl

The Faust Book plot is shaped by the salient features of the Hymn of the Pearl from the Syriac Acts of Judas Thomas. A beautiful allegory of the soul's striving for Gnosis, it is attributed to the third-century school of the Christian Gnostic poet Bardaisan. In it, the consummation of the Gnostic quest is likened to a "robe of glory," a mirror of the soul that, when encountered on the path of life, connects the seeker to the Divine. The Hymn epitomizes the myth of the alien Pilgrim Savior who is redeemed by recalling his divinity. A comparison of highlights from the Hymn of the Pearl and summarized events from the Faust Book shows how the cryptic surface story both conceals and reveals the scripture's message of renewal.

Several symbolic terms the Gnostics used are explained here and, for the most part, are based on Hans Jonas's interpretations. The translation of the hymn is his as well.[5]

FAUST BOOK	HYMN OF THE PEARL
Faustus is raised by a wealthy kinsman in Wittemberg (the center of early radical Lutheranism and occult studies, and in the text comparisons, often a synonym for heaven).	When I was a little child and dwelt in the kingdom of my Father's house [the world of Light] and delighted in the wealth and splendor of those who raised me,
Faustus strays from the godly path and pursues five studies—theology, medicine, astrology, mathematics, and physics.	my parents sent me forth from the East, our homeland, with provisions for the journey [the Gnosis, consisting of five precious substances].
Faustus conjures up a ball of starlight, which changes into the Devil, or a gray material form.	They took off from me the robe of glory, which in their love they had made for me [the divine nature or spiritual body].
Faustus summons the spirit/Devil to his house (the body that encases the soul).	I went down to Egypt [the world of matter or the body that imprisons the soul of Light].
Faustus makes a pact with the Devil in order to receive his hidden knowledge.	I went straightway to the serpent [the evil tempter or the desire nature] and settled down close by his inn until he should slumber and sleep so that I might take the Pearl from him [the divine spark that lies hidden in every man; the deeper knowledge that must be recovered].
Faustus lives alone in his house except for his spirit and a disreputable youth named Christof Wagner whom he adopts and makes his famulus. In the end, he passes on his mission and his silver (inner knowledge) to Wagner.	Since I was one and kept to myself I was a stranger to my fellow dwellers in the inn. Yet saw I there one of my race, a fair and well-favored youth, the son of kings. He came and attached himself to me and I made him my trusted familiar to whom I imparted my mission.
Faustus indulges in food, wine, and sumptuous clothing procured illegally by the Devil.	I clothed myself in [the] garments of the unclean ones [the body or disguise that alienates the soul from its origin] . . . and they ingratiated themselves with me, and mixed me drink with their cunning and gave me to taste of their meat
Faustus tries to change his ways but the Devil tempts him with beautiful women and he forgets his good intentions.	and I forgot that I was a king's son and served their king; I forgot the Pearl for which my parents had sent me.
Faustus falls asleep ("asleep" is a Gnostic term denoting ignorance of the Father) and is flown down to Hell by a devil.	Through the heaviness of their nourishment I sank into deep slumber.

FAUST BOOK	HYMN OF THE PEARL
Faustus lies dreaming in bed one night when he hears a roaring voice call to him, "Get thee up!"	All this that befell me my parents marked. . . . And they wrote a letter to me. . . . Like a messenger was the letter. . . . It rose up in the form of an eagle . . . and flew until it alighted beside me and became wholly speech. [An awakening through a Call from above.]
Faustus jumps out of bed and sees a chariot drawn by two dragons. It carries him up to Heaven where he receives a revelation.	At its voice and sound I awoke and arose from my sleep, took it up, broke its seal and read. I remembered that I was a son of kings . . . remembered the Pearl for which I had been sent down to Egypt,
Faustus performs a variety of magical feats with newly acquired supernormal powers.	and I began to enchant the terrible and snorting serpent . . .
Faustus steals silver (profound wisdom) from the pope's palace.	I seized the Pearl,
Faustus rids a noble lady of an unwanted suitor and separates a knight from his horse.	and turned to repair home to my Father. Their filthy and impure garment I put off and left it behind in their land . . .
Faustus reencounters the bewitching, numinous Helen of Greece (the equivalent of the robe of glory) whom he had conjured up for his students.	My robe of glory which I had put off and my mantle which went over it, my parents . . . sent to meet me. . . . Its splendor I had forgotten, having left it as a child in my Father's house . . . And the image of the King of kings was depicted all over it. . . . I also saw quiver all over it the movements of the gnosis.
Faustus makes Helen his bedfellow and they consummate their love.	And I stretched towards it and took it and decked myself with the beauty of its colors. And I cast the royal mantle about my entire self.
An omniscient child is born from their union. (Faustus has overcome duality and acquired transcendent awareness.)	Clothed therein, I ascended to the gate of salutation and adoration. . . .
The Devil comes for Faustus and dismembers him.	[My Father] received me joyfully and I was with him in his kingdom.

The pilgrim's joyful reunion with his Father becomes Faustus's deadly appointment with the Devil—an example of the Faust Book's use of inversion to both hide and reveal its meaning.

Sophia and Faust

The soteriological foundation of the Faust Book is provided by the Pistis Sophia, a collection of six books containing discourses and a version of Sophia's myth. It purports to be a revelation by the resurrected Jesus to a chosen group of followers in which he reveals mysteries he had not included in his public teaching. In the first two books, he recounts the story of the hubristic goddess Sophia—how she violated the laws of the pleroma [the thirteen highest regions or aeons of the Light world] where ideal forms or stages of awareness—also referred to as aeons—dwell in timeless perfection. Sophia longed to know the unknowable Father directly, to gaze upon his Light, and thinking that she was approaching it, she pursued the Light of a jealous aeon into the darkness beyond the pleroma. There she was hounded and pursued by the forces of darkness until Jesus found her in the chaos, lamenting her wrongdoing and crying to the Light of Lights to save her.

Sophia's story is featured over other fallen deities in the Gnostic pantheon not simply because she personifies wisdom, the goal of the Gnosis, but because the power of her faith and the hope that sustained her inspired her followers and provided a model for human souls who repented and sought salvation. These virtues are expressed in thirteen hymns she sang to the Light as she waited in the Darkness for Jesus to save her. They are scattered throughout the composite myth and accompany stages of awareness taking place in the human transformation encoded in the Faust Book. The hope they express counters the hopelessness that burdens Faustus throughout the story and hints at his eventual release.

In the remaining four books of the Pistis Sophia, Jesus discloses the names of the rulers and regions of the Light world and the workings of a vast, hierarchical system of divine retribution. He reveals how the just may be saved and whether or not there is hope for the damned, the information being drawn from him by questions from the disciples. The question and answer format—which also appears in the Faust Book—is used in the Apochryphon of John and other texts as well and is a familiar form in Gnostic scripture.

It has been suggested that the Pistis Sophia was an attempt to syncretize the various strains of third- or fourth-century religious thought. It combines elements of astrology, magic, Christianity, Gnostic Light physics (a formulated account of the inner workings of the universe based on an inspired vision of atomic structures and processes), docetism (the belief that Christ, a spiritual being, only appeared to be a man, and did not really die on the cross), and emanationism (the flowing forth of extensions of the godhead). It also contains some vivid and bizarre Manichaean cosmological details. (Manichaeaism was a syncretistic, dualist religion that reached its peak in the sixth century and rivaled Christianity for a time. Considered one of the four great world religions, it posits an eternal war between the forces of darkness and the light. Its founder was a Persian visionary named Mani who claimed that he was the thirteenth avatar in a line that included Zoroaster, Buddha, and Jesus.) Like Mani's, the Pistis Sophia's cosmology is complicated, sometimes to the point of incomprehensibility, and has provoked dismay in certain scholarly quarters. In its inclusiveness, however, it is an abundant source for the Faust Book's ecumenical message and provides a certain authority, if not direct inspiration, for Faustus's magical tricks—most notably through the stupendous miracle wrought by Jesus, who reverses the very movements of the heavens. In book five (Ch. 136:359) Jesus makes an invocation, "speaking the name of the father of the Treasury of the Light . . . And in that hour all the heavens went to the west, and all the aeons and the sphere and their rulers and all their powers flew together to the west to the left of the disk of the sun and the disk of the moon . . . And the whole world and the mountains and the seas fled together . . ." (see also chapter 12 of the Faust Book).

Sophia and Creation

Another work of great importance to the Faust Book is the Apochryphon of John, a creation revelation that encompasses the body of Gnostic myth. Its components were accumulated over a period of time beginning before the birth of Christ and its influence extended well into the Christian era—perhaps as late as the eighth century. It is considered a central work of Gnostic scripture and seems to have been understood as such by the Faust Book author, who relied heavily on its inclusive narrative and included many questions it raises about the origin of evil and the fates of different souls.

The Apochryphon includes a version of Sophia's story that complements the one in the Pistis Sophia. While the latter's emphasis is soteriological and focuses on Sophia's repentance and redemption, the Apochryphon of John details her role in creating the material realm. We learn that Sophia's "ignorance" hypostatized into an "abortion" that was cast outside of the pleroma and assumed the form of Yaltabaoth, her hideous son who created the Heavens and the Earth.

Yaltabaoth is the god of the Old Testament—a false god according to this and other Gnostic creation accounts—who fashions Adam as a lifeless prototype of man. Adam comes to life, however, when Yaltabaoth unwittingly blows some of the Light he had received from his mother into the sleeping man's face. This makes Adam luminous, creating envy among the evil powers, who begin to fight with the forces of Light for possession of his soul. The battle takes a number of surprising turns, some of which reverse the temptation account in Genesis. It is the Father, not Satan, for instance, who tempts Eve to eat the forbidden apple, for the fruit is the Father's Word, or the Gnosis.

The cunning archons, rulers of the material realm, give Adam a material body in order to imprison his Light, and they fashion a woman to arouse his desire. This is a setback for the Father's cause, for, as Adam's descendants multiply, a portion of the Father's Light is imprisoned in each of their bodies and forgotten. In response to this wicked stratagem, Christ comes down in successive incarnations to reveal the godhead's glory and remind human beings of their lost inner Light.

This is Faustus's mission, too, as he "circulates" in his various journeys, stealing silver from the pope, and performing amputations, beheadings, and other magical "extractions" that liberate the Light soul from the body.

Sophia and the Logos

Another significant text in the composite myth is the Tripartite Tractate, a creation account that traces the devolution and restoration of the pleroma through the actions of one of its youthful aeons. This is the Logos, Sophia's masculine counterpart, who is given free will to transgress by the Father and thereby to facilitate the divine revelation. The youthful, well-intentioned Logos attempts to grasp the Father's incomprehensibility, but—unable to bear the sight of the Father's Light—looks into the Darkness and doubts. His lower thought remains there, as does Sophia's, and produces a "shadow" realm—a dark reflection of the Light world based on ignorance and error. This evolves into our world, a discordant realm not unlike the hellish kingdom the Devil describes in the Faust Book. Indeed, the Gnostics equated this world with Hell and the god that rules it, with the Devil.

Like Sophia, the Logos repents, arriving at a turning point that leads to his own and the godhead's restoration. It is a critical moment in the Faust Book, too, but Faustus fails to make the turning. Or so the reader is led to believe. His next act, while seemingly arbitrary, proves to be a reflection of the Logos's change of mind. As the latter puts a stop to the emanations of his lower thoughts and returns his higher thought to the pleroma, Faustus suddenly abandons his obsession with Hell, becomes an astrologer, and turns his own thoughts upward to the heavens.

His continuing and disciplined study of astrology coincides with the Logos's creation of an administration whose purpose is to rule and bring order to the chaotic realm he has created. The Logos is aided by a savior who embodies the virtues of the pleroma, and, like Christ in the Apochryphon of John, reveals himself to the warring aeons and their human "copies" in order to remind them of the Father and their own divinity.

The first part of the Tripartite Tractate describes a heavenly trinity consisting of Father, Son, and Church—the Church comprising the aeons of the pleroma, a harmonious grouping whose unity is disrupted by the actions of the Logos. The second part is an account of the fashioning of Man and the suffering he endures according to the Father's plan. His fate is to experience pain so that he may repent and seek salvation.

The third part discusses the three soul types whose prospects for being saved vary according to the amount of Light that is in them. The reader is reminded that repentance, spiritual baptism, and hope will bring "redemption into the Father" for those who are worthy, while those who are not will "receive destruction in every way." In the end, the Logos is redeemed and the pleroma is restored to its original unity. Its restoration is signified in the Faust Book by a sumptuous wedding attended by three young lords who represent the trifurcated Logos.

The World of Hell

The Gospel of Truth derides the "sleeping" or "ignorant" souls whose nightmares of violence and discord are the substance of our world. Its descriptions of those nightmares parallel the descriptions of Lucifer's world in the Faust Book. But it also brings the good news of Jesus's coming and celebrates the souls who awaken. Its message of hope, it says, is its own realization: "In the name of the gospel is the proclamation of hope, being discovery for those who search for him." It praises the Father's Word delivered by Jesus Christ and calls it the "book of the living," which "fills the deficiency" and "abolishes the form of the world." The world, in its view, is a product of "error" or ignorant thought and can be dissolved by a reversal of that thought, that is, through knowledge of the Father. These notions are implicit in the myths of Sophia and the Logos, whose ignorance creates the world and whose remembering, or knowledge of the Father, enables them to leave it behind.

Primal Man and the Battle for Light

Another of the primary underlying texts, the Creation According to Mani, provides some colorful details about the Father's attempt to recapture his Light that was imprisoned in the Darkness. He fashions an elaborate system of cosmic purification that employs the revolutions of the Sun and Moon. The latter transports the particles of Light released by the dead up to the Sun and the Sun returns them to the pleroma. Faustus's round trip flying journeys are, among other things, references to these heavenly revolutions.

In Mani's myth, Primal Man is a counterpart of Sophia and the Logos. He is an emissary of the Father who descends from the Light world to repel an invasion by the Darkness, a strife-ridden kingdom that covets the Light out of envy. The eternal struggle between the opposing principles for possession of the Light begins with a tactic employed by Primal Man who surrenders his armor of five Light powers to the forces of Darkness, thinking that its virtue will dilute their power.

The evil archons capture him anyway and he falls "asleep" in their midst, forgetting his heavenly origin and the mission on which he was sent. He awakens when he is called from on high and, remembering the Father, returns to his kingdom, leaving the armor he surrendered behind. Thus a war begins between the two cosmic forces over the imprisoned parts of Light.

Unlike the transgressions of Sophia and the Logos, Primal Man's descent does not produce the material realm. His role is simply to battle the invading Darkness; the creation results from the greater war between the opposing kingdoms. Their competing and often outlandish stratagems produce a mixture of Darkness and Light that evolves into the cruel material realm. The spirit's description of Hell in the Faust Book is based on a Manichaean hymn expressing the alien soul's terror when confronting the hostile forces of nature.

Mani's myth is not included in the text comparisons, but a number of Faust Book events are clearly analogous to some of its important features. Faustus's corruption reflects Primal Man's imprisonment and "sleep," and his bloody end is based on the death of the Manichaean savior, Jesus patibilis. In his role as a doctor who travels widely to answer requests for help, Faustus represents another aspect of this Jesus that is found in Manichaean hymns. There he is praised as the "Light

Jesus," a beneficent physician who "walks on every road" to heal human souls and bring Light and hope to the world.

The Frame of the Composite Myth

The structure of the myth is similar to that of the Apochryphon of John and the Creation According to Mani. It is based on the form of an ancient Mesopotamian ritual drama in which the transformation of a soul is enacted twice, first on the macrocosmic and then on the microcosmic level. Sophia's story comes first and is enhanced with details from various texts about other divine transgressors. Together, they form a portrait of the fallen cosmic soul in all phases of its initiatory journey.

Sophia's story overlaps the human drama in which the first man, Adam, struggles with the material half of his bitterly divided nature. When the powers of darkness fashion a lifeless Adam, the redeemed Sophia awakens him, and when they battle with emissaries of the Light for the souls of Adam's descendants, Sophia comes down from above to remind them of their inner light. Much speculation accompanies these stories concerning the different soul-types and their prospects for salvation, some passages warning against various evils while others grow rapturous at the joys awaiting the person who receives the Gnosis and experiences the Light directly.

The outline of Sophia's story is visible in the Faust Book plot. Faustus's indulgence in sinful pleasures and consequent torment is a parody of her transgression and her painful exile from the world of Light. While his ending is bloody and seems to negate her joyful rebirth, it is based on the ritual dismemberment of the savior in the Mani myth whose death is implicitly hopeful. The sacrifice of Jesus patibilis—an embodiment of the Light soul imprisoned in Darkness who, as the life force of animals and plants, is slaughtered daily—complements Sophia's redemption, for his cyclical death is followed by rebirth and promises eternal renewal. Indeed, in the human spiritual process encoded in the Faust Book, Faustus's death refers to the "shedding of the body" or extinguishing of ordinary consciousness that attends a spiritual awakening.

While the Faust Book author borrowed material from the Mani myth, he rejected its absolute dualism in favor of a unitary theology compatible with the Hermetic worldview that influences the Faust Book. This theology is attributed to Valentinus, a second-century Christian Gnostic visionary. The Tripartite Tractate and Gospel of Truth—both of which are featured in the composite myth—have been attributed to his school. In these works, Darkness and Light refer to ignorant and enlightened states of mind rather than to antagonistic first principles. The dualistic world emanated from a single source, the mind of an unknowable god the Gnostics called Father, and the whole of creation arose from his generous wish to reveal himself. The material world with its harsh conditions and retributive laws was a paradoxical extension of his loving thought, designed so that ignorant souls might experience pain, seek after him, and receive his revelation.

In a passage from the Gospel of Truth that concludes the underlying myth, a revelation by a savior brings awareness of the Father to a "sleeping" soul and dissolves what it refers to as the "world of oblivion." The Father's imprisoned Light is set free by this act and returns to the godhead to help restore its original unity. The Father's movement toward self-revelation is thus entwined with the human and divine souls' search for enlightenment. In the text comparisons, the godhead's devolution into darkness and matter is matched with Faustus's corruption and loss of faith and with Sophia's fall and suffering. Its restoration is synonymous with their awakening, and events in the Faust Book that signify one of these transformations, signify them all.

FAUST AND SPIRITUAL INITIATION

While the story of Sophia's enlightenment takes place in the context of the underlying myth, the human spiritual initiation it prefigures is encoded in the surface story of the Faust Book. It is indicated by Hermetic and alchemical symbols, symbolic numbers and colors and metaphorical enactments by Faustus and others of repetitious alchemical events. There are also suggestions of Yantric diagrams (linear geometric figures designed to focus consciousness on the inner planes), parodies of sacred sexual acts by Faustus and Helen, and other features peculiar to the transforming spiritual practice of Vajrayama Tantra, the yoga of sex.

It is an Eastern form of kundalini yoga involving the awakening of a universal energy/consciousness residing in the body at the base of the spine. It rises and falls at the yogin's will through an invisible, spiritual channel in the spine. These repetitious movements induce altered states and are designed to reconcile polarities in the body and mind, to unify consciousness and bring about universal awareness. This practice involves worship of the divine feminine through the female body, and includes rituals of sacramental sex that require intensive training and iron self-control.

The alchemical references in the Faust Book complement the tantric process, for their aims and methods are similar and, as we shall see, are based on a similar worldview. Tantric sexual arousal is equivalent to the fire used by alchemists to promote change in their metals, and the goal of both practices is to restore multiplicity to unity by reconciling opposites.

Chinese and Indian alchemists are known to have practiced Tantra, but its use is never mentioned by their secretive European counterparts, although it is strongly suggested by the vivid sexual imagery in their otherwise murky writings. The Faust Book seems to be suggesting with its own symbols and imagery that Faustus is practicing alchemy as well as the yoga of sex.

This surprising notion, appearing as it does in the context of a Sophia-centered Gnostic myth, may be the signature of a hidden Gnostic/Hermetic goddess-worshipping tradition in which alchemy, magic, and sacramental sex played central roles. Since ancient times, in secret cults and brotherhoods in Europe, the Middle East, and elsewhere, worshippers of the divine feminine have sought union with the goddess through rituals involving alchemy and sexual magic. In these sacraments, in which passionate arousal was an analog of the alchemist's transforming fire, the body served as the vessel in which the mystical union took place. Faustus's name is a play on words that connects him to this tradition and to its goddess and her sacraments. We will return to this shortly and to further discussion of alchemy and tantra, but first we must determine which of Faustus's contemporaries he really represents and how they relate to alchemy, to tantra, and to the goddess herself.

Faustus and the Magi

While Faustus is thought to be patterned after the disreputable charlatan whose last name he bears, he actually fits the larger mold of the Gnostic/Hermetic magical alchemist, or magus. The magi were the wonder workers mentioned earlier, throwbacks to the Persian magi and magicians who abounded in the Middle East at the time of Simon Magus, John the Baptist, and Jesus. More recently, they followed in the footsteps of Marsilio Ficino and Pico della Mirandola, fifteenth-century Italian scholars who were inspired by ancient Hermetic texts and Jewish cabala to experiment with magic.

They were all devout Christians, but some of the German and later Italian magi consorted with dark or questionable powers and either practiced alchemy or believed that its processes were aspects of universal truth. While the Italian philosophers sang praises to the divinely seductive figure of Venus, some of their successors, both German and Italian, expressed an inordinate passion for the goddess that bore a suspicious resemblance to the "chaste" eroticism characteristic of tantric sacraments.

Like Faustus, the magi traveled widely; besides understanding cabala, they were versed in mathematical or Pythagorean magic and were familiar with angelic hierarchies and resonances between the spiritual and material planes. They manipulated subtle forces with the help of angels or demons and strove, as Faustus did, to acquire godlike knowledge and power.

Henry Cornelius Agrippa (1486–1535) was, perhaps, the most notorious of the magi. A Hermetic alchemist, he also conducted experiments with talismans, chants, and certain sympathetic substances designed to attract and call down planetary influences. Using cabalistic manipulations and mathematical magic, he aimed to contact stars in the celestial spheres and communicate with angels in the regions beyond the stars. He sought to merge with God through a mediating frenzy for Venus that recalls Faustus's passion for the visualized image of Helen. His relentless pursuit of hidden knowledge and power may have been the model for Faustus's fatal pursuit of the Devil's arcana. Indeed, the Renaissance scholar, Dame Frances Yates, suggested that Agrippa's magic was on Marlowe's mind when he wrote his dramatic adaptation of the Faust Book.[6]

It was John Dee (1527–1608), however, whose influence Marlowe may have been attacking. An enormously influential scholar who was a spy for Queen Elizabeth and secretly promoted the Protestant cause in Europe, Dee was a brilliant and eccentric astronomer, astrologer, mathematician, alchemist, and Hermetic. Like the equally accomplished Faustus, he despaired of gaining wisdom through conventional studies and turned to magic, calling on angels to enlighten him. He and his companion, Edward Kelly, communicated with the archangels Gabriel, Michael, and Uriel, and, while Dee did not profess a passion for Venus, he and Kelly engaged in their own brand of "sacred sex" and "alchemical transmutation": they exchanged their wives with each other periodically (not without the ladies' hesitation) believing as good Hermetics that this "elemental rotation" would transform them all and unite them as One.[7] Dee was a force in Hermetic circles and one of his esoteric treatises may have been an influence on the Faust Book, as we shall see.

Perhaps the most daring and reckless of the magi was Giordano Bruno (1548–1600), an Italian Hermeticist who practiced cabala and powerful Egyptian magic. He ventured further into the arcane arts than the other magi did, openly espousing the Egyptian mysteries and consorting with demonic powers. He cultivated a prodigious memory and a magical system of organizing and storing vast amounts of knowledge in his mind, hoping to acquire the omniscience of a god. This stupendous endeavor surpassed even Faustus's attempts to acquire knowledge, or, as the Faust Book put it, to "seek out the very foundations of Heaven and Earth." Bruno was a celibate whose passion for Venus transported him directly to God. He finally exceeded the limits of Church tolerance and was burned at the stake in Rome.

The magi insisted that their magic was "natural" and that their transformations came about through pious contemplation, but the Faust Book seems to suggest otherwise. By attaching tantric and alchemical symbolism to the magus-like figure of Faustus, and by virtue of his singular behavior, it seems to imply that the magical alchemists engaged in sacramental sex to promote their spiritual development. In chapter twenty-nine of the Faust Book, the Venus whom the magi worshipped appears thinly disguised as the conjured image of Helen of Greece, a traditional symbol for Venus and/or Sophia. In a later chapter, Faustus engages with this goddess image in an act of sacred sexual union, and there she is associated with the white tantric Rupravajra goddesses who are fertile wisdom figures like Sophia. In their hands they hold a mirror that reflects the whole universe, and all aspects of the world are said to reside in their forms.

The magi were not charlatans like Georg Faustus, but their reputations were unsavory and their magic was thought by many to be demonic. Had it been known that they also practiced tantra, as the Faust Book implies, it would doubtless have brought them to ruin. This may not wholly account for the Faust Book's secrecy, however, for cryptic complexity was characteristic of occult writings at that time. Unorthodox thought had to be concealed in an era of political and religious persecution, and secrecy had long been a feature of Hermetic/alchemical literature.

Spiritual Alchemy in the Faust Book

While the alchemists often misled when speaking about their Art, it is clear from their writings that the practice of alchemy rests on two fundamental postulates: one, that all matter is ultimately one substance; and two, that matter is also mutable—that chaotic or unstable substances like lead or tin can be altered and restored to unity (gold) by manipulating or rotating them through the four material elements that govern them. Another basic assumption is that the seed of gold resides in the basest of metals and can be brought forth by the alchemist's Art, just as precious minerals are gestated in the earth.

In pursuit of this goal, they employed two principal agents to promote the metal's transformation. They are feminine Mercury—a volatile, corrosive substance that dissolves the metal and purges it of impurities—and rigid, masculine, form-giving Sulphur, which works in opposition to Mercury's effect. When they are placed together over fire in the alchemist's vessel, they tear at each other viciously, producing the alternations of dissolution and coagulation of the metal that characterizes the alchemical process. Ultimately, Sulphur's form-giving, creative power is released by its purging in Mercury's vitriol, and when Mercury is captured and bound by Sulphur, their "marriage" produces Gold, the most stable of metals.

The Faust Book is divided into four parts, symbolizing the major stages of the alchemical process, and in each part a color is mentioned—black, green, white, and red in that order. Black signals Saturn's phase, the *nigredo,* or dissolution, corruption and putrefaction of the metal, while green (the phase ruled by Jupiter) represents the reforming, or "greening," of the Earth (the metal or Body). The white phase, ruled by the moon, signals the emergence of the feminine principle; and red, the solar phase, represents the culmination of the work where sun and moon are joined in mystical marriage. The Faust Book's forty-five chapters correspond to the symbolic number of "days" it is said are required to complete the Work, and the flying lions, stags, dragons, distilled water, lilies, beheadings, bulls, and apes that appear in the story signify operations taking place in the alchemist's vessel at different stages of the process.

Among their many other roles, Faustus and Mephistopheles play alchemical roles, their actions dramatize all aspects of the Art, but for the most part they represent Sulphur and Mercury. When Mephistopheles seduces and corrupts Faustus, then guides him on transforming journeys, he reflects the actions of Mercury, the dual-natured catalyst that decomposes the imperfect metal before it transmutes it. In their journeys, when he and Faustus fly back and forth to perform healings and miraculous changes, they are imitating the actions of volatile spirits that rise from the decomposed metal and circulate in the vessel, then return to induce a chemical transformation. (By Spirit is meant the essence of the metal that is rooted in the Divine. It is often conflated with Soul when alchemists speak of an essence that arises from the decomposed Body and returns to impregnate it with new life. The Soul is feminine, however, while the Spirit is male, and is connected to the body as a template and a higher form of consciousness. When it is purified it reflects the light of Spirit and receives it in a mystical union of polar opposites.)

Hermetic philosophers maintained that the process of alchemical transmutation underlay the workings of the universe and the Faust Book is based on that assumption. Indeed, like Goethe's great adaptation, it is an alchemical as well as a Gnostic drama. The alchemical process corresponds to stages of the cosmic creation taking place in the myth and for the human transformation encoded in the story. Both involve progressive or ascending levels of awareness that are associated with various stages of the Art. Hermetics also believed that Heaven and Earth are reflections of each other and they attempted to unite them here on earth. Their belief was thought to be validated in the transmutation of metals, for there matter was said to be spiritualized and Spirit was given form. As Faustus and Mephistopheles play first one role and then another from the underlying myth, they demonstrate the mutability of matter that was mentioned above, as well as the link between terrestrial and celestial events. Their changes of behavior, character, and motivation are determined as much by the dissolving, putrefying, circulating and coagulating metal as by the changes in Heaven taking place in the myth.

The spiritual alchemists produced transformations in their metals, not merely by reading the "book of nature" and imitating its processes, but by mastering their inner environments as well. Working deeply on the level of the soul and identifying with the spirits of their metals, they influenced them on a cellular—some say atomic—level, and the transformed metals mirrored back the transformation of their souls.

According to the writings of Eastern tantric alchemists, this process was repeated in their bodies as they raised and lowered the kundalini and entered altered states of consciousness. Both involved a break with ordinary perceptions of reality; even as their metals dissolved, so did their conventional body-minds. Faustus's body-mind is dissolved when he "sleeps" or enters into trances before embarking on the "round trip" flights that also signify the Kundalini's rise and fall. He departs from ordinary reality when he conjures up the Devil and, with him, a universe ruled by different laws where strange, yet familiar, characters participate in extraordinary events.

Among them is the aforementioned enchantress, Helen of Greece, whom Faustus conjures from the past and makes his companion and bedfellow. While in the Gnostic context she represents the goddess Sophia, she is also a reflection of the alchemist's Soror Mystica (spirit woman) who is always with him in his mind. She is the feminine aspect of his psyche, the deeper wisdom that must be developed and united with its opposite, just as feminine Mercury and masculine Sulphur are united in a final conjunction.

TANTRA IN THE FAUST BOOK

Faustus's passion for Helen, as we mentioned earlier, recalls the immortalizing "furor" for Venus experienced by Agrippa and Bruno. Helen's numinous presence seems to be a manifestation of the "divine light" Bruno described, "which takes possession of the soul, raises it and converts it into God."[8] As such it resembles tantric worship of the divine feminine, although the tantrist radically enhances the spiritual methods the magi reported using, intensifying his passion by means of deliberate and controlled sexual stimulation and by arousal of the Kundalini. The nature of kundalini energy/consciousness is both sexual and sublime and, when awakened, can induce transcendent bliss. While references to the Kundalini are carefully disguised in the Faust Book, certain features in the story are readily apparent to the watchful eye as being those of a tantric initiation.

Mephistopheles' contentious, often ambiguous relationship to Faustus is a reference to tantra just as it is to alchemy. It resembles the shifting tactics of a guru who varies his approach to his pupil in order to dissolve his resistances and prepare him for wider states of consciousness. Both

Faustus and the tantric aspirant stimulate and indulge their senses under the guidance of their teachers who encourage them to have sexual encounters with women in their dreams. Both work with magical diagrams or yantras, exhibit extraordinary will, "fly" on visionary journeys, acquire powers of teleportation, invisibility, prophecy, and healing, and have ritual intercourse with women whom they visualize as goddesses. The tantrist is said to become omniscient as a result of his sacred "marriage," and Faustus produces an omniscient child in his union with the visualized Helen, or Sophia.

The tantric yogin indulges in wine, food, and erotic dreams just as Faustus does, but unlike Faustus, he strives to transcend his senses and overcome attachment to pleasure and desire. This goal accords with the efforts of certain magi to rise above carnal love, and with the underlying Gnostic admonition to "cast off the body of desire." It requires strict control of undisciplined thoughts and constant meditation on emptiness.[9] While Faustus seems unwilling to make such an effort, in fact, he practices these disciplines metaphorically. In chapter 12, at the height of his "aphrodesia" he abandons his pursuit of pleasure, studies astrology, and quietly contemplates the heavens, or the "emptiness" on which the yogin meditates.

The tantrist must also learn to control the Kundalini. This awesome life force "sleeps" in an occult center at the base of the spine. It is one of seven whirling energy centers that lie along the invisible channel of the spine and in the cranial vault. Through an invisible network they govern bodily functions and states of awareness. As the Kundalini rises and pierces each chakra, it burns out knots of emotional complexes and opens the yogin to higher levels of consciousness. When the Kundalini is aroused it can be dangerously disorienting, even deadly, for the person who lacks focus or training and cannot control it. Faustus demonstrates this effect in chapter 2 when he conjures up the Devil impetuously and shortly afterward becomes sexually obsessed and emotionally erratic. We will see in that chapter that the Devil is equated both with the Gnostic Logos and with the Kundalini—a device that demonstrates the complexity of these figures. While its force can be destructive, when it is controlled and directed upward to the cranial vault by a massive act of will, it produces the transforming effect mentioned earlier. Its function is similar to the magi's transforming furor for Venus.

For the tantrist the Kundalini power is feminine and he worships it through the mediating image of a goddess[10] that coalesces from the figures he consorts with in his dreams.[11] Like the tantalizing Helen whom Faustus conjures, her beauty is both seductive and divine and promises unparalleled bliss. When the yogin succeeds in arousing and controlling his Kundalini "lover," having mastered a variety of demanding yogic techniques, he is ready to engage with a mortal woman in the uniquely "celibate" act of tantric sexual intercourse. The Faust Book introduces this mortal woman to Faustus's bedchamber in chapter 39 when he unites with Helen, but only as a "portrait," or "copy," of the ideal form of the conjured goddess. This reflects a notion expressed in the Pistis Sophia and in Zostrianos—another of the texts whose highlights are included in the myth—that mortals are copies of ideal forms or aeons of the Light world.

Before the yogin engages in coitus, he consecrates the carnal act by visualizing his partner as a goddess and himself as a god. Then he awakens the Kundalini, and at the moment of climax—using superhuman will—he violently reverses his semen, which is immolated in the intense heat generated by the Kundalini's arousal. Blending in essence with the raging life force, it rushes up an invisible channel paralleling the spine while electric and magnetic, or male and female, currents wind up and around it. They unite in the cranial vault and consummate the physical act on a spiritual plane.

Faustus's journey down to Hell is a version of this process, in which two dragons representing these polarized currents transport him through the "hell" of ejaculatory arrest and the "death" or deep trance that follows it, then submerge him in radiant spiritual waters. With the opposites joined, the yogin achieves a primordial state of unity along with godlike vision, and so it is with Faustus. He emerges from the spiritual waters and finds himself perched on a high, pointed crag, denoting his enlightenment and status as a god.

Through pantomime and imagery such as this, the Faust Book takes us through the raising and lowering of the Kundalini. Faustus's gestures are supported by his perception of flashing lights, percussive and musical sounds, quaking mountains, and so on, as well as other symbols signifying physical, perceptual, emotional, and spiritual experiences that accompany the Kundalini's awakening. In a different context, some of these symbolic forms also have Hermetic/alchemical significance, demonstrating the analogous nature of tantric and alchemical events.

These analogous spiritual practices arose from worldviews that were in many ways similar. Tantrists and alchemists, as well as many Gnostics, envisioned the universe as Mind, or energy—the tantrists, for instance, experiencing it as a vast field of oscillating vibrational patterns, positive and negative polarities[12] that, like Light (Wisdom) and Darkness (Ignorance) emanating from the Gnostic Father, issue from an undivided source.[13] They understood energy, or sound, as the basis of physical forms, and their adepts claimed to have transformed their cellular structures or performed extraordinary feats with the use of mantras as well as controlled breathing, intentional thought, and the exercise of will.

Alchemists and tantrists both utilized the polarities in their work, attempting to reconcile and reunite them: the alchemist repeatedly dissolving and coagulating his imperfect metal, reducing opposites to compatible essences, and the tantrist raising and lowering the Kundalini life force in his body, "killing" and "reviving" his consciousness to purify himself and reconcile his own polarities.[14] Gnostic mythology is predicated on the alternations of opposites, including death and rebirth, and Faustus's transformation also follows this apocalyptic process.

The blending of these systems occurred in the early Christian centuries in and around Alexandria, Egypt, where many religions and cultic practices converged to create new forms of worship. Gnostic "serpent worshippers" or tantrists mingled with Jewish mystics, Egyptian alchemists, magicians, Hermetics, and devotees of Isis, the many-aspected goddess of the Moon. The Gnostics identified Isis with their Sophia, whose sojourn in matter as a "whore," and her subsequent enlightenment, resonated with the sacred sexual rituals of Isian priestesses in which participants were transformed into androgynous gods. Sophia's all-encompassing being—associated with alchemical *prima materia,* the source of all physical forms—further identified her with the fertile moon mother, Isis.

The Favored Ones

Lynn Picknett and Clive Prince, citing a wealth of scholarship in their book, *The Templar Revelations,* have pieced together the outline of a perennial, Johannite goddess-worshipping tradition that seems to have sprung from this beginning. We will avail ourselves of their outline since, surprisingly enough, it includes the features of the Faust Book that we have been discussing and points to Faustus's place in that tradition.[15] It is centered on John the Baptist and Mary Magdalene and includes John the Evangelist and Simon Magus. Curiously enough, the word play in Faustus's name mentioned earlier refers to all of these figures and establishes his link to their movement as well as to its goddess and a secret she represents.

While he bears the surname of the notorious Georg Faustus who is supposed to be his model, it is interesting to note that Faustus's first name was changed to Johannes. This has been attributed to a slip of the tongue by Luther's successor, Philip Melanchthon, who confused Georg with a Johannes Faustus he had known in his youth. The name is thought to have stuck to the charlatan over the years and influenced the author of the Faust Book when he chose his hero's name. But there seems to be another reason for Faustus's name change—one that a simple matter of translation begins to reveal.

Given the Latin meaning of Faustus ("favored one") mentioned earlier and the anglicized version of Johannes, Doctor Faustus's name translates into English as "John, the favored one." As such, it evokes the image of Jesus's beloved disciple, the one whom he favored above all the others and who rested his head on Jesus's breast. It seems unlikely, however, that the Faust Book author should attribute the practice of alchemy and magico/erotic worship of the divine feminine to this eminently Christian John. We will find an explanation for this strange association if we follow the Johannite trail back to Simon Magus and Mary Magdalene, who, like Faustus and John, were also "favored ones."

Simon's reputation as a sex magician survived the concealing of such practices when worship of the goddess went underground. (It is attested to in the Pseudo Clementine literature, a third-century cycle of Peter's travels containing references to Simon that are largely responsible for his reputation) and by the nature of his female companion, Helen. As a reformed prostitute, she was a wisdom figure in the manner of Isis or Sophia, and it is assumed that she and Simon performed the goddess's sacraments together, perhaps as priest and priestess or representations of the Sun (Simon) and Moon (Selene or Helen).[16] Simon was a disciple of John the Baptist and, according to some researchers, so was his Helen, leading them to speculate that the Baptist was also a follower of the goddess and would have been involved in sex magic as Simon and Helen were.

Some early baptismal cults, such as the Mandaeans who were devoted to John and hostile to the Christians, considered Jesus to have been John's rival and condemned him as a devil for having revealed their hidden mysteries. The medieval Cathars—a neo-Gnostic sect that flourished in southern France until its members were massacred by Christian crusaders—seem also to have believed that Jesus and John the Baptist were rivals. In another strand of this tradition it was held that Jesus and Simon were rivals as well—that they competed for John's favor and Simon was the victor, succeeding the Baptist after he was beheaded by Herod. This might account for Simon's being called "the favored one," the cognomen which connects him to Faustus and to John, Jesus's favorite disciple.

The medieval Knights Templar, the Freemasons, and the Rosicrucians also revered John the Baptist and are thought to be part of this feminist strain. The Templars seem to have overlooked Jesus in favor of both of the Johns, who were sometimes conflated in this tradition. The mysterious Temple knights were also rumored to have worshipped a decapitated head and, here again, the "favored" Johns are associated with sacramental sex. While the severed head was thought to signify John's beheading, he and his baptisms may have represented a secret the Templars chose not to disclose. The severed head finds an echo in an anonymous medieval poem that was written during the time of the Templars when the cycle of Arthurian romances mysteriously appeared. It is called *Sir Gawain and the Green Knight* and is a vibrant tantric allegory that concerns itself with keeping one's head. It is clearly a reference to the self-control that is required when raising the Kundalini in the non-orgasmic act of tantric sexual intercourse.

In the poem's erotically suggestive climax, Sir Gawain enters a deep barrow with his spear pointing the way and meets the Green Knight who is waiting inside to cut off his head. He is struck a glancing blow on the neck by the Green Knight's sword, which draws a few drops of blood. The drops represent an intoxicating "nectar" released by the pituitary gland when it is pierced by a tiny protuberance in the pineal gland, or "third eye." The pituitary gland extends when the Kundalini penetrates the sixth chakra.[17] Gawain refuses to flinch at the thrust of this blissful "sword" and manages to "keep his head," or in other words, to maintain his self-control. The image of decapitation would seem to contradict the notion of keeping control but, instead, it signifies the separation of the intellect or higher mind from the body's debasing influence. "To be without a head," says David Frawley in his book *Tantric Yoga,* "is a yogic metaphor for going beyond body consciousness or attachment to the thought composed mind."[18] The headless tantric goddess, Chinnamasta, also represents this form of liberation.

Picknett and Prince pointed out that images of Salome, or even of local priests, carrying John's decapitated head on a platter are found in churches located in areas of southern France where the Templars were quartered. There are often statues of the Black Madonna in those places or churches dedicated to Mary Magdalene, which cover ancient Isis shrines.[19] Both seem to represent the ancient goddess, and it is intriguing that churches dedicated to John the Baptist should be located near to them, as if the Templars recognized John to be a goddess worshipper, a priest/magician like Simon Magus, and Mary to be a priestess who performed the goddess's sacred rites.

In the Faust Book, the spirits take Faustus on a journey that exemplifies the Johannite tradition, escorting him down to Hell and up to the stars where he receives a revelation. This, of course, is a baptism, although not an immersion in water, as the Bible describes John's ablutions. Symbols in the story indicate that Faustus is having a hypnogogically induced death and rebirth experience of the kind John's baptism may represent in this tradition. It is the loss of consciousness and expanded spiritual vision that attends the rise of the Kundalini, whether during ritual intercourse or not.

Esoterically, the Jordan River, where John is reported to have performed his baptisms, is a spiritual stream down which the soul descends into manifestation and then rises to the "promised land." For the Peratae, a second-century Gnostic sect, the downward flow of the river to the Dead Sea represented ejaculation of sperm, while its upward flow indicated the retention of the seed and the Kundalini's rise up the central channel of the spine. Some Gnostic texts insist that the only true rebirth comes from baptism in spiritual, not ordinary, waters, perhaps referring to "dry" or non-ejaculatory sacred intercourse.[20]

Having considered the two Johns' relationship to the goddess's sacraments we turn to Mary Magdalene, another "favored one." She leads us closer to the goddess and her secret by virtue of her many aspects, one of which may be "John, the favorite disciple." According to some of the Christian Gnostic dialogues between Jesus and the disciples, it is she who was Jesus's favorite, not John who is largely absent in these texts. In the Pistis Sophia she overshadows the other disciples with her questioning and Jesus praises her purity and light, while in the Gospel of Mary he is said to love her more than the other disciples (18:15) and "more than the rest of women" (10:1). In the Gospel of Philip he "kissed [her] often on her (presumably) [lips]" (63:35). Seen in this light, the report that John rested his head on Jesus's breast seems to be a disguise for Mary's relationship to Jesus, whether as favorite disciple, wife, consort, or sacramental priestess.

Goddess and Chalice

Two treatises found in the Nag Hammadi collection—one of them Gnostic and the other drawn from many sources—demonstrate Mary's complexity and her similarity to the all-inclusive goddess. The first is the just-mentioned Gospel of Philip, which suggests that Mary Magdalene encompasses all three New Testament Marys—Jesus's mother, his sister, and his companion. "They are all three a Mary," the author concludes, and in the next sentence he or she elevates this composite figure by seeming to associate it with the Holy Spirit. "The Father and the Son are single names," it says, while "the Holy Spirit is a double name," apparently referring to Mary Magdalene who is the only Mary with a double name, and whose inclusive nature is reminiscent of the Holy Spirit's. The latter is "revealed," the Gospel says, "it is below. It is in the concealed: it is above" (59:18). Elsewhere, the writer explains the meaning of "revealed," speaking of "Christ" as a "revealed name." "Christ has everything in himself," it says, "whether man or angel or mystery, and the Father" (56:12).

Mary's name, which derives from the Hebrew *magdala,* meaning "tower," adds to her complexity. The word *tower* is, among other things, a term used by alchemists for the vessel in which the metal is constantly transformed,[21] and for its spiritual analog, a sacred chalice or womb that is the source of all creation. This fertile womb is reminiscent of the Moon goddess, Isis, and of Sophia, whose multifaceted figure appears in several Gnostic self-declarations, attributing many identities, qualities, even dimensions, to itself. In *The Thunder: Perfect Mind,* the second of the two treatises mentioned above, her voice might also be that of Mary Magdalene as she has been variously portrayed by her worshippers and detractors.

> *I am the honored one and the scorned one.*
> *I am the whore and the holy one.*
> *I am the wife and the virgin . . .* (13:17)
> *I am shame and boldness . . .*
> *I am the one who is disgraced and the great one . . .* (14:27)

She goes on to reveal her many aspects.

> *I am the mother and the daughter . . .*
> *I am the barren one and many are her sons.*
> *I am the bride and the bridegroom and it is my husband who begot me.*
> *I am the mother of my father and the sister of my husband and he is my offspring.* (13:21)
> *I am the speech that cannot be grasped,*
> *I am the name of the sound, and the sound of the name.* (20:31)

Mary seems to have acquired many of these aspects as a representation of the goddess in the feminist tradition.

Interestingly enough, Faustus also reflects the goddess's universal, paradoxical nature. He assumes an array of antithetical roles, being male and female, Father and Mother, Devil and Logos, mortal and divine, and—as with Mary and the goddess—is both revered and reviled. Like the fertile Moon mothers Isis and Sophia, he conjures up life forms at will and is further linked to the sacred chalice through John and/or Mary Magdalene, his fellow "favored ones."

In Eugnostos the Blessed, another Nag Hammadi text, this overflowing chalice is androgynous—a reflection of the Father's Light—whose male name is "Begotten, Perfect Mind" and whose female name is "All-wise Begetress, Sophia." Here we have an echo of the other "favored one," Simon Magus (or Mind) with his Helen (Selene or Sophia) whom Faustus and his Helen represent. Presumably, the union of this couple transforms them into androgynous gods as does the union of Faustus and Helen, which begets a miraculous offspring—an omniscient, androgynous Philosophical Child.

Kundalini Sacraments

Given Sophia's importance in the Gnostic myth we should not be surprised to find Faustus identified with her on a level deeper than parody, but he and Sophia both are merely symbols of the true goddess of the magico/erotic tradition. In a recent book called *Tantra: The Cult of Ecstasy,* Indra Sinha also quotes from *The Thunder: Perfect Mind* and her interpretation of the goddess's self-description reveals the latter's real identity.[22] Borrowing a phrase from an early Gnostic sect, she speaks of the tantric act of "coitus reservatus" as "ascent to God in sexual union" and—referring to these words from the goddess—she identifies them as a veiled reference to the Kundalini.

> *I am control and the uncontrollable.*
> *I am the union and the dissolution.*
> *I am the abiding and the dissolving.*
> *I am the one below and they come up to me.*
> *I am the judgment and the acquittal.*
> *I, I am sinless, and the root of sin derives from me.*
> *I am lust in outward appearance*
> *and interior self control exists within me.* (19:10)

This is the tantrist's true goddess—his Kundalini "lover," both in essence and in motion. Her antithetical assertions—besides resembling a mantra in which opposing syllables are recited incessantly to awaken the Kundalini (see chapter 32)—evoke her polarized forces that wind in opposite directions around the spiritual spine. Her lower chakras govern the material elements and produce "the pleasant forms" of the phenomenal world, which the goddess says "men embrace until they become sober."

Kundalini is said to be profound consciousness, a link to universal Mind and the "unstruck sound" of God.[23] She is like the goddess who says: "I am the speech that cannot be grasped, I am the name of the sound, and the sound of the name." When she rises, these substrates of sound/consciousness are absorbed into the unifying bliss that erases dualistic thought and makes humans divine. "When they go up to their resting place," says the goddess, "they will find me there, and they will live, and they will not die again" (21:29).

In a sense, then, all of Faustus's masks are symbols of Kundalini's infinite creativity, and all of the events in the Faust Book represent the rituals and sacraments of her ancient tradition.

The feminine underground strain surfaces from time to time in fairy tales, folklore, and works of art, and out of it have come such tantric and alchemical allegories as the poems of the medieval troubadours, the above-mentioned *Sir Gawain and the Green Knight, Canterbury Tales, Tristan and Isolde, Parzifal, Aeneus,* and other medieval and Renaissance works. While less polished on the surface than the others, the multilayered, far more complex Faust Book seems to be a part of this esoteric literary tradition.

The Monas Hieroglyphica and Transformation

In an age of heroic striving, the Faust Book's ambitious scope was not unusual. The Hermetic magi in particular sought not only to plumb ineffable mysteries, but to transmit them to initiated readers, whether through symbols and allegories, as in the Faust Book, or through charts of angels and celestial spheres or mystifying geometric and cabalistic diagrams.[24] An esoteric treatise by John Dee published in 1564, several years before the Faust Book was written, illustrates this mode of thought—one that is also alchemical. It deciphers a mysterious diagram called the *Monas Hieroglyphica* that was widely studied by occultists and adopted by the Rosicrucians.[25] Whether or not it came to the attention of our anonymous author, the Faust Book reflects its singular construction.

Like the Faust Book, the Monas Hieroglyphica seems simple on the surface but proves to be dauntingly complex. Dee, as we said, shared Faustus's desire to grasp the incomprehensible, and through his Monas, claimed to provide access to universal truth. He called it "a new and sacred art of writing—which spoke of 'all things visible and invisible, manifest and most occult, emanating by nature or art from God himself.'"[26]

It is a geometric figure based on a dot, a line, a circle, and their derivatives and combinations. Except for the dot and the two half circles at the bottom, it resembles the sign for Mercury, which represents the Philosophical Child—the beginning and end, or sum of the alchemical Work (or the "Work" or "Art"). Interpreted cabalistically, it proves to be a hieroglyphic depiction of the alchemical process itself in which diverse elements are reconciled by reducing them to their essences, purifying them, and uniting them over fire.

The alchemists' fire is represented by the two half circles at the bottom of the figure, which form the sign for Aries, the first manifestation of the fiery trigon. The cross above it signifies, among other things, the four elements that are rotated, purified, and etherialized over the fire. The intersected circle above the cross represents the conjunction of the Sun and Moon, the Mystical Marriage in which the essences of the opposing elements are united. The revelation resulting from this union is signified by the Monas itself. These symbols are replicated in chapter 2 of the Faust Book where they introduce the alchemical process.

The Monas can be disassembled and its parts recombined to form the astrological glyphs for the planets (Sun ☉, Moon ☽, Mercury ☿, Venus ♀, Mars ♂, Jupiter ♃, Saturn ♄) demonstrating the connection between astrology and alchemy or, by analogy, the interaction of Heaven and Earth. An extension of the point into a line that rotates and forms a circle indicates how multiplicity arose from unity, and a reinterpretation of the point and circle depicts the zodiac and the heavens that encircle the earth. Cabalistic interpretations and geometric rearrangements of the lines and the numbers they project yield references to natural and celestial phenomena, and to the mystery of the cross and the quaternary; they also demonstrate the harmony that governs creation. Profound contemplation of the Monas reveals the universal path of transformation and, according to Dee, opens the door to eternity.[27] A symbol of the philosopher's stone—the primary alchemical symbol of illumination—multiplies its meaning exponentially.

In the case of the Faust Book, its simple plot serves as the Monas.

It is a metaphorical depiction of the Gnostic cosmic creation and the stages of the alchemical process. The Faust Book characters and events function as the dot, the line, and the circle in the Monas, for when they are "disassembled" or taken from one context and placed in another, they enter different realms and dramatize different processes. They enact the cosmic creation as well as the soteriological ideas that surround it; at the same time they parody tantric and alchemical events. They demonstrate the link between Heaven and Earth and, like the Monas, indicate the path of transformation. Through their interplay with alchemy and the Gnostic myth, they reveal mysteries that the Apochryphon of John says are "hidden in silence"—even beyond those revealed in the Gnostic scripture.

WHO WROTE THE FAUST BOOK?

While it isn't known who the Faust Book author was, there are indications in the story that he or she was associated with the Hermetic Lutherans or the Rosicrucians who were forming underground when the Faust Book was written. They formed a revolutionary movement that hoped to promote the feminine principle and the Hermetic/alchemical philosophy. Its unrealistic dream was to reform society and heal its deep divisions by a radical (or alchemical) spiritual transformation.

The movement burst into public view in 1614 with two manifestos announcing its presence—*Fama Fraternitatus* and *Confessio Fraternitatus*—the one an elliptical account of its founding and organization, and the other an anti-papal statement of its intent and an invitation for others to join them. The manifestos were followed by *The Chymical Wedding of Christian Rosenkreutz,* an openly alchemical drama. While it is pure conjecture, it may be that the Faust Book was an early herald of their appearances. There are symbols in chapter 2 of the Faust Book that are clearly signatures of Hermetic alchemy and that anticipate the opening symbolism in the Rosicrucian "chemical wedding."

There are certain indicators in and out of the Faust Book suggesting this revolutionary underground connection. Heidelberg, a center of radical Hermetic Lutheranism in the last half of the sixteenth century, is located in central Germany where the Faust Book first appeared, and just across the border in Prague the eccentric, mystically inclined Emperor Rudolf II reigned. Along with Heidelberg, his court was a magnet for Hermeticists, cabalists, astrologers, and alchemists who practiced their Art in gloomy dens in the basement of his magnificent castle. John Dee, Giordano Bruno, the Hermetic alchemist, physician, and composer, Michael Maier, the poet Philip Sydney, and other prominent British and continental Hermeticists, Jewish cabalists, Arab scientists, and magicians visited his court to exchange occult ideas or curry his patronage.

Many references in the story indicate that the author was an iconoclast and entertained a bias toward the radical Lutherans and against the established Church. Some associations in the text suggest his political and religious preferences, if not his actual affiliations. Luther's Wittemberg is often matched with heaven in the comparisons, while Munich, a Catholic stronghold at the time, is used as a metaphor for an unenlightened state of mind. The Jews and the pope are equated with the Devil, and a comparison is made between the pope's palace and the alchemist's corrupted metal. The Turkish emperor is cuckolded, while kings and their armies are located at the bottom of Hell. The Rosicrucian *Confesssio* reflects these same biases, condemning "the Pope and Mahomet" and scorning "Romish seducers who have vomited forth blasphemies against Christ."

If, indeed, the Faust Book author was a radical Hermetic Lutheran or goddess-worshipping Rosicrucian, his secrecy proved to have been well advised, for the Catholic powers crushed these movements in 1620, ushering in thirty years of religious wars and a century of strife. Through it all the "alchemical" Faust Book survived and, altering its form through succeeding ages, transformed into the modern myth that reflects the plight of Western man.

PART ONE

Here Beginneth Doctor Faustus

His Vita & Historia

In the beginning of the Faust Book, Faustus is introduced and his superior qualities are noted. He conjures up the Devil who represents the feminine aspect of his nature and adopts a young lout named Christof Wagner who becomes his son. This parallels the beginning of the Gnostic myth in which the world of Light the Gnostics called "Father" is introduced and his infinite virtue is praised, he emanates a female reflection, and together they produce a perfect Son.

The Son in the myth emanates a divine hierarchy of twelve aeons, and Sophia, the youngest of the twelve, is introduced. She commits a transgression that fractures the unity of the Light world, then assumes a material body, forgets her heavenly origin, and succumbs to worldly desires. Faustus reflects Sophia's fall as he makes a pact with the Devil, strays from the godly path, and indulges in wine, women, and other forms of dissipation.

These stories are accompanied by descriptions of the terrors and illusions prevailing here on earth, for—as the text comparisons show—the world of pain and suffering we inhabit is a vast metaphor for inner conflict, both human and divine. The human soul is the major concern of the Gnostic works, however, for human ignorance maintains this hellish world and only human awakening can overcome it. The underlying texts speculate with Faustus on the extent to which various soul types may expect or hope to be saved and declare that humankind's salvation is vital to the godhead's own restoration.

In Gnostic terms, "fallenness" was characterized as "death," "sleep" or "drunkenness," and was typically associated with the search for false pleasure or glittering reflections of the godhead best represented by gold and beautiful women. It was held to manifest in delusions and a scattering of the senses, as Faustus's libidinous pursuit of women and his emotional confusion demonstrate. The stages of "fallenness" were distinguished by the four emotions that Sophia experienced when she was banished from the godhead. They are grief, doubt, fear, and repentance, the first three of which Faustus suffers as part one concludes. He tries to repent as he contemplates the horrors that await him in Hell, but his effort is in vain.

His disorientation reflects the first, or "Nigredo," stage of the alchemical process in which base metal is dissolved and reduced to its essential components. Just as he and Mephistopheles engage in a battle of wills, Mercury and Sulphur struggle for control in the alchemist's vessel. The pact Faustus signs with Mephistopheles represents the first conjunction between the two mineral agents, in which Sulphur captures and "fixes" the volatile Spirit.

The conjuration of the spirit/Devil, Mephistopheles, signifies the appearance of a Logos who embodies the inner mysteries in the underlying myth. It also signals the appearance of the tantrist's guru, who is mystically conflated with the tantric mysteries and has come to enlighten a disciple.

When Faustus conjures up the Devil and enters a different world, certain sights and sounds that are similar to trance-induced perceptions suggest that he is in an altered state. We will encounter these phenomena in chapters 2 and 8 of part one and throughout the story. These altered states coincide with different stages of Faustus's spiritual development and most frequently signify the loss and recovery of consciousness that attends the raising and lowering of the kundalini. His recurring trances also correspond to the dissolutions of the alchemist's metal and to the veils or mists that attend each stage of aeonic creation in the underlying myth.

Introduction to the Faust Book

The Faust Book introduction promises "rare revelations" and reflects the opening passage from the Apochryphon of John,[1] which announces that a revelation of the inner mysteries is about to begin. In this and a number of other Gnostic revelation myths, the Holy Spirit appears to questioning or doubting disciples and discloses secrets about the cosmic creation, the nature and workings of the godhead, and the means of securing human as well as divine salvation. The Faust Book places itself in that genre and addresses all of these mysteries cryptically.

Whenever a direct text comparison is provided in the pages that follow, the Faust Book will appear unabridged in the left-hand column and be matched on its right by one, two, and sometimes three columns of highlights from the Gnostic and Hermetic works. The Faust Book text has been separated into segments to accommodate the different highlights and in order to make the comparisons clear.

A complete reading of the Faust Book text is recommended at the outset of each chapter so the reader may appreciate its full charm and intent. In most cases the mythological highlights that appear in the comparison follow the chronological order of the narratives from which they were taken and constitute sketchy summaries of them. In order to bring them into sharper focus, an attempt will be made to provide missing context for the highlights and to supply other information that may shed light on the sometimes-confusing subject matter.

FAUST BOOK[1]	THE APOCHRYPHON OF JOHN[2]
Historia and tale of Doctor Johannes Faustus, sorcerer, wherein it is described specifically and veraciously his entire life and death.	The teaching of the savior and the revelation of the mysteries, and the things hidden in silence, even these things which he taught John, his disciple.
How he did oblige himself for a certain time to the Devil	It happened one day when John . . . went up to the temple that a Pharisee named Arimanius approached him and said unto him,
and what happened to him	"Where is your master whom you followed?"
And how he got at last his well-deserved reward.	and John said to him, "He has gone to the place from which he came." (1:1–15)
Rare revelations are also included, for these are most useful and efficacious as a highly essential Christian warning and admonition that the laity, in order to protect themselves from similar machinations of the most shameful sort, have especial cause to heed and to avoid such a desperate fate.	

Notice that "sorcerer" is matched with "savior" in the comparison and that Faustus's "well-deserved reward," the fate that awaits sinners, corresponds to the savior's rise to heaven in the Apochryphon of John. Negatives such as these are used frequently in the Faust Book. The first set demonstrates the Gnostic affinity for inversion as well as the author's desire to both hide and reveal his meaning. In the second instance, the negative juxtaposition presents the reader with the choices that confront the divided human being whose nature is both spiritual and material. While on the one hand, Faustus succumbs to pleasures of the flesh and will meet his "well-deserved reward," the disciple in the hidden texts, whose example is the risen savior, will heed the higher call and be saved.

The surface plot, in which Faustus journeys inevitably to his doom, is a gloomy inversion of the underlying message, which holds out hope for a glorious resurrection. It serves as a metaphor for the all-encompassing Gnostic view that the "godless" material world is a negative reflection of the ideal world of Light.

The association of the Pharisee with the Devil may reflect the animosity of certain Gnostic sects toward the Jews for their worship of the "false god" and their acceptance of the laws that govern his oppressive creation. However, prominent and powerful figures such as emperors and popes fare no better in the Faust Book, for they also serve to represent the Devil. The pious warning in the final paragraph is an orthodox sheen that is perhaps satirical, probably intended to obscure the author's heretical intent. Such scoldings appear throughout the Faust Book.

1
Of His Parentage and Youth

This opening chapter introduces the mythological themes that shape the Faust Book plot, as shown by the highlights from the Tripartite Tractate and the Apochryphon of John. As we have seen, the Hymn of the Pearl provides the outline for the composite drama of the fallen cosmic soul whose repentance and return to grace is a model for human spiritual development. In it a hero Savior descends into the realm of matter to rescue the lost Pearl of wisdom—the spark of divinity that lies forgotten in each of us and must be discovered. He fails in his mission, however, for when he crosses the boundary from the world of Light and assumes a material body, he succumbs to its desires, forgets his divine nature, and abandons his soul-saving mission.

This story continues in subsequent chapters of the Faust Book, reflected in other texts with other divine souls, for whether it is Sophia from the Pistis Sophia and the Apochryphon of John, the Logos from the Tripartite Tractate, Primal Man from the Mani myth, or the Pilgrim Savior in the Hymn of the Pearl, all assume the burden of incarnation and fall into "sleep," "drunkenness" or "ignorance." All forget their heavenly origin and must be called to remembrance by a Logos or otherwise awakened in order to return to the world of Light.

The Tripartite Tractate launches the composite creation myth by describing the first principle the Gnostics called Father—the unfathomable, illimitable world of Light that encompasses all potential and emanates from all of creation. In the Apochryphon of John, a doubting disciple is reproached by a Pharisee for succumbing to Jesus's teaching. He will soon receive a revelation from the Holy Spirit, however, a revelation that includes an account of the cosmic creation, a version of Sophia's myth, and secrets of divine and human salvation. For the disciple, access to these mysteries is equivalent to the divine soul's awakening.

At the start of this text comparison, a description of Faustus's virtuous parents is matched with lines from the Tripartite Tractate praising the "good, faultless," and "perfect" Father. Later, after Faustus abandons his faith and sinks into depravity, his friends are condemned for inclining him to magic and other forms of deception. They are compared to Jesus in the Apochryphon of John, whom the Pharisee accuses of seducing the disciple with "deception" and "lies."

Quite aside from its relevance to the underlying texts, Faustus's search for forbidden knowledge reflects the spiritual development of a tantric disciple. We will be following his progress throughout this book, using as our guide an informed summary of the tantric process by Mookerjee and Khanna in *The Tantric Way*. Their book and others supply physiological details about specific tantric practices, which we will compare to some of Faustus's peculiar actions as well as to certain unusual images and events that appear in the Faust Book.

In their summary, Mookerjee and Khanna identify a series of "sharply defined phases" of the tantric process. They characterize the first as "an unwinding" of expansive "inner energies" or the emergence of an impulse "in the newly awakened man" to uncover his "unlimited potential." Thus he breaks the bounds that confine him and seeks out sacred or hidden knowledge. When Faustus abandons his conventional studies, "strays from his godly purpose" and develops a wide-ranging curiosity about magic and other black arts, he is parodying this expansive impulse.

He finds his vocation in sorcery, necromancy, and other forbidden arts in the same way the aspirant "discovers and accepts a belief system—in this case Tantra—in which (he) is going to be actualized."[1] While the belief system Faustus has adopted consists of the Devil's arcana—information about Hell, its rulers and legions, techniques for overcoming the limits of physical laws and the forbidden arts mentioned above—and will contribute to his undoing in the surface story, the practices and beliefs for which it is a metaphor will ultimately "actualize" or transform the tantric disciple, enabling him to acquire the godlike attributes he desires.

The magical "figuroe" and "incantaciones" Faustus studies evoke the tantrist's sacred diagrams or yantras and the potent syllables or mantras they chant to effect their transformations. The "conjuraciones" and "nigromantiae" he practices suggest the powers attributed to tantric adepts who are said to produce plasmic forms out of mind stuff through the projection of sexual energy, to teleport, and to become clairvoyant. Faustus will master these tantric practices and acquire many more as the story progresses.

The magical system he adopts is condemned by the Faust Book author as foreign and blasphemous, labels that have also been applied to tantra, whose worship of the goddess through exotic rituals and explicit sexual techniques clearly runs counter to orthodox norms. Condemned in India by the conservative Brahmans and driven underground in the West by the patriarchal Church, news of tantra has surfaced lately in the speculative environment in which alchemy and Gnosticism are found. Indeed, as we shall see, tantric practices indicated in the "heretical" Faust Book fit comfortably into alchemy's framework and the structure of the Gnostic myth.

FAUST BOOK	TRIPARTITE TRACTATE[2]
Doctor Faustus, the son of a husbandman, was born in Roda in the province of Weimar.	
His parents were god fearing and Christian people	As for what we can say for the things which are exalted, what is fitting is that we begin with the Father,
with many connections in Wittemberg.	who is the root of the Totality. . . . (51:15)
A kinsman who dwelt there was a citizen and possessed of considerable wealth.	
He reared Faustus for the parents and kept him as his own child	he is unbegotten and there is no other who begot him, nor another who created him. . . .

FAUST BOOK

and sent him to school to study theology.

Faustus, however, strayed from this godly purpose and used God's Word vainly.

Therefore we shall blame neither his parents nor his patrons, who desired only the best (as do all pious parents),

nor shall we mix them into this *Historia*.

For they neither witnessed nor experienced the abominations of their godless child. One thing is certain: that these parents, as was generally known in Wittemberg, were quite heartily delighted that their kinsman adopted him. When they later perceived in Faustus his excellent ingenium and memoria, it did most assuredly trouble them, just as Job in the first chapter of that Book was concerned lest they sin against the Lord. Therefore pious parents do sometimes have godless, naughty children, and I point this out because there are many who imputed great guilt and calumny to these parents whom I would herewith pardon. Such distortions are not merely abusive. If they imply that Faustus had been taught such by his parents, they are also slanderous. Indeed certain charges are alleged—to wit: that his parents had permitted wantonness in his youth, and that they had not diligently held him to his studies. It is charged that, so soon as his cleverness—together with his lack of inclination to theology—was perceived, it being further public hue and cry that he was practicing magic, his family could have prevented it.

TRIPARTITE TRACTATE

Not only is he without end . . . but he is also invariable in his eternal existence.

Neither will he remove himself from that by which he is

nor will anyone else force him to produce an end which he has not ever desired.

Thus he is himself unchanged and no one else can remove him from his existence and his identity, that in which he is, and his greatness

so that he cannot be grasped. . . . (52:10–30)

In the proper sense he alone, the good, the unbegotten Father and the complete one, is filled with every virtue and everything of value. And he has more, that is, lack of any malice, in order that (his wealth) may be discovered . . . he gives it, being himself unreachable and unwearied by that which he gives, since he is wealthy in the gifts which he bestows and at rest in the favors which he grants.

He is of such a kind and form and great magnitude that no one else has been with him from the beginning; nor is there a place in which he is or from which he has come forth, or into which he will go; nor is there any difficulty which accompanies him in what he does; nor is there any material which is at his disposal, from which (he) creates; nor any substance within him from which he begets what he begets; nor a co-worker with him on the things at which he works.

FAUST BOOK

All such rumors are *somnia** for the parents, being without guilt, should not be slandered.

But now *ad propositum*.

Faustus was a most percipient and adroit fellow, qualified and inclined toward study, and he performed so well at his examination that the rectors also examined him for the Magister Degree. There were sixteen other candidates, to whom he proved in address, composition, and competence so superior that it was immediately concluded he had studied sufficiently and he became Doctor *Theologiae*.

For the rest he was also a stupid, unreasonable, and vain fellow, whom, after all, his companions always called the *speculator*.

He came into the worst company

for a time laid the Holy Scriptures behindst the door and under the bench, did not revere God's Word but lived crassly and godlessly in gluttony and lust (as the progress of this *Historia* will sufficiently manifest).

Furthermore, Doctor Faustus found his ilk, who dealt in Chaldean, Persian, Arabian, and Greek words, *figurae, characterae, conjuraciones, incantaciones;* and these things recounted were pure *Dardaniae artes, nigromantiae, carmina, veneficii, vatecini, incantaciones,* and whatever you care to call such books, words, and names for conjuring and sorcery. They well pleased Doctor Faustus, he speculated and studied night and day in them.

TRIPARTITE TRACTATE

To say anything of this sort is ignorant.

Rather, (one should speak of him) as good, faultless, perfect, complete, being himself the Totality. (53:5–40)

THE APOCHRYPHON OF JOHN

The Pharisee said to (John,) "With deception did this Nazarene deceive you, and he filled your ears with lies,

---

*Here is an example of the Gnostic use of "sleep" to imply ignorance concerning the Father.

FAUST BOOK

Soon he refused to be called a *Theologus,* but waxed a worldly man,

called himself a *Doctor Medicinae,* became an *Astrologus* and *Mathematicus*—and for respectability, a physician. At first he helped many people with medicaments, herbs, roots, waters, receipts, and clisters.

He became learned besides, well versed in the Holy Scriptures, and he knew quite accurately the laws of Christ:

"He who knoweth the will of the Lord and doeth it not is doubly smitten." Likewise, "thou shalt not tempt the Lord thy God." All this he threw in the wind and put his soul away for a time above the door sill, wherefore there shall for him be no pardon.

THE APOCHRYPHON OF JOHN

and closed your hearts and turned you from the traditions of your fathers. (1:5)

2
How Doctor Faustus Did Achieve and Acquire Sorcery

In this chapter Faustus seeks to plumb the depths of the great mysteries of Heaven and Earth, paralleling the wonder Jesus's disciple expresses regarding the unfathomable Light world called Father and the mysteries of revelation and redemption. In the Tripartite Tractate, the Father puts forth a thought or reflection of himself "out of the abundance of his sweetness" to make himself known to his immanent creation. This heavenly revelation does not appear in the text comparison—perhaps because it is ineffable—but an earthly version of it does. In the Pistis Sophia and Apochryphon of John, Jesus and the Holy Spirit, who are both reflections of the Father, appear in triple-aspected fields of light and reveal his glory to frightened disciples. In the Faust Book's quaint version of these revelations, a ball of fire gushes from intersecting circles Faustus draws at a crossroads; then two forms emerge and coalesce into a third—a spirit, or devil—in front of the equally frightened Faustus. The spirit with three forms is a reflection of the triple-aspected light fields in the underlying texts and, as such, is a Logos, or revelation of the triple-powered godhead.

There are many symbols in this chapter and we will focus on four at the outset—the fire, the crossroads, the intersecting circles, and the number three—leaving the others for the end. The first three replicate John Dee's Monas Hieroglyphica ☿, the alchemical diagram described earlier, and introduce the alchemical and spiritual processes about to begin in the Faust Book.

The intersecting circles ⚭ are a variation of the circle intersected by a crescent in the Monas ♉, which, we may recall, represents the union of Sun and Moon, or Heaven and Earth. The figure of a cross arising from the image of the crossroads is, of course, the same as the one in the Monas, which signifed a rotation of the four material elements. The fire is reflected by the fire sign Aries in the Monas, or the two half circles at its base. The area where the intersecting circles overlap ⋈ is called the *Vesica Piscis* in esoteric geometry. It denotes a sacred space where Heaven and Earth embrace and spirit is revealed, and has the same significance as the Monas. When we arrange these symbols in the proper order, the figure that emerges ⚲ is almost identical to the Monas ☿ and tells the same story. As in the Monas, the cross of the elements is placed over fire and the elements are rotated, purified, and reduced to their essences. Then they are united, as the intersecting circles imply, and the spirit is revealed in the Vesica.

While the devil's three forms indicate the triple-powered godhead, their appearance together with the crossroads is also a signature of Hermetic alchemy. It anticipates the symbolism found in an opening scene of the *Chymical Wedding of Christian Rozenkreutz,* an early seventeenth-century alchemical drama.[1] Roland Edighoffer's description makes this clear:

> At the beginning of his pilgrimage, Christian Rosenkreutz comes to a strange crossroad, which stands explicitly under the sign of Hermes. It is well known that Hermes was worshipped as the protector of crossroads and that the so-called Hermai—that is to say, Hermes stones—were used to mark out ways. At the crossroad of our story stand three cedars . . . the number 3 [being] connected with Hermes Trismegistus and with the alchemical triad of sal, sulphur, and mercurius.

He points out that a marginal note defines one of the cedars as *arbor Mercurialis,* and another as *tabula Mercurialis,* referring to the "alchemical doctrine of the four elements."[2] Thus, the crossroads and the number 3, or trio of cedars in the Chemical Wedding, are Hermetic signatures and introduce the alchemical process just as the crossroads and the triple-form spirit do in the Faust Book.[3]

Finally, if we perform some "cabalistic" magic and extract another figure from the circles at the crossroads, we arrive at an esoteric symbol for the Earth, ⊕, which tells us that a spiritual initiation has begun. Here, the cross refers to the four directions or pull of opposing forces that both animate and burden the world and which Man must reconcile within himself. In spiritual alchemy, the directions are associated with stages of awareness related to the qualities of the elements, and the circle signifies the "fiery wheel," or crucible of transformation into which Faustus is about to plunge. We infer from this symbol, then, and from the Vesica Piscis in the intersecting circles, that Faustus has received a revelation and is embarking on a process of transformation in which opposites must be transcended and Heaven and Earth, or spirit and flesh, made one.

FAUST BOOK

As was reported above, Doctor Faustus's complexion was such that he loved what ought not to be loved, and to the which his spirit did devote itself day and night, taking on eagle's wings and seeking out the very foundations of Heaven and Earth.

APOCHRYPHON OF JOHN

When I, John, heard these things I turned away from the temple to a desert place. And I grieved greatly in my heart, saying, "How, then, was the savior appointed, and why was he sent in to the world by his Father, and who is his Father who sent him, and of what sort is that aeon to which we shall go? For what did he mean when he said to us, 'This aeon to which you will go is of the type of the imperishable aeon,'

PISTIS SOPHIA[4]

FAUST BOOK

For his prurience, insolence, and folly so pricked and incited him that he at last resolved to utilize and to prove certain magical vocabula, figuroe, characters, and conjurationes in the hope of compelling the Devil to appear before him. Hence (as others also report and as indeed Doctor Faustus himself later made known) he went into a dense forest, which is called Spesser Wald and is situated near Wittemberg. Toward evening at a crossroads in these woods he described certain circles with his staff, so that, beside twain, the two which stood above intersected a large circle.

APOCHRYPHON OF JOHN

but he did not teach us concerning the latter of what sort it is."

PISTIS SOPHIA

It came to pass, when Jesus had risen from the dead, that he passed eleven years discoursing with his disciples . . . [but he] had not told [them] the total expansion of the emanations of the Treasury, [or] of what type are the five Helpers, nor into what region they are brought, nor had he told them how the great light hath expanded itself . . . But he had discoursed with them generally . . . [and] for this cause they have not known that there were also other regions within that mystery . . .

FAUST BOOK	APOCHRYPHON OF JOHN	PISTIS SOPHIA
		but in teaching them, he said unto them:
Thus in the night between nine and ten o'clock he did conjure the Devil.		"I am come forth from that mystery."
Now the Devil feigned he would not willingly appear at the spot designated, and he caused such a tumult in the forest that everything seemed about to be destroyed. He blew up such a wind that the trees were bent to the very ground. Then it seemed as were the wood with devils filled, who rode along past Doctor Faustus's circle; now only their coaches were to be seen; then from the four corners of the forest something like lightning bolts converged on Doctor Faustus's circle, and a loud explosion ensued.	Straightaway while I was contemplating these things, behold, the heavens opened and the whole creation, which is below heaven shone, and the world was shaken. (1:15–30)	It came to pass, then, when the disciples were sitting together on the Mount of Olives . . . [that a] Light-power came down over Jesus [and] he soared into the height, shining most exceedingly . . . [And] when he had reached the Heaven . . . all the powers of the Heaven fell into agitation, and all were set in motion one against the other, they and all their aeons and all their regions, and the whole earth was agitated and all they who dwell thereon. . . .
When all this was past, it became light in the midst of the forest and many sweet instruments, music and song could be heard. There were various dances, too, and tourneys with spears and swords.		And all the angels and their archangels and all the powers of the height, all sang praises to the interiors of the interiors so that the whole world heard their voices without ceasing till the ninth hour of the morrow. (Ch. 3)
Faustus, who thought he might have tarried enough now, considered fleeing from his circle,	I was afraid,	But the disciples sat together in fear and were in exceedingly great agitation and were afraid because of the great earthquake which took place.

FAUST BOOK	APOCHRYPHON OF JOHN	PISTIS SOPHIA
but finally he regained his godless and reckless resolve and persisted in his former intention, come whatever God might send. He continued to conjure the Devil as before, and the Devil did mystify him with the following hoax. He appeared like a griffin or a dragon hovering and flattering above the circle, and when Doctor Faustus then applied his spell the beast shrieked piteously. Soon thereafter a fiery star fell right down from three or four fathoms above his head and was transformed into a glowing ball.		While they . . . wept together . . . the heavens opened and they saw Jesus descend, shining most exceedingly,
This greatly alarmed Faustus, too, but his purpose liked him so well, and he so admired having the Devil subservient to him that he took courage and did conjure the star once, twice, and a third time. Whereupon a gush of fire from the sphere shot up as high as a man, settled again, and six little lights became visible upon it. Now one little light would leap upward, now a second downward until the form of a burning man finally emerged. He walked round about the circle for a full seven or eight minutes. The entire spectacle, however, had lasted until twelve o'clock	and behold, I saw in the light a youth who stood by me. . . . While I looked at him he became like an old man. And he changed his likeness again becoming like a servant. There was not a plurality before me, but there was a likeness with multiple forms in the light, and the likenesses appeared through each other and the likenesses had three forms. (2:1–10)	and there was no measure for his light in which he was . . . it shot forth light rays in great abundance. It was of threefold kind. . . . The second, that in the midst, was more excellent than the first which was below. The third, which was above them all, was more excellent than the two which were above. And the first glory, which was placed below them all, was like to the light which had come over Jesus before he had ascended into the heavens, and was like only itself in its light. And the three light modes were of divers light-kinds and they were of divers type . . . (Ch. 4)

FAUST BOOK	APOCHRYPHON OF JOHN	PISTIS SOPHIA
in the night. Now a devil, or a spirit, appeared in the figure of a gray friar, greeted Doctor Faustus, and asked what his desire and intent might be. Hereupon Doctor Faustus commanded that he should appear at his house and lodging at a certain hour the next morning, the which the devil for awhile refused to do. Doctor Faustus conjured him by his master, however, compelling him to fulfill his desire, so that the spirit at last consented and agreed.		

As Doctor Faustus conjures the Devil, the latter mystifies him by appearing "like a griffin or a dragon hovering above the circle," and then, like a burning man who walks around it for several minutes. In the Valentinian Light-physics system, the visionary aeonology mentioned previously, the universe is conceived of as a polarized energy field, which devolves in a pattern based on geometric solids, and according to the sacred number sequences of Pythagorus. Here, the great turn of the twentieth-century Gnostic scholar George (G. R. S.) Mead describes the unfolding of the cosmos in terms of this vision, a process based on the interaction of polarized energies that resembles the strange occurrences in the Faust Book.

> The aetheric spaces destined to be the home of the future system are void and formless. From the fullness of potential energy, the Pleroma, there comes forth the stream of power, the spiral vortex—the Magna Vorago, or vast whirlpool of Orpheus. It is the fiery creative power; there is as it were the purification of spaces by fire. He enters into the formlessness and becomes the thing which it lacked,

> the spiral life force or primordial atom; he also fashions it without. The mother substance becomes a sphere, irradiate with life, a swirling mass of stardust. The "atom" becomes the "flying serpent," the comet, which as it were first hovers over the mother substance, the newborn system. It is the spermatozoon and ovum of the solar embryon.[5]

In this system a veil or mist is said to attend each stage of aeonic creation, and even the soul's Light grows dim when it condenses into matter. In the Faust Book, the creative vortex coalesces into the form of a burning man and then darkens, forming the figure of a gray friar. "See how the splendor of the alien man is diminished," says a Mandaean text, "the living force in him became changed. His splendor was impaired."[6] In the Faust Book, this alien man is Mephistopheles who has come to instruct Faustus, not lead him to his doom as the surface story suggests. When he emerges from the circles at the crossroads, he is "crucified" in time and space and burdened with a body—the life force diminished and controlled.

The six little leaping lights that arose from a fiery star carry on the process of creation and demonstrate the triple-powered godhead's tendency to reproduce itself in threes. Here is Mead's description of the first emanations produced by the Father's female reflection: "Ennoia, the negative sphere," having multiplied, "is now the type of 'seven robed' Isis. . . . The negative sphere is now seven spheres (herself and six like unto herself and the positive sphere) that is, three pairs of aeons."[7]

Some Sethian Gnostics envisioned the Primal Trichotomy as three roots or aeons containing varying quantities of spiritual Light. Descending from these roots were three minds and three men. The three types of men were said to be the wholly spiritual pneumatics who were assured of salvation, the psychics—part spirit and part matter—whose destiny it was to serve their fellow men in the hope of being saved; and finally, the hylics—those wholly material souls who were destined for eternal damnation. Here the number three raises the issue of salvation and who may hope to be saved, a matter of great concern to Faustus.

In the final paragraph, as Faustus commands the devil to appear at his "house and lodging . . . the next morning," his simple act conceals a deeper meaning. Hans Jonas tells us that "lodging may refer to the body, which is eminently the house of life . . . a passing earthly form encasing the soul."[8] Is Faustus commanding the spirit to appear next morning and enter him? There are many such examples in the Magical Papyri—a collection of fourth-century Egyptian spells, rituals, ceremonies—and other methods of evoking spirits in the suprasensible world—and Morton Smith has suggested a few:

> I conjure you, spirit, because I wish you to enter me. (PGM IV 320 5 ff)

> Come to me, air walking spirit, called by symbols and names not to be uttered . . . and enter his soul that it may receive the imprint of thine immortal form. (PGM VII 559 ff.)

> I conjure these divine names that they may send me the divine spirit, that he may do whatever I have in mind and desire. (PGM 131 2 ff.)[9]

While the magical literature provides a model for this most unusual act, some of the texts underlying the Faust Book reveal that the spirit's entrance into a supplicant may produce not merely crass or evil magic, but a divine revelation. In the Paraphrase of Shem, the Divine Pymander,[10] and a number of other Gnostic works, when a spirit descends on a disciple he is caught up in a heavenly rapture and accorded a glimpse of the inner ordering of things.

In the Pistis Sophia, too, when Jesus performs a mysterious magical rite using symbol and incantation, he ushers in a revelation for the disciples. Listing worldly and otherworldly rulers and entities over whom they will tower when they receive the full Gnosis, he promises they will be one with him and receive his miraculous powers. This seems to be the stuff of Faustus's desire as he commands the spirit to enter and inform him.

While the spirit's appearance in the Faust Book is equivalent to a revelation in the Gnostic context, it also signifies the tantric disciple's first encounter with his guru, which, in a certain sense, is also a revelation. The appearance of the spirit signals the second stage in a tantric disciple's initiation. According to Mookerjee and Khanna, after he has accepted a belief system that seems valid, his next step is to search for a guru who will instruct him and guide him on the path he has chosen.

Like Faustus's triple-form spirit, the guru may have many aspects. While some are simply projections of the disciple's unconscious—as in the case of the Tibetan master, Naropa, who saw his guru, Tilopa, as "a leprous woman, a butcher, and in many other forms before he saw him as himself"—the lack of clarity is also a function of the ambiguous nature of the guru. According to Guenther and Trungpa, "the term [guru] does not refer so much to a human person as to the object of a shift in attention which takes place from the human person who imparts the teaching to the teaching itself."[11]

Apparently this identification is mystical as well as perceptual, and at some point includes the disciple himself. This is illustrated in the Apochryphon of John where the figures of a servant, a youth, and an old man appear and then dissolve into each other in the field of light. They are at once the teacher, the one who is taught, and the teaching or revelation that the light field represents. These figures appear in the Faust Book, too, as the spirit/servant, Mephistopheles, a youth named Wagner to whom Faustus will bequeath his knowledge, and an enlightened old man who manifests the Word of God. As mystical entities, they personify and promote Faustus's spiritual transformation.

According to Mookerjee and Khanna, after the disciple finds his guru he begins to experiment with various physical and mental techniques and disciplines designed to focus concentration and center his energies. Among the techniques they list are drawing and meditating on a yantra, a geometric diagram of a deity or the function it represents, and of vibrational patterns in the cosmic energy field. The linear components of a yantra are arranged in such a way that they act as "cosmic cross points"[12] between realities, affording the viewer a glimpse of another dimension. While the intersecting circles Faustus draws at the crossroads are Hermetic or Pythagorean devices that resemble the mystical diagrams of Giordano Bruno and other Renaissance magi, they are created and utilized in the same way as a yantra. Faustus's diagram summons figures from another realm just as the yantra allows the disciple to enter "unusual states of mind."[13] The reader may have noticed that the descriptions of the intersecting circles in the Faust Book and of Jesus's Light rays in the Pistis Sophia are vague and confusing in a similar way. Faustus's circles seem to have evoked the image of the Devil in the same way the light field prefigured Jesus.

Another practice Mookerjee and Khanna mention is *pranayama,* or controlled and prolonged breathing whose paramount purpose "is to stimulate the center of paranormal consciousness in the brain for the arousal of the Kundalini." Daily practice of this and other disciplines strengthens the disciple's ability to enter into "unusual states of mind."[14] Certain features of the conjuration suggest that Faustus is practicing this kind of breathing, has entered an altered state, and may have awakened the Kundalini. Following is a description by Omar Garrison, a tantric adept whose book, at the time of its publication was hailed as the only one in English that makes tantra clear to a western audience—of an exercise called the "Yoga of Ascendancy," whose resemblance to Faustus's conjuration of the Devil is worth noting. It is designed, Garrison says, to manifest "on the material plane anything (that is) strongly desired."[15]

The role of will power is vital in an exercise like this, says Garrison, and many tantrics "employ images and mystic diagrams to help create the proper frame of mind." (Faustus begins by inscribing intersecting circles at the crossroads.) The yogin commences slow, deep breathing, focusing on the center of the naval chakra and visualizing "a tiny, intensely brilliant tongue of flame. . . . He thinks of his lungs as a bellows, stoking the glowing tongue of fire until it incandesces more and more." (Faustus visualizes the fiery star.) "At that point the yogin substitutes for his image of the fire a mental image of the thing or condition desired by him." (Faustus visualizes the Devil disguised as a circling dragon.) "Then, by breathing in and out in short, staccato spurts, he causes his abdomen to move back and forth in quick, spasmodic motion . . . he lowers his head, expels all the air and shakes the solar plexus violently." (The Devil blows a powerful wind and it causes a tumult in the forest.)

"This portion of the exercise lasts for perhaps two minutes during which the sadhaka, or aspirant, concentrates intensely upon the desired objective. . . ." (Faustus conjures the star "once, twice, and a third time.") "Holding the breath for a count of seven, the yogi visualizes the tumo flame passing upward toward the crown of the head." (The glowing sphere shoots up a gush of fire "as high as a man.") "With it, he sends the mental substance of his desire." (The figure of a burning man emerges from the fire.) "As he exhales, he imagines his desire to be outside himself. It has now become an exteriorized, living thought form, objective and real."[16] (The "Devil, or a spirit, appears in the figure of a gray friar, greets Doctor Faustus and asks what his desire and intent might be.")

Elsewhere, Garrison mentions some perceptions accompanying a profoundly altered state that resemble other things Faustus saw or heard in the forest. He speaks of "plenary and intense" sounds coming from the lower chakras that are perceived in the early stage of meditation or sweet musical sounds like stringed instruments and flutes that come at a deeper stage.[17] (Faustus hears "a loud explosion" and "many sweet instruments, music and song.") Finally, according to Mookerjee and Khanna, when the yogin enters a dream state, he may perceive "dots of light, flames, geometric shapes" ("something like lightning converged on Faustus's circle") and when the meditation is more advanced, the previous perception of flashing lights "dissolve into an inner radiance of intensely bright, pure light."[18] ("When all this was past," says the Faust Book, "it became light in the midst of the forest.")

We will encounter the Devil's blast of "wind" again in subsequent chapters along with the other features that appear here. Then Faustus will experience great heat—a sign of the Kundalini's awakening—and will engage in activities that involve rising and falling, such as running up and down stairs, flying and landing, and so on, which represent the raising and lowering of the Kundalini. For now, however, Faustus seems to have stirred the fiery force through his deep meditation but failed to raise it. Otherwise, the Logos might have appeared in the glorious form described in the myth instead of in a gray friar's somber garb. Nevertheless, Faustus has made a first contact with his "guru"—the Kundalini power that will elevate his consciousness, or the "lover" who will bring him unparalleled bliss.

As a neophyte, he may have lacked the iron will and steady focus required for raising the Kundalini. Indeed, when he hesitates between fleeing the circle and continuing to conjure the Devil, he dramatizes the disciple's tendency to let his focus wander at one moment, and at the next, to control the powerful force he has aroused. His struggle is signified by the presence of bent trees and swords that, as gender opposites, represent a vacillation between feminine passivity and the exercise of active will. The feminine and masculine symbols also signify tendencies to devolve into gross manifestation or evolve into higher spiritual forms. These are Hermetic symbols which, along with the intersecting circles, serve as interfaces between tantric and alchemical aspects of this chapter.

3

Here Followeth the Disputatio Held By Faustus and the Spirit

In this chapter Faustus demands obedience from the Spirit and requests certain information from him. He receives in return a description of the hellish kingdom ruled by the spirit's master, Lucifer, and by his government of demons. This parallels and parodies descriptions in the Gnostic texts about the creation of this world and its ignorant rulers who subjugated men and kept them enslaved.

Another of the Gnostic texts underlying the Faust Book, On the Origin of the World, provides details about the cruel material universe the grandiose Yaltabaoth fashioned.

> Now the prime parent Yaltabaoth, since he possessed great authorities, created heavens for each of his offspring . . . and in each heaven he created great glories, seven times excellent . . . and also mighty armies of gods and lords and angels and archangels—countless myriads—so that they might serve.
>
> Now, when the seven rulers were cast down from their heavens onto the earth, they made for themselves angels, numerous, demonic, to serve them.
>
> And the latter instructed mankind in many kinds of error and magic and potions and worship of idols and spilling of blood and altars and temples and sacrifices and libations to all the spirits of

> the earth . . . all men upon earth worshipped the spirits. . . . Thus did the world come to exist in distraction, in ignorance and in a stupor.[1]

These passages clearly inspired the spirit's description of Lucifer's kingdom in this chapter and demonstrate the broad Gnostic belief that hell is this world and the devil is its god.

The Gospel of Truth implies that the hellish kingdom the spirit refers to really is our world, and that men's damnation results from godlessness. It is the substance of the world we live in—the "world of oblivion" created by ignorance of the Father. The Tripartite Tractate says this alienation from God must be acknowledged and the pain experienced so that human beings will seek the Father and be saved.

In this and other chapters of the Faust Book where comparisons are made between this world and Lucifer's kingdom, they are accompanied by speculation in the underlying texts about the problem of ignorance or evil. A solution is touched on briefly in On the Origin of the World where we learn that the Father is constantly sending blessed spirits down to our world.

> Since the immortal Father knows that a deficiency of truth came into being amongst the eternal realms and their universe, when he wished to bring to naught the rulers of perdition through the creatures they had modeled he sent your likenesses down into the world of perdition, namely, the blessed little innocent spirits. (124:1–15)

The mission of the "blessed little innocent spirits" who assume the burden of incarnation is to serve and instruct other souls. The spirit who serves and instructs Faustus both represents and parodies these divine emissaries, an association he confirms by implying that he was sent to make Lucifer "subservient." The blessed spirits bring the Word that sets men free: knowledge of the Father that dissolves the "world of Oblivion."

In the Apochryphon of John, the Light world has divided and the Father's female reflection, Barbelo, has appeared:

> The Father's thought performed a deed and she came forth, namely she who had appeared before him in the shine of his Light. This is the first power, which was before all of them and which came forth from his mind . . . her Light shines like his Light—the perfect power which is the image of the invisible, virginal Spirit who is perfect. The first power, the glory of Barbelo, the perfect glory in the aeons. [2]

As Faustus receives the devil's hellish instruction, she requests certain knowledge and powers from the Virginal Spirit which seem to comprise the Gnosis, or the Word the blessed spirits bring. In the Pistis Sophia, Jesus has come down from the Light world like one of the blessed spirits to impart a revelation of the inner mysteries to the disciples. He awaits permission from the "four-and-twentieth mystery" to begin his instruction.

FAUST BOOK	PISTIS SOPHIA	APOCHRYPHON OF JOHN
Doctor Faustus returned home and later that same morning commanded the spirit into his chamber, who indeed appeared to hear what Doctor Faustus might desire of him.		And Barbelo performed a deed and she came forth . . . she who had appeared before him in the shine of his Light . . . (4:25–30)
(And it is most astounding that a spirit, when God withdraws his hand, can so deceive mankind.)	It came to pass, then, (that the disciples) said: "Lord, if it be thou, withdraw thy Light-glory into thyself that we may be able to stand; otherwise our eyes are darkened . . ."	

FAUST BOOK	PISTIS SOPHIA	APOCHRYPHON OF JOHN
Doctor Faustus again commenced his machinations, conjured him anew, and laid before the spirit these several articles, to wit: Firstly, that the spirit should be subservient and obedient to him in all that he might request, inquire, or expect of him throughout Faustus's life and death. Secondly, that the spirit would withhold no information which Faustus in his studies might require. Thirdly, that the spirit would respond nothing untruthful to any of his interrogationes.		She requested from the invisible virginal Spirit . . . to give her foreknowledge. . . . (5:10) And she requested again to grant her indestructibility . . . (5:20) and Barbelo requested to grant her eternal life . . . (5:30) and she requested again to grant her truth. (5:35)
The spirit immediately rejected the articles, refused Faustus	Then Jesus drew to himself the glory of his Light. . . .	
and explained his reason: that he had not complete authority except in so far as he could obtain it from his lord who ruled over him. He spake: "Sweet Fauste, it standeth neither within my election nor authority to fulfill thy desires, but is left to the Hellish God."	[and said to them:] "It came to pass when I sat a little removed from you on the Mount of Olives, that I thought on the order of the ministry for . . . which I was sent, that it was completed, and that the . . . four-and-twentieth mystery from within . . . had not yet sent me my Vesture . . . which I had left behind in it. . . ." (Ch. 6)	
	"Until the time should be completed to put it on and I should begin to discourse with the race of men . . ." (Ch. 7)	

FAUST BOOK

Faustus replied: "What? How am I to understand thee? Art thou not thine own master?"

The Spirit answered: "Nay."

Faustus then said to him: "Sweet Spirit, explain it to me then."

"Now thou shalt know, Fauste," said the spirit, "that among us there is a government and sovereignty, just as on earth, for we have our rulers and governors and servants—of whom I am one—and we call our kingdom Legion.

"For although the banished Devil Lucifer brought about his own fall through vanity and insolence, he raised up a Legion nevertheless, and a government of devils,

and we call him the Oriental Prince, for he had his sovereignty in Ascension. It is thus a sovereignty in Meridie, Septentrione, and Occidente as well.

"Certainly we have never revealed to men the real fundament of our dwelling place, nor our rule and sovereignty.

GOSPEL OF TRUTH

When the totality went about searching for the one from whom they had come forth . . . the incomprehensible, inconceivable one who is superior to every thought—

ignorance of the Father brought about anguish and terror; and the anguish grew solid like a fog, so that no one was able to see. For this reason error became powerful; it worked on its own matter . . . not having known the truth. It set about with a creation, preparing with power and beauty the substitute for the truth. (1:5–20) Thus it had no root, it fell into a fog regarding the Father, while it was involved in preparing works and oblivions and terrors, in order that by means of these it might entice those of the middle and capture them. (1:30–36)

TRIPARTITE TRACTATE

The Father . . . has such greatness and magnitude, that, if he had revealed himself suddenly . . . to all the aeons . . . they would have perished. (64:30) This one, however, stretched himself out, and it was that which . . . gave a foundation and a dwelling place for the universe. (65:5)

The expulsion . . . was made for (man) when he was expelled from the enjoyments of the things which belong to the likeness. (107:20)

FAUST BOOK	TRIPARTITE TRACTATE
"No one knoweth what doth occur after the death of the damned human who learneth and experienceth it."	This the Spirit ordained when he first planned that man should experience the great evil, which is death, that is complete ignorance of the Totality, and that he should experience all the evils which come from this and, after the deprivations and cares which are in these, that he should receive of the greatest good, which is life eternal. (107:26)
Doctor Faustus became alarmed at this and said: "Then I will not be damned for thy sake."	
The spirit answered: "Wilt not agree? For thee no plea, thou must come with me. Thou wost it not when we hold thee. Yet come thou must with me, nor helpeth any plea: an insolent heart hath damned thee."	
Then Doctor Faustus said: "A pox take thee! Hence! Be gone!"	
Even in the moment when the spirit was about to withdraw, Doctor Faustus did change his vacillating mind.	
He conjured the spirit to appear at the same place at vespers to hear what else he would require.	
The spirit granted this and disappeared from before him.	

The partnership between the spirit and Faust is based on the dissolutions and coagulations of the alchemical process and on nature's own process of death and renewal. Hermetic philosophers recognized that their imperfect metals had to be dissolved and freed of impurities before they could be transmuted into nobler form. Mercury was the agent that promoted the dissolution and the spirit in the Faust Book has a similar function. In the chapters that follow, he will tempt and goad Faustus and bring him to his knees as a prelude to the transformation promised him in the underlying texts. For now, however, Faustus resists the spirit's plan.

His insistance that the spirit be "subservient to him in all that he might request, require, inquire, or expect of him throughout his life or death," is a demand far different in tone from the disciples' humble requests to Jesus in the Pistis Sophia. His attitude here reflects the behavior of Sulphur as it begins to grapple with Mercury in the alchemist's vessel.[3]

Sulphur is a form-giving agent that tends toward rigidity and whose nature is to delimit and control, as in the human exercise of will. While it must be dissolved before its full creative power can be realized, it resists Mercury's corrosive action and works instead to capture and fix the volatile Spirit. From the beginning, Faustus has attempted to impose his will on his own elusive spirit, but, like the volatile Mercury, the spirit has escaped his control.

The myth of Sophia follows the alchemical formula, too, for she was tempered by degradation and purified by suffering. Faustus's vacillation at the mention of Lucifer's fall heralds the appearance of her story in chapter 8. Like Lucifer, she was the jewel in Heaven's crown, and his banishment from Heaven reflects her fall from grace. She is also associated with the ruler of Hell by way of her ignorant son, Yaltabaoth, the material god who rules his own "hellish" kingdom. Thus her story is referred to indirectly here, and at the very moment when Faustus exhibits the first erratic behavior that will lead to his own dissolution and fall.

Introduction to Chapters 4–7

In these chapters the spirit returns after reporting back to the "Hellish God." He offers to instruct Faustus if he will be "his, the spirit's own property" after a certain number of years. The number specified in the pact is twenty-four, which has a special meaning in the mystical tradition. Since twenty-four hours is the time the Sun takes to make its rounds each day, both "day" and "twenty-four" connote completion of a cycle. For the alchemists, a "day" was also a "year," for just as a day marks a complete revolution of the earth on its axis, a year completes the passage of the earth around the Sun. "Twenty-four," "day," and "year," then, all signify completion.

In the Pistis Sophia, when Jesus refers to the highest mystery as the "four-and-twentieth mystery, the completion of completions," he adds the notion of enlightenment to the number twenty-four. The alchemists, too, speak of a twenty-four-unit cycle, or a "day," as the time it takes to complete their Work and the process of spiritual transformation. We may thus infer that when the spirit binds Faustus to a term of twenty-four years he pledges him to complete the effort of self-transcendence.

While completion of a cycle connoted fulfillment for the Gnostics, the cycle itself or the passing of time was held to be a misfortune. Where Plato sang praises to time as "the moving image of eternity," the Gnostics scorned it as an "error." A Valentinian source accuses the false god who created the material world of embodying eternity in "times, epochs, and great number of years under the delusion that by quantity of times he could represent their infinity."[1] For the Gnostics, this burdensome imitation of the Light world's changeless perfection was the false god's greatest curse, for it measured out in moments their sojourn in the body and, hence, their separation from God. The twenty-four years of Faustus's pact, then, dramatize his separation and imprisonment in matter even as they promise him fulfillment.

In tantric yoga, the number twenty-four is implied in a successful Kundalini ascent, according to the renowned scholar, Arthur Avalon (Sir John Woodroffe), in his book *The Serpent Power.* He speaks twenty-three *tattvas*—metaphysical categories or cosmic principles that, through meditating centers associated with the chakras govern physical, mental, and spiritual manifestation—are absorbed by the Kundalini in its rise to the twenty-fourth, or spiritual plane. As it passes through the chakras, he writes, referring to the Kundalini as female:

> She absorbs into Herself the regnant Tattvas of each of these centers. . . . [and] As the ascent is made, each of the grosser Tattvas enters into the Laya state and is replaced by the energy of Kundalini . . . for, whereas, in the Muladhara [the first chakra] She is the Sakti [goddess] of all in their gross or physical manifested state . . . at the stage of Ajna [the sixth chakra] She is the Sakti of the mental and psychic or subtle body . . . and in the region of the Sahasrara [the crown chakra] She is the Sakti of the spiritual plane.

"In Her progress upwards," says Avalon, "[Kundalini] has thus . . . absorbed in Herself the twenty-three Tattvas starting with the gross elements, and then, remaining Herself Sakti as Consciousness . . . unites with Paramasiva, [the highest manifestation of the male principle] whose nature is one with hers."[2] Thus, infinite awareness is achieved when a "marriage" takes place in the final or twenty-fourth stage.

In the *Amanaska Yoga,* a tantra hatha yoga source, twenty-four years is the time of completion for the disciple who has mastered the practice of breath control. David White, author of *The Alchemical Body,* an exhaustive and indispensable book about the tantric alchemists of India, reports that "the length of time one holds one's breath determines the degree of success one realizes, in a mounting progression." He offers a list of powers the yogin accumulates with every second, minute, hour, day, month, and year of practicing uninterrupted breath retention.

Starting with one full breath which "establishes the life force in the body," the list includes such things as "the development of supernatural olfactory powers" after a day, the power of "television" after four days, "after ten days, visions of hidden wonders . . . after twenty-eight days, one bends the universe to one's will . . . after nine months, a diamond body and mastery over the element earth," and after years of gaining mastery over the other elements, "He who practices uninterrupted breath retention for twenty-four years gains dominion over the goddess Sakti" and will retain "his integrity and inviolability even after the universal resorption of the gods Brahma, Visnu, and Siva."[3]

In Faustus's allotted time he will gain all of these powers and in his twenty-fourth year he will become immortal.

Up to this point, the composite creation myth has introduced the unfathomable god the Gnostics called Father and described the emanation and empowerment of his female reflection. Now, he moves to manifest a Son whose divinely simple but complex form personifies the infinite potential of the Father who makes himself known through the Son.

Faust Book chapters 4 through 7 refer to this process. They culminate in a pact between Faustus and the Devil in which the former's blood is drained into a crucible to be transformed over the hot coals, or fire of experience. This resembles the eucharistic blood offering of magical practice in which the ritual offering of wine or the magician's blood is designed to promote a transformation by mingling the spirit that it represents with the magician's famulus or other recipient. By virtue of his transformation, the recipient serves as a manifestation of the magician's power in the same way that the Son's divinely infused form embodies and reveals the Father. The blood pact in the Faust Book reflects this notion of union as revelation, for there Faustus gives his body or "form" to the spirit and acquires the spirit's knowledge.

4
The Second Disputatio with the Spirit

In chapter 4 the spirit reappears and offers Faustus his obedience. This coincides with the appearance of the Son in the Apochryphon of John: after the positive Light sphere called the Father has emanated Barbelo, his negative reflection, they produce a Son. The Son "attends the Father" and sings praises to him, whereupon the Father anoints him with his goodness and he becomes perfect. The spirit pledges that Faustus will gain many powers, but attaches deadly conditions to his offer. This mockery of the Father's loving gift of perfection to the Son establishes Mephistopheles as an evil force—a necessary development in the negative surface story.

As Faustus and the spirit negotiate the terms of a pact, a similar exchange is taking place in the alchemist's vessel. Mercury has begun to exert its corrosive influence on Sulphur, whose attempts to capture and fix the volatile Spirit have failed. Now Sulphur succumbs to Mercury's vitriol and, as it slowly dissolves, it soaks up its own liquid and begins to expand. Titus Burckhardt's description of this process accords with the cat-and-mouse negotiations taking place between Faustus and the spirit.

At first Mercury "works at cross purposes with Sulphur, wresting" out his "substance," writes Burckhardt, but then she offers "herself to him as a newer, unlimited, more receptive substance."[1] The elusive spirit plays a similar game with Faustus. He offers him his "obedience and subservience in all things," then "wrests out Faustus' substance" by demanding that he renounce his Christian faith. Shifting again, he offers in exchange for Faustus's sacrifice "a spirit's form and powers," or, as Burckhardt says, a "newer, unlimited" form. Thereupon, the deluded scholar begins to swell like Sulphur in the vessel, "puffing up" at chapter's end "in pride and arrogance."

While this puffing and swelling takes place in the Faust Book, the Son in the Apochryphon receives his powers and the godhead increases in number and glory. In the Pistis Sophia, the disciples learn that they have received certain powers from Jesus, "which he had taken from the twelve saviors of the Treasury of Light and transmitted to the disciples when they were in their mothers' wombs." Whether Faustus's "puffing up" is a play on this as well, the reader may decide.

FAUST BOOK	APOCHRYPHON OF JOHN	PISTIS SOPHIA
At Vespers, or at four o'clock in the evening, the flying spirit again appeared unto Faustus	And (the Father) looked at Barbelo with the pure Light, which surrounds the invisible spirit, and with his spark, and she conceived from him. He begot a spark of Light with an Light resembling blessedness,	
and proffered his obedience and subservience in all things	But it does not equal his greatness. This was an only-begotten child of the Mother-Father, which came forth; it is the only offspring, the only-begotten one of the Father, the pure Light. (6:10–20)	
if so be that Faustus would tender certain articles to him in return. Would he do that then his desires	And it attended him as he poured upon it. And it glorified the Holy Spirit. (6:3)	

FAUST BOOK	APOCHRYPHON OF JOHN	PISTIS SOPHIA
These following were the several articles required by the spirit: Firstly, that he, Faustus, would agree to a certain number of years, at the expiration of which he would promise and swear to be his, the spirit's own property. Secondly, that he would, to the further confirmation thereof, give himself over with a writ to this effect authenticated in his own blood. Thirdly, that he would renounce the Christian faith and defy all believers.		
Should he observe all such points, every lust of his heart would be fulfilled.		"Rejoice then and exult and rejoice more and more greatly, for to you it is given that I speak first with you from the beginning of the Truth to its completion. . . . (Ch. 7:10)
	And the invisible, virginal Spirit rejoiced over the Light, which came forth, that which was brought forth by the first power of his forethought which is Barbelo.	
"And" (spake the spirit) "thou shalt be immediately possessed of a spirit's form and powers."	And he anointed it with his goodness until it became perfect. (6:20–5)	"for when I set out for the world, I brought . . . with me twelve powers (which) I cast into the womb of your mothers . . . those which are in your bodies today. . . . For the power which is in you is from me; your souls belong to the height." (Ch. 7:11)

FAUST BOOK

Puffed up with pride and arrogance, Doctor Faustus (although he did consider for a space) had got so proud and reckless that he did not want to give thought to the weal of his soul, but came to terms with the evil spirit, promised to observe all his articles, and to obey them. He supposed that the Devil might not be so black as they used to paint him, nor Hell so hot as people say.

The initiate who has not prepared mentally and physically for a rigorous spiritual practice may be thrown off balance by the archetypal energies it can arouse. He or she may become vulnerable to distortions of perception or self-aggrandizement such as Faustus is beginning to experience. Julius Evola, author of *The Hermetic Tradition,* summarizes the words of the alchemist George Gichtel, who described the ego inflation that may result from a careless awakening of the primal forces.

> [He] speaks of the danger that appears at the moment when the power of the virgin is transmitted to the "Igneous Soul," because this last may then depart from humility and fall back in love with itself, turning thereby into an egotistic and puffed up demon. Nor can the Virgin help because her husband [the Soul] can neither be liberated nor dissolved but always becomes exalted, and repels anything that is not fire; so that Sophia retreats into her principle of Light and darkens the fire of the soul, which thereupon falls into a state of sin.[2]

Sir George Ripley, a fifteenth-century alchemist, had a vision that describes the "aggrandizement" that afflicts the alchemist's Sulphur when it imbibes the "virginal power" of Mercury:

A toad full ruddy I saw, did drink the juice of Grapes so fast,
Till over-charged with the broth, his Bowels all to brast;
And after that, from poyson'd bulk he cast his Venom fell,
For Grief and Pain whereof his members all began to swell.[3]

Faustus has also "drunk the juice of Grapes too fast" in the form of the spirit's enticements and has lost his sense of proportion. Now he supposes the Devil "might not be so black as they used to paint him, nor Hell so hot as people say." Black, as we have noted, symbolizes the first stage of the alchemical process, and its mention here is a signal that dissolution and putrefaction of the metal has begun. The fire at this stage is mild—like the temperature Faustus now imagines in Hell—or the warmth that Benedictine monk and alchemist Antoine Joseph Pernety describes: "It is like the hen when hatching her eggs, or like the natural heat digesting the food to convert it into the substance of the body, or like that of horse dung, or, in fine, similar to that of the Sun in Aries."[4]

Faustus is complacent now, but he will be less so when the temperature increases later on.

5

Doctor Faustus's Third Colloquium with the Spirit, Which Was Called Mephistopheles—Concerning Also the Pact Which These Two Made

In the Apochryphon of John, the Son requests certain of the Father's powers for himself and, in the first of a series of mysterious emanations from the Invisible Spirit, Mind and Will oblige him and come forth. In the Faust Book the spirit appears at Faustus's command in an equally mysterious way. While Faustus pledges fealty to the Devil, the Son and his powers attend and glorify the Father. In each instance sounds and words signal or produce these events.

Another of the underlying texts of the Faust Book is Allogenes, an account of a spiritual revelation, which contains information concerning the secrets of the Light world. In it Allogenes tells his son, Messos, about a revelation he received from the deity, Youel, concerning the creation of a Logos similar to the Son in the Apochryphon of John. It demonstrates that a certain "silent" sound is a central feature of the divine revelation:

> Since your instruction has become complete and you have known the Good that is within you, hear concerning the Triple-Powered One those things that you guard in great silence and great mystery. . . . (52:15–20)
>
> That One moved motionlessly in that which governs. . . .
>
> And he entered into himself and he appeared . . . (53:10–15)
>
> Whereas there is no possibility for complete comprehension he is nevertheless known.
>
> And this is so because of the third silence of Mentality and the second undivided activity which appeared . . . that is, the aeon of Barbelo. . . . And the power appeared by means of an activity that is at rest and silent, although it uttered a sound thus: "zza, zza, zza." (53:20–35)
>
> But when [Barbelo] heard the power [she said] "Thou art Solmis! . . .
>
> "Thou art great! . . . Thou art One . . ." (54:1–10)[1]

This creative vibration also appears in the Gospel of the Egyptians, another soteriological history, which describes the emergence of the aeons of the godhead:

> Then there came forth from that place the cloud of the Great Light. . . . And she gave birth to him whose name I name, saying "ien ien ea ea ea" three times. For this one, Adamas, is a light which radiated from the Light . . . for this is the first man. . . . Then the Great Logos, the divine Autogenes [the Son who embodies the Father and brings his revelation to the world] and the incorruptible man Adamas mingled with each other. A logos of a man came into being. However, the man came into being through a Word. (61:1–23)[2]

This Word is one of the Father's many names. According to the Tripartite Tractate, it is the means by which he conceives of himself and through which he makes himself known. In the Faust Book the word is "Mephistopheles," as we shall soon see. The sounding of his name has the same transforming power as "ien ien ea ea ea" has in the Gospel of the Egyptians, where the Word separates the light from the Light and causes a mingling of the primary powers outside of the godhead. Its very mention in this chapter separates Faustus from God and prompts him to pledge fealty to, or "mingle" with, the Devil.

FAUST BOOK	APOCHRYPHON OF JOHN
Now as for the pact it came about in this wise. Doctor Faustus required the spirit to come before him on the next morning	And (the Son) requested to give it a fellow worker which is the Mind,
commanding him to appear	and he consented. . . . And the Mind came forth (6:35)
so often as he might be called,	and it attended Christ glorifying him and Barbelo.
in the figure, form and raiment of a Franciscan monk	
and always with a little bell to give certain signals withal, in order that it might be known when he was approaching.	And all these things came into being in silence.
Then he asked the spirit his name and the spirit answered: "Mephistopheles"—	And the Mind wanted to perform a deed through the word of the invisible spirit.
Even in this hour did the godless man cut himself off from God and creator	And his Will became a deed
to become a liege of the abominable Devil,	and it appeared with the Mind;
whereto pride and arrogance did bring and seduce him.	and the Light glorified it. (7:1–10)
Afterwards, in audacity and transgression, Doctor Faustus executed a written instrument and document to the evil spirit. This was a blasphemous and horrible thing, which was found in his lodging after he had lost his life. I will include it as a warning to all pious Christians, lest they yield to the Devil and be cheated of body and soul (as afterward his poor famulus was by Doctor Faustus to this devilish work seduced).	

FAUST BOOK

When these two wicked parties contracted with each other, Doctor Faustus took a penknife, pricked open a vein in his left hand (and it is the veritable truth that upon this hand were seen graven and bloody the words: "O homo fuge id est (O mortal fly from him and do what is right)," drained his blood into a crucible, set it on some hot coals and wrote as here followeth.

Not mentioned in the text comparison is an inscription in the Pistis Sophia "zama zama ozza rachama ozai," that appeared on Jesus's vesture when he came down from the Light world and told the disciples "The power which is in you is from me." There again, a mysterious "word" is associated with a mingling of powers and a separation of "light from the Light." The unusual number of z's in Jesus's inscription suggests the vibratory sound in Allogenes—the creative Word that manifests the aeon of Barbelo.

The notion that a word may have creative or transforming power can be traced back to ancient India, where Hindu seers divined that there existed specific resonances for the various energy waves that underlie and shape material forms. The fifty letters of the Sanskrit alphabet were held to be the sounds of these "silent" vibrations and, in concert, were the harmony of God. Yogis use these seminal sounds in mantras to arouse the sleeping life force and create a spiritual body in imitation of the godhead's primal creative act.

Faustus seems to be using a mantra in this chapter—one that was given to him by Mephistopheles when he sounded his catalytic name. The passing of a sound, or mantra, from a guru to his disciple is a significant event in tantric initiation. The act constitutes a transfer of power and is intended to bestow on the recipient the attributes of the deity that the particular letters of the mantra encase. It is a deity the guru has chosen for the disciple—one that accords with his or her "divine aspect," or essential nature. When the mantra is recited incessantly, it can induce an altered state and enable the aspirant to access a higher consciousness, as exemplified by the spirit that Faustus summons here.

In sounding his name to Faustus, Mephistopheles imitates the guru who, Mookerjee and Khanna say, "whispers the mantra . . . into the disciple's ear." Only in this way does it acquire its transforming power. The mantra, thus awakened, "activates vibration channels and produces certain superconscious feeling states which aid the disciple in his sadhana. The very sound of the mantra . . . has the capacity to arouse the divine forms or their energies."[3]

The speed with which the spirit appears at Faustus's command attests to the mantra's power. While uttering it, the disciple is instructed to concentrate on a single object or figure and thus Faustus focuses on the Franciscan monk. The latter's frequent comings and goings, however, suggest that Faustus's ability to concentrate is not yet well developed.

The little bell that accompanies the spirit's appearances is designed to assist Faustus in this effort. It suggests a practice central to Vajrayama Tantra, in which the disciple repeatedly reminds himself to generate himself as a deity by ringing a ritual bell. According to tantric master Geshe Kelsang Gyatso, "he thus strives to attain the holy body (of his deity) and a holy mind that is inseparable from the great bliss and emptiness."[4] The bell is rung at least six times a day, or, as in the Faust Book, "so often as the spirit might be called."

There is also an inner bell, writes Gyatso, calling it "the wisdom directly realizing emptiness."[5] Listening for this "unstruck sound," says Omar Garrison, "is a creative act."

> It forms one of the most important of the tantric disciplines. For leaving all thoughts and all strivings, meditating upon sound alone, [the yogi's] mind merges into sound, finally to pass beyond into the ether of pure consciousness . . . as inner attunement becomes more refined, the yogi perceives directly the subtle modes of cosmic sound, like a distant tinkling of bells, a flute, a bee.[6]

Ultimately, the figure the tantric disciple seeks is his sacred consort. Even in his dreams he maintains watch for figures that come and go, knowing that his goddess can appear in various forms. Eventually, says Garrison, these shifting figures "will give way to a direct relationship with another person or being, usually of the opposite sex."[7] The Franciscan monk, who appeared previously as a gray friar and a spirit, or devil, reveals himself now as the servant Mephistopheles. In time, however, he will appear in Faustus's dreams in the guise of seductive women. They will coalesce in moments of revelation around a single dazzling figure—the legendary Helen of Greece whose classic image symbolizes Sophia, and the tantric Rupravajra goddess who is born from wisdom.

Psychologically, Faustus's inward journey suggests the *opus contra naturam,* which an alchemical dictionary calls a "turning back to the divine source against the outward thrust of nature." Its purpose is to "experience pure consciousness and acknowledge the dark aspect of the psyche."[8] With the signing of the devilish pact, Faustus will acknowledge his "dark aspect" and pave the way for the period of his dissolution. But before it begins he will return to the "divine source." In chapter 7 he cohabits with Mephistopheles and a disreputable youth named Wagner, making a threesome, which the underlying texts identify as the triple-natured godhead itself.

6
Doctor Faustus's Instrumentum, or Devilish and Godless Writ Obligatio

In this chapter Faustus and the spirit sign a blood pact in which Faustus bequeaths his body to the spirit after his death in exchange for the spirit's knowledge. This parallels a transubstantiation taking place in the Apochryphon of John where the Son, having received all of his powers, now stands before the invisible virginal Spirit as Christ, its divine embodiment. This is the heavenly Eucharist in which the unknowable Father is made manifest.

In the last chapter Faustus's pact was referred to as "a blasphemous and horrible thing," a characterization that captures the flavor of an event under way in the alchemist's vessel. There Sulphur and Mercury, the hitherto antagonists, form a conjunction. Sir George Ripley discusses it in the Fourth Gate of his compound of Alchemy.

After the chapter of natural separation
By which elements of our Stone are dissevered
The chapter here follows of secret Conjunction;
Which repugnant natures join to perfect unity . . .

Just as an exchange of body for knowledge seals the pact in the Faust Book, an exchange of chemical substances brings about the conjunction.

The metal has been dissolving under the steady fire and Mercury's corrosive action, and now, as Sulphur and Mercury are reduced to compatible substances, Sulphur fixes the volatile Spirit.

And so them knit that none from the other may flee;
When they by fire shall be examined,
So they be together surely joined.

It should be noted that the Tripartite Tractate refers to the Father's relationship to the Son as "something which is fixed."

Ripley calls the conjunction "a copulation of dissevered bodies" and, for its complete success, he offers three prescriptions, the first of which has been satisfied by the pact between Faustus and the spirit.

But manners there be of this conjunction three,
The first is called by philosophers, Dyptative,
Betwixt the agent and the patient which must be
Male and Female, Mercury and Sulphur vive.[1]

Locked in their first conjunction, Sulphur and Mercury lie together at the bottom of the vessel, a black, oily mass. In the following chapter the second and third conditions for a true conjunction will be met.

The text comparisons weaken or fade away entirely in this chapter, perhaps reflecting the mysterious nature of the heavenly event that has occurred. Following, however, is one fragile comparison—a passage from the Tripartite Tractate whose lines sometimes blend with the Faust Book in an interesting way. It discusses the terms and conditions of a pact, or a divine union-in-separation such as the ones mentioned above.

Faustus rather pompously signs the pact "Adept in the Elementa and Church Doctrine," an additional reason for associating this chapter with the passage from the Tripartite Tractate, for it reflects the special knowledge of the mysteries of Church doctrine the author of the Tripartite Tractate seems privy to. And this despite the amusing declaration by Faustus, "I still cannot comprehend," at a point corresponding to the enigmatic assertion in the Tripartite Tractate that the Father who is a unity has an only Son who is a brother to himself! Here we see the paradoxical emergence of the preexisting Son.

FAUST BOOK	TRIPARTITE TRACTATE
I, Johann Faustus, Dr.,	Just as the Father exists in the proper sense, the one before whom there was no one else, and the one apart from whom there is no other unbegotten one,
	so too the Son exists in the proper sense, the one before whom there was no other, and after whom no other son exists. Therefore he is a first-born and an only Son, "firstborn" because no one exists before him and "only Son" because no one is after him.
Do publicly declare with mine own hand in covenant and by power of these presents:	
Whereas, mine own spiritual faculties having been exhaustively explored	Furthermore he has his fruit, that which is unknowable because of its surpassing greatness.
(including the gifts dispensed from above and graciously imparted to me)	Yet he wanted it to be known, because of the riches of his sweetness. And he revealed the unexplainable power and he combined it with the great abundance of his generosity.
	Not only did the Son exist from the beginning, but the Church, too, existed from the beginning. Now he who thinks that the discovery that the Son is an only Son opposes the statement about the Church—because of the mysterious quality of the matter it is not so. For just as the Father is a unity and has revealed himself as father for him alone, so too the Son was found to be a brother to himself alone, in virtue of the fact he is unbegotten and without beginning.
I still cannot comprehend.	

FAUST BOOK

And whereas, it being my wish to probe further into the matter, I do propose to speculate on the elementa;

And whereas mankind doth not teach such things:

Now therefore have I summoned the spirit who calleth himself Mephistopheles, a servant of the Hellish Prince in Orient, charged with informing and instructing me, and agreeing against a promissory instrument hereby transferred unto him to be subservient to me in all things.

I do promise him in return that, when I be fully sated of that which I desire of him,

twenty-four years being past, ended and expired,

he may at such a time and in whatever manner of wise it pleaseth him order, ordain, reign, rule and possess all that may be mine:

body, property, flesh, blood, and so on,

herewith duly bound over in eternity

and surrendered

by covenant by mine own hand

by authority and power of my mind, brain, intent, blood, and will.

I do now defy all living beings, all the Heavenly Host and all mankind, and this must be.

In confirmation whereof I have drawn out mine own blood for certification in lieu of a seal.

Doctor Faustus, the Adept in the Elementa and in Church Doctrine.

TRIPARTITE TRACTATE

He wonders at himself along with the Father,

and he gives himself glory and honor and love.

Furthermore, he too is the one whom he conceives of as Son,

in accordance with the dispositions: "without beginning" and "without end."

Thus is the matter something which is fixed.

Being innumerable

and illimitable,

his offspring are indivisible

Those which exist have come forth from the Son and the Father like kisses,

the kiss being a unity

although it involves many kisses. (57:10–30)

In tantra, the transfer of fluids may take another form and is designed to transform the disciple into a "manifest Siva, or enlightened being." Various tantric sources refer to it as "initiation by penetration" and, according to David White, it consists of a "'procreative' transfer of yogic seed between guru and disciple": "The guru having meditated on the heart of the disciple, transfers from his own mouth into the mouth of the disciple . . . transformed sexual fluid. . . . [The transfer] is characterized by a powerful seminal flow in both guru and disciple that spreads through their bodies and rises to [their] cranial vaults."[2]

Piercing of the cranial vault brings union with the Absolute and bestows godlike attributes and powers. Ingestion of perfected Mercury can do the same, just as wine can take the place of the magician's blood; in all cases the purpose is to manifest a higher form.

7
Concerning the Service That Mephistopheles Used Toward Faustus

A threesome now appears in the Faust Book. Faustus has domiciled with a young lout named Christof Wagner and the spirit Mephistopheles. In the Apochryphon of John and the Tripartite Tractate the Holy Trinity has been established and—in the former—the Son has emanated a hierarchy of four Light powers and twelve aeons and now creates the perfect Man as well as Seth, the perfect Man's son. They all glorify and praise the triple power. In the Tripartite Tractate, the Son extends himself into aeons and totalities, and they produce glories for the Father and the Son. Meanwhile, Faustus and Wagner receive "glories" of their own—luxuries they acquire with the aid of the spirit through sorcery and theft.

Another relevant Gnostic text is the badly fragmented Zostrianos that, nevertheless, offers an exhaustive report on the realms and rulers of the upper world. In it, the disciple Zostrianos ponders this matter of abundance and wonders how so many aeons and lower emanations could have come from a Spirit that is undivided.

> It came upon me alone as I was setting myself straight, and I saw the perfect child. . . . Many times and in many ways he appeared to me as a loving father when I was seeking the male father of all who are in

> a thought, a perception, in a form, a race, a region, in an All which restrains and is restrained, in a body yet without a body, in essence, matter and those that belong to all these. It is with them and the god of the unborn Kalyptos and the power in them all that existence is mixed.
>
> About existence: How do those who exist, being from the aeon of those who exist, come from an invisible, undivided, and self-begotten Spirit?
>
> Are they three unborn images having an origin better than existence? . . .
>
> How has the existence, which does not exist, appeared from an existing power?[1]

In the alchemist's vessel a trinity has also been formed, fulfilling a second requirement for a true conjunction. Here is Ripley again.

> *The second manner is called Tryptative,*
> *Which is conjunction made of things three,*
> *Of Body, Soul and Spirit till they not strive,*
> *Which Trinity must be brought to perfect unity,*
> *For as the Soul to the Spirit the bond must be;*
> *Right to the Body the Soul to him must knit . . .*

The third requirement reflects the fourfold hierarchy the Son has emanated.

> *The third manner and also the last of all,*
> *Four elements together which join to abide,*
> *Tetraptative contently philosophers do it call. . . .*
> *In our conjunction four elements must be aggregate,*
> *In due proportion first which asunder were separate.*[2]

The conjunction having been formed, the oily mass must now be dissolved and reduced to pure ash before a stable one can be achieved.

As Faustus succumbs to the Devil's seduction, he will mirror the metal's dissolution as well as Sophia's fall from grace.

FAUST BOOK	APOCHRYPHON OF JOHN
Doctor Faustus having with his own blood and in his own hand committed such an abomination unto the spirit, it is certainly to be assumed that God and the whole Heavenly Host did turn away from him.	And from the foreknowledge of the perfect Mind, through the revelation of the Will of the invisible Spirit and the Will of the Autogenes, the perfect Man appeared, the first revelation, and the truth.
He dwelt in the house of his good Wittemberg kinsman who had died and in his testament bequeathed it to Doctor Faustus.	[The virginal Spirit] placed him over the first aeon with the mighty one, the Autogenes, the Christ . . . (8:30–35)
With him he had a young schoolboy as famulus, a reckless lout named Christof Wagner.	And he placed his son Seth over the second aeon in the presence of the second light Oriel. (9:15)
Doctor Faustus's game well pleased Wagner, and his lord also flattered him by saying he would make a learned and worthy man of him. A tune like that appealed to him (youth being always more inclined toward wickedness than toward goodness).	And the invisible one gave him a spiritual, invincible power. And he spoke and glorified and praised the invisible Spirit, saying . . . "I shall praise and glorify thee and the Autogenes and the aeons . . .
Now Doctor Faustus, as I have said, had no one in his house save his famulus and his spirit, Mephistopheles, who in his presence always went about in the form of a friar and whom Doctor Faustus conjured in his study, a room which he kept locked at all times.	the three: the Father, the Mother, and the Son, the perfect power." (9:5–10)
	TRIPARTITE TRACTATE
Faustus had a superfluity of victuals and provisions,	[The Son] was given to the Totalities for enjoyment and nourishment and joy and an abundance of illumination. (65:20)
for when he desired a good wine the spirit brought it to him from whatever cellars he liked (the doctor himself was heard to remark that he made great inroads on the cellar of	They offered glory worthy of the Father

FAUST BOOK	TRIPARTITE TRACTATE
his Lord the Elector of Saxony as well as the Duke of Bavaria and of the Bishop of Salzburg).	from the pleromatic congregation which is a single representation although many,
He likewise enjoyed cooked fare every day, for he was so cunning in sorcery that when he opened a window and named some fowl he desired it came flying right in through the window.*	because it was brought forth as a glory for the single one . . . (68:30–35) having come forth from the living aeons, being perfect and full
His spirit also brought him cooked meat of a most princely sort from the courts of nobility in all the territories round about.†	because of the one who is perfect and full, it left full and perfect all those who have given glory. . . . For, like the faultless Father, when he is glorified he also hears the glory which glorifies him, so as to make them manifest as that which he is. (69:1–15)
The fabrics for his apparel and that of his boy (he went sumptuously clothed)	It is possible for them to see [the Son] and speak about that which they know of him, since they wear him while he wears them . . . (63:1–15) [he] is called and is, in fact, the Son, since he is the Totalities and the one of whom they know both who he is and that it is he who clothes . . . (65:25)
the spirit had to steal by night in Nuremburg, Augsburg, or Frankfort.	. . . his powers and properties are innumerable and inaudible because of the begetting by which he begets them. . . . (67:20)
A similar injury was done to the tanners and cobblers.	All those who came forth from him . . . being emanations and offspring of his procreative nature . . . have given glory to the Father. . . . (68:1)

*Julius Evola speaks of the marvelous elevating properties of wine: "Among other stimulants," he says, "wine may have been used to release the fire of desire for the transcendent." He quotes an alchemical writer Gerhardt Dorn on the subject: "By dint of its continuous circulating movement [wine has the power] to extract . . . any other spirit from its body, be it vegetable, mineral or animal. . . . [It] attracts the vires of all beings infused in it: loosening them from the elements through dissolution of the natural ties: enabling the spirits by appetence and reaction, to elevate themselves above the passive resistances."

†Included in David White's list of powers acquired by prolonged breath retention are: "supergustatory powers after a day" and "the attainment of all one desires" after twenty-two days (*The Alchemical Body*, 317).

FAUST BOOK	TRIPARTITE TRACTATE
In sum, it was all wickedly borrowed goods, so that Doctor Faustus' meat and clothing was very respectable but godless.	
Indeed, Christ our Lord doth through John call the Devil a thief and a murderer, and that is what he is.	They are silent about the way the Father is in his form and his nature and his greatness, while the aeons have become worthy of knowing through his Spirit that he is unnameable and incomprehensible. . . . (73:1)
The devil also promised to give Faustus twenty-five Crowns a week, which amounts to 1300 Crowns a year	Just as the present aeon, although a unity, is divided . . . into years, and years are divided into seasons, and seasons into months, and months into days, and days into hours, and hours into moments,
and that was his year's emolument.	so, too, the aeon of the Truth, since it is a unity and multiplicity, receives honor . . . according to the power of each to grasp it. (73:30–35)

Introduction to Chapters 8–11

In these chapters we see Faustus being torn by numerous temptations even as he longs for salvation. His confusion or scattering is a necessary part of the development of the spiritual initiate, whose path corresponds to the process of cosmic evolution. In the Gnostic cosmocreation, as we have seen, the godhead's division led to a proliferation of its parts. The original syzygies, or pairs of aeons—called in some systems Mind-Truth, Word-Life, and Man-Church—multiplied and became twelve in number. In the Valentinian Light-physics system, as polarization increased, a split occurred—a whirling out of orbit, so to speak, of one of its parts. In Gnostic myth, this split is mythologized as the transgression and fall of the goddess Sophia, the last created of the twelve, for it amounts to a cosmic fall from grace.

Several of the underlying texts correspondingly begin Sophia's story. In the Pistis Sophia, Jesus tells it to the disciples after he returns from his journey to the heights. He had come upon her "grieving and mourning" just below the thirteenth aeon, the Light World's outermost limit. Much of this account is devoted to the thirteen repentances that Sophia hymned as she waited for her savior to redeem her. These hymns express the hope that sustained her in her deepest despair. They act as inspiration for the psychic soul (the soul that is part spirit and part matter) who serves humanity and struggles for perfection, hoping one day to receive the Father's grace.

Many of the underlying texts link their Sophia-Yaltabaoth accounts to discussions concerning the prospects of the various soul-types for salvation. The psychic, servant, or seeking soul receives the texts' major attention. Its dual nature embodies the cosmic split between Darkness and Light, and is the final arena chosen by the Father in which the battle for cosmic salvation must take place. While the wholly spiritual and wholly material souls are duly mentioned by virtue of their relative fates and functions in the cosmic scheme of things, they lack the inner tension or pull of opposing forces that causes the psychic soul to evolve as well as to suffer, and hence are of little soteriological or dramatic interest.

Beneath the composite Faustian character, then, the psychic soul is really the hero of the Faust Book. And while Faustus appears to be fated for the damnation reserved for material souls we find that this may not really be so. In chapter 11, the word *hope* appears thirteen times in a discourse by the spirit that seems to foreshadow Faustus's doom. It reminds us that, like the fallen Sophia, he has hope and, indeed, expects to be saved.

8
Concerning Doctor Faustus's Intended Marriage

In this chapter, Faustus suddenly defies the Devil and threatens to marry. In the text comparison, his threat is matched with the hubristic acts of Sophia and the Logos that lead to their banishment and fall. The Pistis Sophia and the Apochryphon of John recount the myth of Sophia, the youngest aeon, while the Tripartite Tractate, tells the story of the Logos, Sophia's male counterpart, who is also the youngest of the aeons who falls from grace. He creates a realm of his own in imitation of the Father, and his state of mind, like Sophia's in certain versions of the myth, forms the substance of the material realm.

In the Tripartite account of creation, the Father plans the Logos's transgression in order to effect a long-range plan.

> This aeon was the last to have been brought forth by mutual assistance, and he was small in magnitude. And before he begot anything else for the glory of the will and in agreement with the Totalities (the aeons of the pleroma) he acted magnanimously, from an abundant love, and set out toward that which surrounds the perfect glory, for it was not without the will of the Father that the Logos was produced, which is to say, not without it will he go forth. But he, the Father, had brought him forth for those about whom he knew that it was fitting, that they should come into being. (76:14–31)

The pairing of Faust's threat to marry and the stories of the willful god and goddess reflect a Gnostic view that marriage promotes fallenness, a notion expressed in the doctrinarily strict and rigidly ascetic Testimony of Truth, a bitter polemic against the Catholic Church. It condemns procreation and praises "the man who subdues desire" and turns away from the things of this world. In the author's view, that man will gain power and wisdom and eventually bear witness to the truth. These words underlie the spirit's objection to Faustus's sudden desire to marry and the latter's abrupt abandonment of habitual self-indulgence.

The Testimony of Truth is not included in the text comparison, but is referred to in this chapter by two key phrases. When the Devil insists that Faustus not marry, saying, "a man cannot serve two masters, God and us too," he is clueing the reader to the following passage, which condemns the Catholic law promoting marriage: "For no one who is under the Law will be able to look up to the Truth, for they will not be able to serve two masters. For the defilement of the Law is manifest; but undefilement belongs to the Light" (29:21).

The Devil also commands Faustus, "be henceforth steadfast. I tell thee, be steadfast," referring to another passage in the Testimony of Truth that exhorts the reader to remain virginal.

> But those who receive him to themselves with ignorance, the pleasures, which are defiled, prevail over them. It is those people who used to say, "God created members for our use, for us to grow in defilement, in order that we might enjoy ourselves." And they cause God to participate with them in deeds of this sort; and they are not steadfast on the earth. Nor will they reach heaven. (38:30)[1]

These passages express the belief of certain Gnostic sects that marriage was evil since it led to procreation. The birth of more bodies, they reasoned, imprisoned more souls in matter and further debased and scattered the Father's Light. These radical groups sought to undermine the false god's strategy by ceasing to reproduce altogether.

While Faustus's willful and erratic behavior mimics the hubris of

Sophia and the Logos, it also dramatizes the uncertain condition of the alchemical conjunction of Sulphur and Mercury. Because the two were in a chaotic or unstable state before they were united, the conjunction itself is unstable. Alchemists call it "confused Body" or "confused Matter." As a result, the mixture must be dissolved and separated again before the two can form an enduring bond. The alchemist must work adroitly with his elements here, making them "hug and kiss," as Ripley puts it, "and like as Children play them up and down"[2] lest they solidify or rubify prematurely, in which case, all would be lost.

A tantric guru who is guiding a disciple must also be nimble in his training. Mephistopheles' clever handling of Faustus to prevent him from marrying or being "conjoined" is a caricature of the fluid tactics a guru uses to keep the disciple on the path. Mookerjee and Khanna point out that, while many yogic practices require firm guidance by the guru, the disciple is given freedom to determine when it is appropriate.

> It is imperative that an aspirant should not turn into a blind follower of a guru but have an open mind. . . . No guru . . . can help a sadhaka unless he helps himself by his own efforts and willingness. Having learnt what he can learn, the sadhaka should be prepared to question and if necessary introduce experimental verifications by working on himself.[3]

Faustus's desire to marry is matched in the comparison with the Logos's "attempt to grasp the incomprehensibility." It represents a search for profound inner wisdom, not by "withdrawing from life," as Mookerjee and Khanna put it, but "through the fullest possible acceptance of our desires, feelings and situations as human beings."[4] As we shall see, Faustus is exercising his freedom in this regard with a premature and unsuccessful attempt to raise the Kundalini.

FAUST BOOK	APOCHRYPHON OF JOHN	TRIPARTITE TRACTATE	PISTIS SOPHIA
While he lived thus day in and day out like an epicure—or like a sow—			And Jesus said unto his disciples: "It came to pass, when Pistis Sophia was in the thirteenth aeon, in the region of all her brethren the Invisibles . . .
			by command of the First Mystery (she) gazed into the height. She longed to reach to that region, and she could not. . . .
with faith neither in God or the Devil,			"But she ceased to perform the mystery of the thirteenth aeon and sang praises to the Light of the height.
Doctor Faustus's aphrodesia did day and night so prick him that he desired to enter matrimony and take a wife.	And the Sophia of the Epinoia, being an aeon, conceived a thought from herself and the conception of the invisible spirit and foreknowledge. She wanted to bring forth a likeness out of herself	It came to one of the aeons that he should attempt to grasp the incomprehensibility. . . . (75:20)	
He questioned his spirit in this regard, who was sure to be an enemy of the matrimonial estate as created and ordained by God.	without the consent of the Spirit—he had not approved—and without her consort and without his consideration.	His intent was good. When he had come forth, he gave glory to the Father, even if it led to something beyond possibility,	"It came to pass, then, when she sang praises to the region of the height, that all the rulers in the twelve aeons who are below, hated her, because she

FAUST BOOK	APOCHRYPHON OF JOHN	TRIPARTITE TRACTATE	PISTIS SOPHIA
			had ceased from their mysteries, and because she had desired to go into the height and be above them all.
The spirit answered: “Well, what is thy purpose with thyself?” Had Faustus forgot his commitment, and would he not hold to the promise wherein he had vowed enmity to God and mankind? If so, then neither by chance nor by intent dare he enter matrimony.		since he had wanted to bring forth one who is perfect, from an agreement in which he had not been, and without having the command. (76:1–12)	
“For a man cannot serve two masters” (spake the devil), “God and us, too. Matrimony is a work of the Lord God. We, who take our profit from all that pertains to and derives from adultery and fornication, are opposed to it. Wherefore, Fauste, look thou to it: shouldst thou promise to wed, thou shalt then most assuredly be torn into little pieces by us. Sweet Fauste, judge for thyself what unquiet, antipathy, anger and strife result from matrimony.”			

FAUST BOOK	APOCHRYPHON OF JOHN	TRIPARTITE TRACTATE	PISTIS SOPHIA
			“It came to pass, then, thereafter . . . by command of the First Commandment, that the great triple-powered Self-Willed . . . pursued Sophia in the thirteenth aeon, in order that she should look toward the parts below, so that she might see in that region his lion-faced Light power and long after it and go to that region, so that her Light might be taken from her. . . . (Ch. 30:41) thereafter . . . she looked below and saw his Light-power . . . and she knew not that it is that of . . . Self-Willed. . . .
Doctor Faustus considered various sides of the matter, his monk constantly presenting objections. At last he said: “Well, I will wed, let come what may!”	And though the person of her maleness had not approved, and she had not found her agreement, and she had thought without the consent of the Spirit and the knowledge of her agreement, (yet) she brought forth. (9:2)	For the freewill which was begotten with the Totalities was a cause for this one, such as to make him do what he desired, with no one to restrain him. (75:35)	“And she thought to herself: ‘I will go into that region without my pair and take the Light and thereout fashion for myself Light aeons, so that I may go to the Light of Lights which is in the Height of Heights.’
When Faustus had uttered this resolve, a storm wind did fall upon his house and seemed			

FAUST BOOK	APOCHRYPHON OF JOHN	TRIPARTITE TRACTATE	PISTIS SOPHIA
about to destroy it. All the doors leaped from their hooks, and at the same instant his house was quite filled with heat,	And because of the invincible power which is in her, her thought did not remain idle	The Logos himself caused it to happen, being complete and unitary . . .	
just as if it were about to burn away into pure ashes.		but those whom he wished to take hold of firmly he begot in shadows and copies and likenesses. (76:12–2)	
Doctor Faustus took to his heels down the stair,		He was not able to bear the sight of the Light, but he looked into the depth and he doubted. (77:18)	“This then thinking, she went forth from her own region, the thirteenth aeon, and went down to the twelve aeons. . . . (Ch. 30)
but a man caught him and cast him back into the parlor		The one whom he himself brought forth as a unitary aeon rushed up to that which is his	
Round about him everywhere sprang up fire		and this kin of his in the pleroma abandoned him. . . . (78:1)	And she went forth also from the twelve aeons, and came into the regions of the chaos
He thought he would be burned alive and he screamed to his spirit for help, promising to live in accordance with every wish, counsel, and precept.			

FAUST BOOK	APOCHRYPHON OF JOHN	TRIPARTITE TRACTATE	PISTIS SOPHIA
Then the Devil himself appeared unto him, so horrible and malformed	and something came out of her which was imperfect and different from her appearance. . . . (10:1)	From that which was deficient in itself there came those things . . . from his thought and arrogance likenesses, copies, shadows and phantasms, lacking reason and the Light,	and drew nigh to that lion-faced Light power to devour it.
that Faustus could not look upon him.	She cast it away from herself, outside that place, that no one of the immortal ones might see it . . . (10:7)	these which belong to the vain thought, since they are not products of anything. Therefore their end will be like their beginning: [they are] from that which did not exist, and are to return once again to that which will not be. (Ch. 78:15, 30)	
Satan said: “Now tell me, of what purpose art thou?” Doctor Faustus gave him short answer, admitting that he had not fulfilled his promise in that he had not deemed it to extend so far, and he did request Grace. Satan answered him equally curtly: ”Then be henceforth steadfast. I tell thee, be steadfast.”			

FAUST BOOK	APOCHRYPHON OF JOHN	TRIPARTITE TRACTATE	PISTIS SOPHIA
After this, the spirit Mephistopheles came to him and said unto him: “If thou art henceforth steadfast in thy commitment, lo, then will I tickle thy lust otherwise, so that in thy days thou wilt wish naught else than this—namely: if thou canst not live chastely, then will I lead to thy bed any day or night whatever woman thou seest in this city or elsewhere. Whoever might please thy lust and whomever thou might desire in lechery, she shall abide with thee in such figure and form.”			But all the material emanations of Self-Willed surrounded her, and the great lion-faced Light power devoured all the Light powers in Sophia and cleaned out her Light and devoured it, and her matter was thrust into the chaos.
Doctor Faustus was so intrigued by this that his heart trembled with joy and his original proposal rued him. And he did then come into such libidinous dissipation that he yearned day and night after the figure of beautiful women in such excellent forms, dissipating today with one devil and having another on his mind tomorrow.			When then this befell, Sophia became very greatly exhausted, and that lion-faced Light power set to work to take away from Sophia all her Light powers, and all the material powers of Self-Willed surrounded Sophia at the same time and pressed her sore. (Ch. 31)

The reader may find it strange that the spirit urges Faustus to be both lecherous and chaste but a tantric disciple might not, for these are elements of a paradoxical tantric practice that involves simultaneous sexual arousal and control. The yogin is trained to block the discharge of sexual energy that he has purposefully and systematically stimulated over a period of time. In so doing, he reverses the rush of orgasmic energy, forcing the male and female polarities of the Kundalini up the invisible spine where they unite in the cranial vault. A nectar released by this marriage of opposites floods the body and produces a blissful, superconscious awakening. One of the methods of prior stimulation involves visualizing intimate interactions with seductive women, a pleasurable pursuit that requires enormous control in order for the energy aroused not to be expended in ejaculation. Little wonder then that the spirit urges Faustus to "remain steadfast" and not "marry," or yield to the "defiling" procreative act.

The "storm wind" that buffets Faustus's house and the urgent events that follow in its wake suggest that the disciple is attempting to raise the Kundalini. We have encountered this wind before and have identified it as pranayama or a controlled breathing technique used to awaken the sleeping "goddess." The leaping doors and intense heat Faustus experiences while running down and being thrown back up the stairs are analogous to physiological and psychic sensations perceived by the yogin when the Kundalini awakens. Mookerjee and Khanna's description of these sensations accords with Faustus's experience:

> In the preliminary stages, the body trembles and the yogi can feel the explosion of psychic heat passing like a current through the Sushumna, the central of three invisible channels in the body through which the polarized energy courses. Ramakrishna describes his own experience of the leaps and bounds of this phenomenon as "hopping," "pushing up," "moving," "zigzag."[5]

Faustus is shocked at the intensity of the heat—reported to stimulate the reproductive hormones and organs—and presumably has difficulty controlling the direction of the energy he has aroused. He is thrown into the parlor, which perhaps represents the Muladhara, or first chakra, where the Kundalini resides and from where it ascends unless a failure of will allows it to rush downward and force an ejaculation. Faustus's immobility—"he could move neither hand nor foot"—suggests the loss of body consciousness or deep trance that occurs when the Kundalini awakens.

Garrison reports the difficulty a tantric master has with young disciples who cannot or will not control their sexual energy. He quotes a guru to that effect:

> One of the boys, a Pashtu, infected with the taint of the Kali Age, did not restrain his bindu as I have taught him. Instead he is spending his seed like one devoid of all dharma. Shiva! Shiva! Even a worse thing. To the others he is saying "This is very jolly. Let us indulge."[6]

For Faustus, this experience was not so jolly, for it seems to have acted as a dangerous stimulant, "pricking" him with an uncontrollable "aphrodesia." Garrison warns that if the Kundalini is not properly controlled, "it may rush downward, bringing union with a lower order of creation. The carnal appetites are then vastly intensified. Worldly ambitions are likewise stimulated, together with the will to satisfy them at any cost. Lust, anger, greed—the whole catalogue of evil passions—take over."[7]

Some of these passions have begun to grip Faustus already, but the spirit's prescription of wine and women will actually turn out to be the antidote he requires. It is an ancient remedy and, according to Garrison, one that should not be dismissed.

> There is no doubt that the concrete rituals, including those that require wine and women, set forth in the original tantric scriptures, were meant to be taken literally. Indeed, the stated purpose of the Shastra was to provide the spiritual dwarfs of the Kali Age with a ready means of sublimating animal tendencies.[8]

Faustus is apparently not able to control the Kundalini yet, let alone to engage with a real woman, so the spirit directs him back to the stimulating but less challenging practice of consorting with visualized women. Thus he offers him "whatever figure," "form," or "she devil" he might desire. It is possible, however, that the "she devils" he offers Faustus may prove to be more dangerous than the real ones he has been ordered to avoid. As Garrison warns:

> It has been reported that some of the less enlightened "brothers of the hidden life" practice sex union with . . . she devils, with discarnate human beings; and with phantoms whom they materialize for the purpose. . . . tantric literature contains many warnings to the novice concerning the perils inherent in such intercourse. He is admonished that if these fiends escape his control, they may do him great harm, both physically and spiritually.[9]

Whether Faustus's dream figures are goddesses in disguise or demons of the "hidden life," he will not control either without first controlling himself.

9
Doctor Faustus's Quaestio of His Spirit Mephistopheles

In this chapter of the Faust Book, Faustus has read the Devil's "book"—a treatise on sorcery and necromancy—and now he receives the Devil's "Word." It is a vivid account of the evils Lucifer visited on humanity. It parallels and makes pale the reports in the Apochryphon of John concerning the evils that are native to this world. The Apochryphon attributes them to a counterfeit spirit fashioned by the false god who rules this realm. The mission of the evil spirit is to lead people astray by polluting, deceiving, and enslaving them and hardening their hearts. In a later passage the Lord returns to the Darkness as Pronoia and suffers along with humankind, but as "the remembrance of the pleroma," he carries the unquenchable Light of hope.

The Gospel of Truth tells us that the conflicts and terrors that afflict the world are produced by ignorant souls who have not been "named" by the Father and cannot reach out to him and read the "living book," that is, receive his Word in their hearts.

Even as Mephistopheles' words make Faustus despondent, the heat in the alchemist's vessel and the metal's own internal heat are causing it to decompose. "Now beginneth the Chapter of Putrefaction," says Ripley,

> *Without which Pole no seed may multiply,*
> *Which must be done only by continual action*

Of heat in the body, moist, not manually,
For bodies else may not be altered naturally.[1]

Faustus is feeling the heat, too, and soon Mephistopheles' terrifying descriptions of Hell will cause him even greater despair.

FAUST BOOK	GOSPEL OF TRUTH	APOCHRYPHON OF JOHN
Now after Faustus had carried on such a fine matrimony with the Devil (as was reported above), his spirit committed unto him a great book containing all manner of sorcery and nigromantia, wherein he indulged himself in addition to his devilish wedlock	Jesus, the Christ, enlightened those who were in darkness through oblivion. . . . (18:15) There was manifested in their hearts the living book . . . the one written in the thought and mind of the Father. . . . (19:35)	
(these *dardanioe artes* later being found with his famulus and son Christof Wagner).	No one could have become manifest from among those who have believed in salvation unless that book had appeared. . . . (20:10)	
	Just as there lies hidden in a will, before it is opened, the fortune of the deceased master of the house, so it is with the totality, which lay hidden while the Father . . . was invisible, being something which is from him. . . . (20:15)	
Soon his curiosity did prick him and he summoned his spirit Mephistopheles, with whom he desired to converse	But those who are to receive teaching are the living who are inscribed in the book of the living. It is about themselves that they receive instruction,	And I said, "Lord, from where did the counterfeit spirit come?"

FAUST BOOK	GOSPEL OF TRUTH	APOCHRYPHON OF JOHN
and to whom he said: "Tell me, my servant, what manner of spirit art thou?"	receiving it from the Father, turning again to him. (21:5)	
The spirit answered and spoke: "This disputatio and question if I am to elucidate it for thee, Lord Fauste, will move thee somewhat to discontent.	When the Word appeared, the one that is within the heart of those who utter it—it is not a sound alone but it became a body—a great disturbance took place. . . . (26:5) All the spaces were shaken and disturbed because they had no order nor stability. Error was upset, not knowing what to do: it was grieved, in mourning, afflicting itself because it knew nothing. (26:15)	
"But I must obey thee.	Truth appeared; all its emanations knew it. They greeted the Father in truth with a perfect power that joins them with the Father. (26:30)	
"Thou shalt know therefore, that the banished angel at the time of his fall was still graciously and kindly disposed toward man who had just been created.	This is the manifestation of the Father and his revelation to his aeons. He manifested what was hidden of him; he explained it . . . (27:5)	
	and he gives a name to him and brings it about that . . . before they come into existence, (they) are ignorant of him who fashioned them. I do not say then that they are nothing at all . . . (27:25) but the fruit which is not	

FAUST BOOK	GOSPEL OF TRUTH	APOCHRYPHON OF JOHN
	yet manifest does not know anything . . . for he who has no root has no fruit either . . . but though he thinks to himself, "I have come into being," yet he will perish by himself.	
"But soon the leaf did turn	What then did he wish to think of himself? This: "I have come into being like the shadows and phantoms of the night." When the light shines on the terror, which that person had experienced, he knows that it is nothing. (28:5)	
and Lucifer, become the enemy of all mankind, did presume to work all manner of tyranny upon men—	Since it was terror and disturbance and instability and doubt and division, there were many illusions at work . . . as if they were sunk in sleep and found themselves in disturbing dreams.	
as is every day manifest when one falleth to his death; another hangeth, drowneth or stabbeth himself; a third is driven mad, and the like other cases which thou might have observed.	Either there is a place to which they are fleeing or without strength they come from having chased after others, or they are involved in striking blows . . . or they have fallen from high places.	
		Then he said to me, "The Mother-Father . . . (27:30) he raised up the offspring of the perfect race and its thinking and the eternal Light of man.

FAUST BOOK	GOSPEL OF TRUTH	APOCHRYPHON OF JOHN
"Because the first man was created so perfect by God, the devil did begrudge him such.		"When the chief archon realized that they were exalted above him in the height and that they surpass him in thinking—then he wanted to seize their thought [and] . . . He made a plan with his authorities. . . . (28:5)
"He beset Adam and Eve and brought them with all their seed into sin and out of the grace of God. Such, sweet Fauste, is the onslaught and tyranny of Satan. Likewise did he Cain. He caused the people of Israel to worship him, to sacrifice unto strange gods and to go lustfully in unto the heathen women.		"They created a counterfeit spirit who resembles the Spirit who had descended, so as to pollute the souls through it. And the angels changed themselves into . . . the likeness of their mates, filling them with the spirit of Darkness. . . . (29:25) And they took women and begot children out of the Darkness according to the likeness of their spirit.
"It was one of our spirits who pursued Saul and drave him unto madness, pricking him on till he took his own life. Another spirit is among us, as Asmodeus, who slew seven men in lechery.		
Then there is the spirit Dagon, who caused 30,000 men to fall away from God, so that they were slain and the Ark of God was captured. And Belial, who did prick David's heart that he began to number the people and 60,000 perished.	Again, sometimes it is as if people were murdering them, though there is no one even pursuing them, or they themselves are killing their neighbors, for they have stained with their blood. (29:5–25)	

FAUST BOOK

"It was one of us who did send Solomon a-whoring after false gods. Without number are our spirits that do insinuate themselves among men and cause them to fall. To this very day we still distribute ourselves all over the world, using every sort of guile and rascality, driving men away from the Faith and urging them on to sin and wickedness, that we may strengthen ourselves against Jesus by plaguing his followers to death. We possess, to be sure, the hearts of the kings and rulers of this world, hardening them against the teachings of Jesus and of his apostles and followers."

Doctor Faustus answered and spake: "So hast thou possessed me also? Sweet fellow, tell me the truth."

The spirit answered: "Well, why not? As soon as we looked upon thy heart and saw with what manner of thoughts thou didst consort, how thou couldst neither use nor get another than the Devil for such an intent and purpose, lo, we then made those thoughts and strivings yet more impious and bold, and so prurient that thou hadst no rest by day nor by night, all thine aspirations and endeavors being directed toward the accomplishment of sorcery. Even while thou didst conjure us, we were making thee so wicked and so audacious that thou hadst forsaken thy purpose. Afterward, we encouraged thee yet further until we had planted it into thy heart not to falter in thy cause until thou hadst a spirit subservient to thee. In the end, we persuaded thee to yield thyself to us finally and with body and soul."

APOCHRYPHON OF JOHN

"And they closed their hearts and they hardened themselves through the hardness of the counterfeit Spirit until now. (30:5)

"And they steered the people who had followed them into great troubles by leading them astray with many deceptions. . . ." (29:30)

"And thus the whole creation became enslaved forever, from the foundation of the world until now. (30:5)

"I, therefore, the perfect Pronoia of the all, changed myself into my seed, for I existed first, going on every road. For I am the richness of the Light;

FAUST BOOK

"All this, Lord Fauste, canst thou learn from thyself."

"It is true," quoth Doctor Faustus, "there is no turning from my way now. I have ensnared myself. Had I kept to god-fearing thoughts, and held to God in prayer, not allowing the Devil so to strike root within me, then had I not suffered such injury in body and soul. Ay, what have I done, and so on."

The spirit made answer: "Look thou to it."

Thus did Doctor Faustus take his despondent leave.

APOCHRYPHON OF JOHN

I am the remembrance of the pleroma.

And I went into the realm of Darkness and I endured." (30:15)

10
A Disputatio Concerning the Prior State of the Banished Angels

Faustus despairs after hearing the account of the evils visited upon human beings by Lucifer, and his suffering mirrors Sophia's after she created an "abortion" and cast it away from herself outside the pleroma. In the Apochryphon of John Sophia is staggered by the implications of her act and experiences a variety of painful emotions. This is a seminal moment in the soteriological schema, for the material world destined to test human souls is soon to be created out of her hypostatized emotions.

In most accounts her emotions are said to be grief, fear, doubt, and repentance, although in others they may vary. Doubt may be replaced by shock or bewilderment, supplication may replace repentance, and laughter may be added,[1] but in all events they represent a descent of consciousness into deepening layers of ignorance.

There is no text comparison here, but as the torn and divided Faustus contemplates his own transgressions, the four words signifying Sophia's passion are stated openly or strongly suggested by his lamentations. Here again the mention of Lucifer is a veiled reference to Sophia. The chapter opens with a description of his brilliance before his self-exaltation and banishment from heaven—a brilliance, as we mentioned earlier, that equals Sophia's glory before she committed her transgression.

FAUST BOOK

Doctor Faustus again undertook a discourse with his spirit, asking: "How, then, did thy master, Lucifer, come to fall?"

This time, Mephistopheles asked of him a three-day prorogation, but on the third day the spirit gave him this answer: "My Lord Lucifer (who is so called on account of his banishment from the clear light of Heaven) was in Heaven an angel of God and a cherub. He beheld all works and creations of God in Heaven and was himself with such honor, title, pomp, dignity, and prominence to be the exemplary creature before God, in great perfection of wisdom, yea, in such brilliance that he outshone all other creatures and was an ornament beyond all other works of God, gold and precious stones, even the sun and stars. For so soon as God created him He placed him upon the Mount of God as a sovereign prince, and he was perfect in all his ways.

"But so soon as he rose up in insolence and vanity and would exalt himself above the Orient he was driven out from the House of Heaven, thrust down into fiery brimstone, which is eternally unextinguished and tormenteth him forever. He had been honored with the crown of all heavenly pomp. But since he sat in spiteful council against God, God sat upon his Throne of Judgment and condemned him to Hell, whence he can never more rise up."

And now Faustus suffers:

Grief

Doctor Faustus, having heard the spirit concerning these things, did now speculate on many different tenets and justifications. He went in silence from the spirit into his chamber, laid himself upon his bed and began to weep and to sigh, and to cry out in his heart. For the account by the spirit caused him this time to consider how the Devil and banished angel had been so excellently honored of God, and how, if he had not been so rebellious and arrogant against God, he would have had an eternal heavenly essence and residence, but was now by God eternally banished.

Fear

Faustus spake: "O woe is me and ever woe! Even so will it come to pass with me also, nor will my fate be the more bearable, for I am likewise God's creature, and my insolent flesh and blood have set me body and soul into perdition, enticed me with my reason and mind so that I as a creature of God am strayed from him and have let the Devil seduce me to bind myself unto him with body and soul, wherefore I can hope no more for grace, but must needs be, like Lucifer, banished into perpetual damnation and lamentation. Ah woe and ever woe! To what perils I am exposing myself! What is my purpose with myself? O, that I were never born!"

Doubt

Then Faustus would have betaken himself to church and followed Holy Doctrine, thereby offering resistance. Even if he had been compelled to yield up his body here, his soul would nevertheless have been saved. But he became doubtful in all his tenets and opinions, having no faith and little hope.

Repentance/Supplication

Thus did Doctor Faustus complain, but he would not take faith, nor hope that he might be through penitence brought back to the grace of God. For if he had thought: "The Devil doth now take on such a color that I must look up to Heaven. Lo, I will turn about again and call upon God for grace and forgiveness, for to sin no more is a great penance."

In both the Sophia and Logos myths, the defective lower realms evolved from their ignorant or arrogant thoughts. They acted in misguided imitation of the Father, whose loving thought produced Barbelo, his shining reflection. Some versions of the Sophia myth give details of this cosmic process in which mind alone is the agent of creation and destruction. Sophia's passions were banished beyond the pleroma, but being of divine nature they were given substance and later shaped by the Christ into fire, air, earth, and water, the basic elements of the physical realm. According to a version described by Hippolytus—an influential third-century Christian bishop whose Refutation of All Heresies summarized unflatteringly the doctrines and practices of some twenty Gnostic sects—her fear evolved into fire and contracted into the psychic plane, while her grief became earth and solidified into matter. Her doubt led further down into grosser forms while her repentance was the "turning" or tendency upward.

In this speculation the psychic substance, or fire, is the power that forms the physical realm. Thus the world itself is a product of mind and, ultimately, of a particular state of mind, that is, ignorance. In Sophia's myth, this psychic substance is her son, Yaltabaoth, who is called the "fiery god." The world was created from his ignorant thought just as he was created from Sophia's.

11
A Disputatio Concerning Hell; How It Was Created and Fashioned; Concerning Also the Torments in Hell

In this chapter Faustus appeals to the spirit to resolve his own conflicted state. He asks about the damned who are in Hell, hoping to be frightened by their fates into feeling contrition. The spirit's response echoes some of Sophia's hymns in the Pistis Sophia, in which she describes the trials she endured at the hands of the lion-faced Self-Willed Light power who rules in the Darkness beyond the pleroma. In others she protests her innocence, denounces her oppressors, and demands their punishment. She proclaims her faith and implores her lord to return the Light power Self-Willed had taken from her and devoured. All the while she is being tormented and pursued by Self-Willed and the other emanations the Father produced in order to punish her.

This is a test of Sophia's faith and endurance and, ultimately, a triumph of the hope that sustains her. As the disciples hear her songs of hope from Jesus, they interpret her trial as a model for human souls "submerged in the slime of the abyss," whose faith and hope will enable them to rise above the worldly forces that afflict them. Sophia, herself, does not appear in the text comparisons for this chapter but the word *hope* appears thirteen times in the Faust Book as if in reference to her hymns and to this phase of her story. The Logos from the Tripartite Tractate carries on the myth here, appealing for help from a savior to stem the discord in the defective realm he had created. Like Sophia, the Logos repents, but Faustus is unable to make the turning.

The Gospel of Truth appears in this comparison too, continuing its discussion of the evils that arise from ignorance, or "sleep." As Faustus dreams of the Devil and Hell, it speaks of the Father's Word, which dispels illusion and awakens those who are dreaming. It reminds us that the Father can never be known directly, even as the spirit tells Faustus that the mortal soul can never comprehend Hell.

He obliges Faustus, however, by delivering a gloomy report on the horrors of Hell where the damned can never be freed. It is here that the word *hope* appears thirteen times, like points of light in the darkness. This repetition points to a soteriological dissertation in the Tripartite Tractate in which *hope* also appears thirteen times. As for poor Faustus, faith and repentance have been denied him, but he still has hope that he will be saved.

FAUST BOOK	GOSPEL OF TRUTH	TRIPARTITE TRACTATE
Doctor Faustus had no doubt contrition in his heart at all times.		The Logos was a cause of those who came into being and he continued all the more to be at a loss and he was astonished. Instead of perfection he saw a defect; instead of unification he saw division; instead of stability he saw disturbances; instead of rests, tumults. Neither was it possible to make them cease from loving disturbance, nor was it possible for him to destroy it. He was completely powerless, once his totality and his exaltation abandoned him. . . . (80:12–25)

FAUST BOOK	GOSPEL OF TRUTH	TRIPARTITE TRACTATE
But his contrition was the contrition of Cain and Judas. Indeed, there was contrition in his heart, but he despaired of the grace of God, it seeming to him an impossibility to gain God's favor; like unto Cain who also despaired, saying his sins were greater than could be forgiven him. It was the same with Judas. And it was the same with Doctor Faustus.		Until he judged those who came into being because of him contrary to reason . . . he struggled against them unto destruction, that is, the ones who struggled against the condemnation and whom the wrath pursues,
I suppose he looked up to Heaven, but his eyes discerned naught therein.	When those who are going through all these things wake up, they see nothing, they who were in the midst of all these disturbances, for they are nothing.	
They say that he dreamt of the Devil and Hell.	Such is the way of those who have cast ignorance aside from them like sleep, not esteeming it as anything, nor do they esteem its works as solid either, but they leave them behind like a dream in the night. . . . (29:25–30)	
That means that when he recalled his transgressions he could not help thinking that frequent and much disputation, inquiry and discourse with the spirit would bring him to such a fear of the consequences of sin that he would be able to mend his ways, repent his sins, and sin no more.	Good for the man who will return and awaken. And blessed is he who has opened the eyes of the blind. And the Spirit ran after him, hastening from waking him up. Having extended his hand to him who lay on the ground, he set him up on his feet, for he had not yet risen. He gave them the means of knowing the knowledge of the Father and the revelation of his Son. (30:15–30)	while the wrath accepts and redeems them from their false opinion and apostasy, since from it is the conversion which is also "metanoia."

FAUST BOOK	GOSPEL OF TRUTH	TRIPARTITE TRACTATE
Thus Doctor Faustus again decided to hold discourse and a colloquium with the spirit.		The Logos turned to another opinion and another thought.
Asking him: "What is Hell?" Further, how was Hell created; thirdly, about the manner of wailing and lamentation in Hell;		Having turned away from evil he turned toward the good things.
and fourthly, whether the damned could come again into the favor of God and be released from Hell.		Following the conversion came the thought of the things which exist and the prayer for the one who converted himself to the good. (81:10–30)
The spirit gave answer to none of these questions. "As concerns thy purpose, Lord Fauste, thy disputatio on Hell and Hell's effects on man, thy desire for elucidation—		
"I say to thee, 'what is thy purpose with thyself?' If thou couldst ascend directly to Heaven, yet would I fling thee down again,		This is the thought which calls out from afar, bringing him back. (82:10)
for thou art mine, walking my path toward Hell		Once he had prayed, he both raised himself to the good
even in thy many questions about Hell.		and sowed in them a predisposition to seek and pray to the glorious preexistent one, and he sowed in them a thought about him and an idea . . . although they did not understand what it was. . . . (83:15–25)

FAUST BOOK	GOSPEL OF TRUTH	TRIPARTITE TRACTATE
		Those had not humbled themselves. . . . They thought that they were beings originating from themselves alone, and were without a source . . . the two orders assaulted one another, fighting for command because of their manner of being . . . the vain love of glory draws all of them to the desire of the lust for power
"Sweet Faust, desist. Inquire of other matters. Believe me, my account will bring thee to such remorse, despondency, pensiveness, and anxiety that thou wilt wish thou hadst never posed this question."		while none of them has the exalted thought or acknowledges it. (84:1–25)
Doctor Faustus spake: "And I will know it or I will not live, and thou must tell me."		While the mind of the Logos was open to a revelation of the hope which would come to him from above. (85:15)
"Very well," quoth the spirit, "I will tell thee. It costeth me little.	The Father manifested what was hidden of him, he explained it. (27:10)	
"Thou wouldst know what Hell is, but the mortal soul is such that all thy speculations can never comprehend Hell, nor canst thou conceive the manner of place where the wrath of God is stored.	For who contains if not the Father alone? All the spaces are his emanations. They have known that they came forth from him like children who are from a grown man. They know that they had not yet received form nor yet . . . a name. . . . Then when they receive form by his knowledge, though truly within him, they do not know him.	

FAUST BOOK	GOSPEL OF TRUTH	TRIPARTITE TRACTATE
"The origin and structure is God's wrath, and it hath many titles and designations: House of Shame, Abyss, Gullet, Pit, and Dissensio.	But the Father is perfect, knowing every space within him. If he wishes he manifests whomever he wishes by giving him form and giving him a name. (27:25–30)	
		The one in whom the Father is and . . . in whom the Totalities are was created before the one who lacked sight. He instructed him about those who search for their sight, by means of the shining of that perfect Light. (88:10–15) But to those who came into being because of him he revealed a form surpassing them. (88:30)
"For the souls of the damned are also shamed, scorned, and mocked by God and his Blessed Ones, that they are thus confined in the House of the Abyss and Gullet. For Hell is an insatiate Pit and Gullet, which ever gapeth after the souls, which shall not be damned. This is what thou must understand, good Doctor.		The beings of the likeness, however, were exceedingly afraid since they were not able to hear about him in the beginning, that there is a vision of this sort. Therefore they fell down to the pit of ignorance which is called "the Outer Darkness" and "Chaos" and "Hades" and the "Abyss."
"So soon as my master was fallen, and even at that moment, Hell was ready for him and received him. It is a darkness where Lucifer is all banished and bound with chains of darkness, here committed that he may be held for judgment.		They were worthy of ruling over the unspeakable darkness, since it is theirs, and is the lot which was assigned to them. (89:10–35)

FAUST BOOK

"Nought may be found there but fumes, fire, and the stench of sulfur. But we devils really cannot know in what form and wise Hell is created, either, nor how it be founded and constructed by God, for it hath neither end nor bottom."

TRIPARTITE TRACTATE

It was on account of the depth that they received error, the depth of the one who encircles all spaces while there is none that encircles him. It was a great wonder that they were in the Father, not knowing him. (22:20–30)

As the chapter continues "hope" weaves through the spirit's depressing report on whether the damned in Hell can be saved.

FAUST BOOK

That is my first and second report, which thou hast required of me. For the third, thou didst conjure me and demand of me a report as to what manner of wailing and lamentation the damned will find in Hell. Perchance, my Lord Fauste, thou shouldst consult the Scriptures (they being withheld from me). But now even as the aspect and description of Hell is terrible, so to be in it is an unbearable, acute agony. In as much as I have already given account of the former, thy hellish speculations on the latter will I also satisfy with a report. The damned will encounter all the circumstances which I recounted afore, for what I say is true.

The pit of Hell, like womb of woman, and earth's belly, is never sated. Nevermore will an end or cessation occur. They will cry out and lament their sin and wickedness, the damned and hellish hideousness of the stench of their own afflictions. There will then be at last a calling out, a screaming and wailing out unto God, with woe, trembling, whimpering, yelping, screaming and pain and affliction, with howling and weeping. Well, should they not scream woe and tremble and whimper, being outcast, with all Creation and all the children of God against them, bearing perpetual ignominy while the blessed enjoy eternal honor? And the woe and trembling of some will be greater than that of others, for, as sins are not equal, neither are the torments and agonies the same.

We spirits shall be freed. We have *hope* of being saved. But the damned will lament the insufferable cold, the unquenchable fire, the unbearable darkness, stench, the aspect of the devils, and the eternal loss of anything good. Oh, they will lament with weeping of eyes, gnashing of teeth, stench in their noses, moaning in their throats, terror in their ears, trembling in their hands and feet. They will devour their tongues for great pain. They will wish for death, would gladly die, but cannot, for death will flee from them. Their torment and agony will wax hourly greater and acuter.

There, my Lord Fauste, thou hast thy third answer, which is consonant with the first and second. Thy fourth question pertaineth to God: whether He will receive the damned into his grace again. Thanks to thine other related inquiries, and mine own views concerning Hell and its nature, how it was created of God's Wrath, we have been able to clarify certain fundamentals in advance. Thou shalt now receive one further, specific account (in spite of the fact that it will be in direct violation of thy contract and vow).

Thy last question is whether the damned in Hell can ever come again into the favor and Grace of God, and mine answer is: 'No.' For all who are in Hell are there because God banished them there, and they must therefore burn perpetually in God's wrath and severity, must remain and abide in a place where no ***hope*** can be believed. Yea, if they could eventually gain the grace of God (as we spirits, who always have ***hope*** and are in constant expectancy) they would take cheer, and sigh in anticipation. But the damned have even as little ***hope*** as have the devils in Hell of transcending their banishment and disgrace. They can have no more ***hope*** of salvation than can they ***hope*** for a twinkling of light in Hell's darkness, for refreshment with a drink of water in hellfire's heat and anguish, or for warmth in Hell's cold. Neither their pleading, nor prayer, their crying nor their sighing will be heard, and their conscience will not let them forget.

Emperors, kings, princes, counts, and other such regents will lament: had they but not lived all in violence and lust, then they might come into the favor of God. A rich man: had he but not been a miser. A frivolous man: had he but not been vainglorious. An adulterer and philanderer: had he but not indulged in lechery, adultery, and fornication. A drunker, glutton, gambler, blasphemer, perjurer, thief, highwayman, murderer, and their ilk: "Had I but not filled my belly daily with sumptuousness, pleasure, and superfluity of drink and victual, had I but not cheated, blasphemed God in my heart, had I but not scolded wickedly and wantonly against God at every opportunity, had I but not borne false witness, stolen, sacked, murdered, robbed, then perhaps I could still ***hope*** for grace. But my sins are too great and cannot be forgiven me, wherefore I must suffer this hellish torment. Hence may I, damned man, be sure that there is no Grace for me."

Let it be understood then, my Lord Fauste, that the damned man—or the soul, if you will—can no more attain grace than can he ***hope*** for an end to his sufferings or a tide wherein he might perchance be removed from such anguish. Why, if they could be given the ***hope*** of dipping water day by day from the sea at the seashore until the sea were dry, then that would be a redemption. Or if there were a sand heap as high as Heaven from which a bird coming every other year might bear away but one little grain at a time, and they would be saved after the whole heap were consumed, then that would be a ***hope***. But God will never take any thought of them. They will lie in Hell like unto the bones of the dead. Death and their conscience will gnaw on them. Their firm belief and faith in God—oh they will at last acquire it—will go unheeded, and no thought will be taken of them. Thou thinkest perhaps that the damned soul might cover itself over and conceal itself in Hell until God's wrath might at last subside, and thou hast the ***hope*** that there might come a release if thou but persist in the aim of ***hope*** that God might still take thought of thee—even then there will be no salvation. There will come a time when the mountains collapse, and when all the stones at the bottom of the sea are dry, and all the raindrops have washed the earth away. It is possible to conceive of an elephant or a camel entering into a needle's eye, or of counting all the raindrops. But there is no conceiving of a time of ***hope*** in Hell.

Thus, in short, my Lord Fauste, hast thou my fourth and last report. And thou shalt know that if thou ask me more of such things another time thou shalt get no audience from me, for I am not obligated to tell thee such things. Therefore leave me in peace with further such probings and disputationes.

Again Doctor Faustus departed from the spirit all melancholy, confused, and full of doubt, thinking now this way, now that, and pondering on these things day and night. But there was no constancy in him, for the Devil had hardened his heart and blinded him. And indeed when he did succeed in being alone to contemplate the word of God, the Devil would dizen himself in the form of a beautiful woman, embrace him, dissipating with him, so that he soon forgot the Divine Word and threw it to the wind.

The language and imagery of the spirit's report seems to have been inspired by a Manichaean vision of Hell, or life in this world without knowledge of God, as expressed by this anguished Parthian hymn.

Who will redeem me from all the pits and prisons
Where terrible lusts are contained? . . .
Who will save me from being sucked up by the heights,
(And) from being swallowed by the depths which are pure
Hell and distress? . . .
Who will offer to save me from the pit of destruction,
And from the dark valley where all is harshness,
Where all is anguish and the stab of death?
There is no helper and friend there.
It is all full of darkness and fume-filled fog.
(It is) full of wrath and there is no pity there.
All who enter are pierced by wounds.

(It is) dry from drought, and parched by hot winds.
Not one golden drop is ever found there . . .
Who will transport me far away from all the distress of Hell?
Not one of all the lusts, nor the comforts of wealth will help
them in that hellish place.
Not one of all their idols, altars, or images can save them from
that Hell. . . .
No one who enters there can find a way out . . .
Neither demons nor the Devil give them any peace.
They shrink and implore the righteous Judge . . .
He does not answer to help them . . .
They are forever hungering inside, within that Hell . . .
That devouring deep where hope is unknown.[1]

Curiously enough, in the midst of this crushing hopelessness, it is the spirit who has hope: "We spirits shall be freed. We have hope of being saved. . . . Yea, if they could eventually gain the grace of God (as we spirits who always have hope and are in constant expectancy) they would take cheer and sigh in anticipation." The spirit here is the psychic or servant soul who is guiding a disciple through a difficult period in his initiation and who, like the disciple, hopes to receive God's grace.

Mephistopheles' vision of Hell is apparently designed to shock Faustus out of complacency. He follows a practice of the tantric guru who tests the disciple repeatedly to break down his or her pride and remove any preconceptions that may be impeding true understanding. We have seen Faustus demand answers from the spirit and be refused, while at other times the answers he receives simply confused him. When he "puffed up" with pride and decided to marry, the spirit brought him down, not only by assigning him simpler tasks, but by reporting on Hell in a way that unsettled him.

Guenther and Trungpa refer to this back-and-forth process as "an oscillation between success and failure," and use Naropa's experience with his guru as an example.

> In the beginning, Naropa failed to understand the process in which he was involved. The inner growth that was already being prepared and taking root in him was still obscured by the many preconceptions he had. . . . Only after the testing period did any real answers emerge. . . . No amount of words would have achieved the result that came after exposure to rough treatment, the shock treatment, to which Tilopa subjected him. At the very moment in which he would think that at last he had understood, that at last these endless trials were over—at that very moment he would realize that he had again failed to see.[2]

Faustus repeatedly asks Mephistopheles for information and then does not understand what he is told. He is as confused and discouraged as Naropa, and the spirit's description of Hell reflects his state of mind as well as it does the chaos in Lucifer's kingdom.

In this final chapter of part one, as the spirit speaks of Hell, two of his comments anticipate the odor of putrefaction that begins to seep from the alchemist's vessel: "Naught may be found there but fumes, fire and the stench of sulfur. . . . They will cry out and lament their sin and wickedness, the damned and hellish hideousness of the stench of their own afflictions."

As Mephistopheles' vision of Hell brings Faustus to the point of total despair, the alchemist's heat steadily dissolves the metal and sends the elements to "Purgatory," where, as Ripley puts it, they "purg ther fylth orygynall."[3] In part two, Faustus will be "purged" when he journeys down to Hell and is baptized.

PART TWO

Doctor Faustus His Historia

Here Followeth the Second Part, Adventures & Sundry Questions

Part two is about baptism and revelation—for human and divine souls as well as for the alchemist's corrupted metal. At the end of part one, we left Faustus suffering and anticipating the horrors of Hell after being led astray by Mephistopheles. Now he makes an abrupt turnaround. He accepts the limits of his influence on the spirit, abandons the volatile life he has been leading, and with the latter's cooperation, returns to his studies with an unaccustomed steadiness of purpose. His newfound discipline is preparing him for the baptism he will receive when he journeys down to Hell in chapter 15.

In the Pistis Sophia, as Sophia sings her hymns and affirms her faith, the angels Gabriel and Michael draw her devoured Light from the emanations of Self-Willed, who had stolen it from her, and pour it back into her half-dead body. By means of this spiritual baptism her sins are forgiven and she is cleansed and renewed. Like Sophia, Faust will be washed in spiritual waters and, according to the underlying texts, will receive a revelation and experience an expansion of awareness.

Even as Faustus sets out on his initial journey, the metal in the alchemical vessel is also being "baptized." It releases the captive spirits that "rise amid odorous smokes and winds," then circulate and return to penetrate, corrupt, and transform it. At the end of seven "bathings," it will acquire new form and reveal its spiritual essence. This part of the process still falls under Saturn's restrictive rule, as indicated by the muted colors on the flying dragons that carry Faustus up to the stars. Their yellows, blues, and mottled browns are tones that precede the desired blackening of the metal, and their appearance gives assurance that the process is progressing as it should.

Baptism in the Spirit involves a massive inner struggle to awaken the "sleeping" life force and set it free. We saw indications in part one that this force is the Kundalini, the "serpent power" that induces an ecstatic revelation when awakened, dissolves the dualistic world, and bestows supernormal powers on the yogin. Indeed, by the end of part two, Faustus will have demonstrated some of these powers, having acquired them in his first two transforming journeys.

The Kundalini power is linked to the very ground of being, and its awakening requires a plunge into a hypnogogic state in which the ego's control is diminished, although not beyond its capacity to maintain a degree of watchfulness. Such practice demands unwavering focus lest the awesome force inundate the organizing structure and obliterate consciousness or scatter it to the winds. The difficulty lies in the need to control the Kundalini force on the one hand, and on the other, to let it have its way. This is the challenge that Faustus will face when he plunges into Hell and meets elemental forces that threaten to overwhelm him.

Clearly, extraordinary preparation is required for such a task, and Faustus's newfound discipline and focus on the stars attests to that. Another Gnostic text, the *Exegesis of the Soul,* speaks of baptism as a turning inward, and helps us to understand Faustus's sudden shift of purpose.

> As long as the soul keeps running about everywhere copulating with whomever she meets and defiling herself, she exists suffering her just desserts. But when she perceives the straits she is in and weeps before the Father and repents, then the Father will have mercy on her and will make her womb turn from the external domain and will turn it again inward, so that the soul will regain her proper character. . . . So, when the womb of the soul, by the will of the Father, turns itself inward, it is baptized and is immediately cleansed of the external pollution which was pressed upon it. . . . (131:15–35)

Thus, while Faustus's sudden turnaround seems arbitrary in the surface story, this and the texts that underlie part two suggest that he is, in fact, heeding the Father's call and is preparing himself to be baptized and redeemed.

In the Tripartite Tractate, the Logos who has repented begins to undo the evil his error had created, and, as Faustus begins to put his life in order, the Logos creates an administration to govern and bring order to his discordant realm.

12
His Almanacs and Horoscopes

Faustus suddenly abandons the dissolute life he has been living and, with the spirit's guidance, turns to the study of astrology. The heavens he studies represent the eternal truths the disciple Allogenes meditates on as he prepares himself for a revelation. With apparent diligence and focus Faustus develops an unerring skill at prediction, which is matched with the visionary powers Allogenes acquires after an extraordinary period of preparation.

> Now after the all-glorious One, Youel, said these things to me, she separated from me and left me. But I did not despair of the words that I heard.
>
> I prepared myself therein and I deliberated with myself for a hundred years. (57:25)
>
> When the completion of one hundred years drew nigh, it brought me a blessedness . . . by (whose means) I saw all those about whom I had heard. . . . And I saw holy powers by means of the Luminaries of the virginal male Barbelo, telling me that I would be able to test what happens in the world. . . . (59:1–10)

Even as Faustus and the spirit reach a new accord, Sulphur and Mercury are conjoined again, and they lie together at the bottom of the alchemist's vessel stewing over a steady fire. They are "engendering a seed" by their new marriage, which will have to be nourished in order to "grow and bear fruit." The mixture should be left for six weeks, says Ripley, "not rising that while," and "shall swell and burble, settle and putrefye."[1] The period of the metal's gestation is a time of turning inward for Faustus as he studies and absorbs the meanings of the stars.

And so it is with a disciple who—after being deflated by his or her guru—has gone back to the basics and is working to acquire new understanding as well as the skills and discipline needed to raise the Kundalini successfully. Mookerjee and Khanna tell us that in this stage of training the aspirant must follow a "continuous and uninterrupted physical and mental discipline," and allow the methods involved "to infiltrate into his life and actions." They use a term that identifies this stage with the metal's gestation: "He will absorb the techniques in a process analogous to incubation, until their daily performance and observance becomes as natural to him as breathing."[2]

While the skills and disciplines the disciple and Faustus are "incubating" may differ, the end they both desire is the same—the omniscience Allogenes acquires after preparing himself for "a hundred years."

FAUST BOOK

Doctor Faustus being no longer able to obtain answers from the spirit concerning godly matters, now had to rest content and desist from his purpose.

It was in those days that he set about making almanacs and became a good astronomus and astrologus.

He gained so much learning and experience from the spirit concerning horoscopes that all which he did contrive and write won the highest praise among all the mathematici of that day.

His tables and almanacs were praised above others because he set down naught in them but what did indeed come to pass. When he presaged fogs, wind, snow, [they] were quite certain.

His almanacs were not as those of some unskilled astrologi who know of course that it gets cold in the winter and hence forecast freezes, or that it will be hot in the summer, and predict thunderstorms. Doctor Faustus always calculated his tables in the manner described above, setting what should come to pass, specifying the day and the hour and especially warning the particular districts—this one with famine, that one with war, another with pestilence and so forth.

The Testimony of Truth offers assurance of similar revelations to the man who would turn inward, cleanse his soul of transgressions, and enter into the truth.

> No one knows the God of truth except solely the man who will forsake all of the things of the world. . . . He has set himself up as a power; he has subdued desire every way within himself. . . . (41:5–15) [He has fought] against [thoughts] of the Archons and the Powers and the Demons. . . . He did not give them place in which to rest, but he struggled against their passions. (41:25)
>
> He cleansed his soul from the transgressions which he had committed with an alien hand . . . he turned toward the parts of the right, and he entered into the truth, having forsaken all things pertaining to the left. (43:1–15)
>
> He began to keep silent within himself until the day when he should become worthy to be received from above. (44:1–10)
>
> He was filled with wisdom. He bore witness to the truth . . . and he went into imperishability having left the world which has the appearance of the night and those that whirl the stars in it. (44:20–30)

The Testimony of Truth seems to scorn those who look to the planets for guidance. "Through the agency of the wandering stars," it says, "they say they have 'completed' their futile course. . . . They do not have the Word which gives life" (34:5–25). In the Pistis Sophia, Jesus condemns astrologers, too, but spares the ones who are skilled, that is, those who do have this Word. He exposes the ignorance of the others when, in hastening cosmic purification, he alters the workings of the heavens they interpret. He takes away "a third from the power of the rulers of all the aeons" and changes their Fates and their spheres. . . . "It came to pass then," he says,

> that I have set them facing left six months and accomplishing their influences, and I have set them turned another six months to the right and accomplishing their influences (Ch.16). I have changed their squares and their triangles and their octagons . . . (Ch. 21:30) in order . . . that they may be confounded in confusion and deluded in delusion . . . (Ch. 21:32) and yield up the power which is in the matter of their world and which they fashion into souls. (Ch. 23)

In the six months when the spheres are turned to the right, the predictions of ignorant astrologers will go astray; whereas astrologers who "invoke the mysteries of the magic of the thirteenth aeon" (Ch. 20:30) will perform their calculations accurately.[3] Jesus's act of cosmic purification anticipates his cleansing of Sophia and prefigures the baptism awaiting Faustus.

13

A Disputatio or Inquiry Concerning the Art of Astronomia, or Astrologia

Mephistopheles continues to instruct Faustus in preparation for his baptism. We learned in the last chapter that astrologers whose calculations were correct were souls who had the "Word which gives life" while inaccurate astrologers did not. In this chapter, skilled and unskilled astrologers are compared again. There is no apparent text comparison here, but the spirit seems to be making a broad reference to a Tripartite Tractate passage in which different soul types are compared critically, just as he compares astrologers.

FAUST BOOK

One time after Doctor Faustus had been contriving and producing such horoscopes and almanacs for about two years he did ask his spirit about the nature of *astronomia* or *astrologia* as practiced by the *mathematici*.

The spirit gave answer saying: "My Lord Fauste, it is so ordained that the ancient haruspices and modern stargazers are unable to forecast anything particularly certain, for these are deep mysteries of God which mortals cannot plumb as we spirits can, who hover beneath Heaven where we can see and mark what God hath predestined. Yes, we are ancient spirits, experienced in the heavenly movements. Why, Lord Fauste, I could make thee a perpetual calendar for setting of horoscopes and almanacs or for nativity investigations one year after the other. Thou hast seen that I have never lied to thee. Now it is true that the patriarchs who lived for five and six hundred years, did comprehend the fundamentals of this art and become very adept. For when such a great number of years elapse a luni-solar period is completed, and the older generation can apprise the younger of it. Except for that, all green inexperienced astrologi have to set up their horoscopes arbitrarily according to conjecture."

The "ancient haruspices and modern stargazers" that the spirit dismisses as inaccurate appear to represent the divided souls spoken of by the Tripartite Tractate who cannot understand "the causes of things without instruction." As a result, they produce a multitude of mistaken explanations. The Hebrew prophets were the exceptions, says the author. These "righteous ones . . . did not say anything from imagination or through a likeness or from esoteric thinking, but each one spoke by the power which was at work in him, and while listening to the things which he saw and heard" (111:10–16).

The ancient spirit in the Faust Book who plumbs the "deep mysteries of God" and can "mark what [he] hath predestined" has similar powers, and—while he says that mortals cannot plumb the mysteries as spirits can—we learned in the last chapter that he has, in fact, passed his predictive powers on to Faustus.

In the Tripartite Tractate the Hebrew prophets also received their powers through transmission—through the "testimony and confession . . . made by their fathers," and it is suggested there that all who preserve the confession as they did will receive a dispensation to proclaim the Truth. "(For) in them is sown the seed of prayer . . . it appears to draw them to proclaim these things as pertaining to a unity. And it was a unity which worked in them when they spoke" (111:35).

Apparently Faustus has received an ancient testimony and confession from the spirit. His unerring skill at prediction seems to transcend mere "knowledge of the visible elements" as if its source, indeed, may be a higher power. Mention in the Faust Book of the five- and six-hundred-year-old patriarchs who passed on inauthentic information seems to be little more than a reference to the Tripartite Tractate's disparagement of the Jews who altered the words of the prophets and established "heresies" (112:17) and "teachers of the Law" (113:5).

At the chapter's end, Mephistopheles speaks of "green astrologi" who must be instructed by their elders. Green is the color alchemists designate for fecundity and refers to the gestating Body in the vessel whose seed is being nourished. Faustus, as the "green astrologus," is being nourished or "fed" knowledge by the spirit.

On the eve of Faustus's descent into Hell and flight to the stars—which, we will see, mimic the up and down movements of the Kundalini—much of his instruction involving the comparison of opposites suggests the oscillating rhythms of the polarized energies that underlie the tantric process. Many of the focusing techniques that prepare the initiate to raise the Kundalini are based on these rhythms of opposition, such as methods of controlled breathing, the chanting of certain mantras whose phonemes encase opposing qualities, and the alternating dissolutions and coagulations of stubborn or fickle thought, which work to still and then transform the alchemist's mind.

"When the yogin penetrates the void," says David White of the tantric alchemist, "he falls prey to the residues of prior thoughts, acts, events and impressions. [He] coagulates these residues into a single mass which he then melts down or liquidates through meditation on the circle of Kalis, [representations of the goddess who is associated with purification by immolation]. Through successive coagulations and liquifications these are ultimately annihilated, permitting the yogin to penetrate the ineffable void."[1]

"The process of becoming is not unilinear" rather, "it is dialectical," say Mookerjee and Khanna,[2] and so is the spirit's instruction to Faustus. By repeatedly posing opposites he guides Faustus's mind to the center, or the "void" that the heavens he studies represent.

14
A Disputatio and False Answer Which the Spirit Gave to Doctor Faustus

On the eve of his baptism, Faustus asks the spirit how God created the earth and how humankind came into being. While the answers he receives from the spirit are cryptic if not thoroughly confusing, highlights from the underlying texts attempt to answer his questions. They also seem to be readying Faustus for his baptism and the revelation that will follow it.

On the Origin of the World answers Faustus's question about how the world came into being by describing the first movements of Sophia's "error" as it creates the world of matter.

> How well it suits all men, on the subject of the chaos, to say that it is a kind of darkness! But in fact it comes from a shadow. . . . And the shadow comes from a product that has existed since the beginning. It is, moreover, clear that the product existed before chaos came into being, and that the latter is posterior to the first product. (98:1)
>
> The shadow perceived that there was something mightier than it, and felt envy . . . suddenly it engendered jealousy (which was) found to be an abortion without any spirit in it. Like a shadow it came into existence in a vast watery substance.

> Then the bile that had come into being out of the shadow was thrown into a part of chaos. . . .
>
> Since that day a watery substance has been apparent.
>
> And what sank within it flowed away, being visible in the chaos . . . matter came into being out of shadow and was projected apart. (99:5–20)

This is a realm whose watery substance is the very darkness that the savior in the Tripartite Tractate has come to dispel. He appears as lightening in the text comparison even as Faustus asks how humankind became subservient to God.

In Zostrianos the disciple receives a series of revelations concerning the mysteries of creation and the identities of the baptismal powers. Even though the text is fragmented, it is clear that a good bit of Zostrianos's instruction as he moves through ascending planes of consciousness focuses on the origins and natures of the different soul types and their relative fitness for baptism. The ungenerable aeons of the Light world are held up unfavorably against their "copies," which are inferior aeons crafted by Sophia's ignorant son. Some of the "copies" are illuminated by the light that is in them, however, and they are worthy of being baptized.

> I was baptized for the fourth time. . . . I became a perfect angel. (7:20) Then I said "Why are people different from one another? . . . And in what way are they human?"
>
> Authrounios said to me, "Are you asking about those whom you have passed by? And about this airy earth—why it has a cosmic model? . . ." (7:20–8:5)
>
> "The airy earth came into being by a word, yet it is the begotten and perishable ones whom it reveals by its indestructibility. (9:1)
>
> "Its ruler . . . (was) a model of the world . . . and an origin of matter begotten in lost darkness. (9:15)
>
> "(He) saw a reflection. . . . In relation to the reflection, which he saw in it, he created the world. With a reflection of a reflection he

> worked at producing the world, and then even the reflection belonging to visible reality was taken from him." (9:30)
>
> "I called upon the Child of the Child Ephesech. . . . (13:10) And I said, 'I have asked about the . . . power . . . in which we receive baptism.' (3:15) He said '(They are) three . . . Existence (Kalyptos), Blessedness (Protophanes), and Life (Autogenes). . . . (14:15) But the name in which they wash is a word of the water . . . for the Invisible Spirit is a fountain of them all. . . .'" (17:5–15)

As always in Gnostic thought, lower forms and processes are reflections of divine prototypes, and thus we see that the "bile," or material realm, that arose from dark waters in On the Origin of the World is an inversion of the redeeming baptismal waters that flow from the fountain of the Invisible Spirit spoken of in Zostrianos. Similarly, when Faustus inquires about the original birth of humankind, the Tripartite Tractate takes us beyond that mortal event to creation of a savior in whose image humans were formed.

FAUST BOOK	TRIPARTITE TRACTATE
The spirit, finding Faustus all sorrowful and melancholy, did ask him what his grievance might be and what was on his mind.	The Logos which moved had the hope and expectation of him who is exalted
When he saw that Doctor Faustus would give him no answer	since they fight against him.
he became importunate and pressing, demanding to know the nature of Faustus's thoughts.	As for those of the shadow he separated himself from them in every way
Doctor Faustus answered saying: "Well, I have taken thee unto me as a servant and thy service doth cost me dear enough. Yet I cannot have my will of thee as would be a proper servant."	and are not at all humble before him.
	As for one who is set up in this way and who is within the exalted boundary remembering the one who is defective,

FAUST BOOK	TRIPARTITE TRACTATE
The spirit spake: "My Lord, thou knowest that I have never opposed thee, but have ever humored thee. Except on one occasion when I withheld information on one specific subject and under certain express terms, I have ever been submissive to thee. Now wilt thou not reveal thy desires? What is on thy mind?" With such talk the spirit stole away the heart of Faustus and he confessed that he had been wondering how God created the world, and about the original birth of mankind.	the Logos brought him forth, in an invisible way. . . . The stumbling which happened to the aeons . . . was brought to them as if it were their own, in a careful and non-malicious and immensely sweet way.
The spirit now gave Faustus a godless, unchristian and childish report on the subject.	It was brought to the Totalities so that they might be instructed about the defect by the single one, from whom they all received strength to eliminate the defect. (85:35–86:5)
"The world, my Lord Fauste, hath never experienced birth and will never know death and the human race has always existed. There is not any origin or beginning of things.	
"The earth subsists as always of itself	
"The sea arose from the earth	
"and the two got along so very well one would think they had carried on a conversation	They gathered together, asking the Father with a beneficent intent that there be aid from above since the defective one could not become perfect in any other way. (86:15–20)
"in which the land required his realm from the sea, the fields, the meadows, woods, grass, and trees; and that the sea likewise demanded his own realm of water with the fish and all therein.	They brought forth the fruit . . . revealing the countenance of the Father. (86:25) They came forth in a multifaceted form. For the father has set the Totalities within him. . . . He was capable of doing it. He revealed those which he had placed within him. (87:35, 88:1)
"Now they did concede to God the creation of mankind and of Heaven,	He directed the organization of the universe according to the authority

FAUST BOOK	TRIPARTITE TRACTATE
	which was given to him from the first and according to the power of the task. (88:5)
	The one . . . in whom the Totalities are was created before the one who lacked sight. (88:10) He sowed in him in an invisible way a word which is destined to be knowledge. . . . (88:20) Thus he made himself manifest to him. . . . (88:20–30)
"and this is the way they finally became subservient to God."	Suddenly he revealed himself to them, approaching in the form of lightning. . . . He exists before them, and they have sown within them an attitude of amazement at the exalted one who will become manifest. Therefore they welcomed his revelation and they worshipped him. (89:10)
"Thou wilt observe that I have explained how from one realm there finally arose four: air, fire, water, and earth.	
"I know none other, nor briefer way of instructing thee."	
Doctor Faustus speculated on these things but could not comprehend them, for in the first chapter of Genesis he had read how Moses had told it otherwise. For this reason, he made no comment.	

The mention of Moses at the end of this chapter of the Faust Book clues us into a passage from the Apochryphon of John that answers Faustus's question about the original birth of humankind—something the spirit clearly failed to do. In this account, as told to John by the Holy Spirit, the false god surveys his heavens and powers and boasts that he is the true god, that there is no other god than he. His ignorance of the Father disturbs Sophia and she begins to "move to and fro." The disciple is as confused by this as Faustus was by the spirit's answer, and he asks the Holy Spirit, "What does it mean that she moves to and fro?" The smiling Lord gives John this cryptic answer, "Do not think it is as Moses said, above the waters." The Spirit seems to have moved beneath the waters, not above them, as the Bible says. In this Gnostic version of creation, Sophia's moving to and fro caused the waters "which are above matter" to be illuminated with her image, inspiring Yaltabaoth—who saw it from down below—to create the first man in its likeness.

We can also share Faustus's bewilderment at the spirit's account of how fire, air, earth, and water arose from one realm. A number of Gnostic texts shed light on this matter, however. They introduce a variety of fourfold primary powers that issue from the original unity of the godhead and reproduce themselves in increasing levels of density. The four material elements are apparently a gross manifestation of one set of these quaternities. In the Zostrianos text there are four baptismal powers—the invisible Spirit who is the "fountain" of all mercy and forgiveness, and the divinities through whom his spiritual "waters" flow: Autogenes (Life), Protophanes (Blessedness), and Kalyptos (Existence). In the Apochryphon of John, four powers attend Autogenes, the Son who embodies the Father and brings his revelation to the world. Another four baptismal powers issue forth from Jesus and the First Mystery in the Pistis Sophia to cleanse the suffering goddess after she completes her thirteenth hymn. In *Eugnostos the Blessed,* the fourfold power consists of the Father and three androgynous sons, the last of whom is the savior who enlightens and redeems.

Pitted against these baptismal powers are four primary powers that are evil. Karen King, in the introduction to the *Gospel of Mary,* speculates that these may be antecedents of the four material elements. In the Gospel of Mary their names are The Darkness of Death, Desire, The Foolish Wisdom, and Ignorance, some of which can be recognized as afflictions of the fallen cosmic soul. Indeed, as we have seen, in some versions of the Sophia myth the four passions arising from her ignorance were hypostatized into fire, air, earth, and water and were used by the false god and his three androgynous sons (negative counterparts of the Father and his three sons) to create the material universe.

Thus, two lines of creation descend from the godhead in groups of four—one conceived in ignorance, leading to the darkness of matter, and the other bringing the light of forgiveness. They clash, of course, in the ultimate arena of cosmic salvation, the divided human soul. The spirit's mention of fire, air, earth, and water, is a reminder of this dual and contentious process of creation and of the choice that confronts the psychic soul. It is one that Faustus will face when he journeys to Hell—whether to inhabit the carnal body that stems from ignorance, or to shed it for the body that rises from the living waters.

15
How Doctor Faustus Traveled Down to Hell

Now Faustus is baptized. As he journeys down to Hell he encounters terrifying creatures in a menacing landscape, then finds himself submerged in mysterious waters that seem not wet, but radiant. These are spiritual waters, not the water of ordinary, or "errant," baptism, according to the Paraphrase of Shem, a non-Christian revelation involving a soul-saving mission, some of whose features resemble the descent of Primal Man. While in a deep trance, Shem is instructed by Derdekeas, the Son of Light, who describes his attempt to redeem the Mind of Darkness. He descended into the waters of Hades to reveal the cleansing light of the spirit to souls who had been deceived into practicing baptism with water alone.

His words offer assurance that a divine presence watches over those who receive spiritual baptisms.

> Then by the will of the Majesty I took off my garment of Light. I put on another garment of fire. . . . (18:1)
>
> I went down to the chaos to save the whole Light from it. (18:12)
>
> The gates of fire and endless smoke opened against me. All the winds rose up against me. The thunderings and the lightning-flashes for a time will rise up against me. And they will bring their wrath upon me. . . . And many who wear erring flesh will go down to

> the harmful waters through the winds and the demons. (36:10–30)
>
> I have taken the light of the Spirit from the frightful water. . . . [and] I shall appear in the baptism of the demon to reveal with the mouth of faith a testimony. . . . (31:10–20)
>
> [And] I shall come up from the water having put on the Light of faith. (32:5)
>
> Then he said to his disciples: "Have I not told you that like a visible voice and flash of lightning the good will be taken up to the Light?" (135:5–25, 136:1–10)[1]

In this chapter, one of the underlying texts, the Dialogue of the Savior, makes its only appearance as an important source for Faustus's journey down to Hell. It is a Christian work, a collection of Jesus's sayings in dialogue form, some of which are echoed in the Synoptic Gospels. Jesus is not referred to by name, however, but is called "the Lord" throughout. He offers the disciples a vision of the baptism they are about to receive and warns them about the perils they will face—the darkness, the power of fear that could engulf them, and the terrible crossing place "whose depth is great and whose height is enormous." The Faust Book uses this imagery along with certain features of the alien Manichaean landscape to construct the Hell that Faustus encounters.

It is a dark, forbidding place and Faustus is, indeed, engulfed by fear. The challenging heights and depths are features that also appear in a dialogue involving two of the Lord's disciples who tremble at the spiritual tests they will encounter in their coming baptism. The Lord assures them that he will guide them when their hour of darkness is at hand and adds that salvation comes to those who "set their souls on high." As the disciples are reminded that the good will be taken up to Heaven, Faustus's spirit comes down, sets him on his chariot, and flies him up and away. In the Pistis Sophia, as the repentant goddess suffers in the chaos, the angels Gabriel and Michael bathe her in a stream of spiritual waters that will protect and ultimately redeem her.

As well as dramatizing the challenges a disciple confronts in a soul separation or baptismal descent, Faustus's journey also represents an important event in the yogic disciple's path. According to Mookerjee and Khanna, a disciple enters the next stage of his initiation when "He has struck a balance between external aids and his inner rhythm," and now "he must learn to control his inner mind." The methods they describe consist of difficult and frightening challenges—"periods of panic stricken tension" induced in ritual—that are a necessary part of the process. They force the aspirant to come to terms with his own inconsistencies and to reconcile the conflicting aspects of his nature: "These confrontations are a source of renewal. . . . They help to obliterate distinctions between the objects of attraction and revulsion and stress that all extremes, the individual's conscious and unconscious self with its contradictions, the ostensibly positive and negative aspects of existence, form an inseparable unity."

Tantric rituals designed for this purpose are shamanic in nature, and for the "civilized" mind, particularly terrifying. They may involve sitting on human skulls and contemplating impermanence or maintaining solitary nighttime vigils in cremation grounds. In such places, say the authors, "the aspirant's heart itself becomes a cremation ground—pride and selfishness, status and role, name and fame are all burnt to ashes."[2]

In Faustus's journey, which is no less demanding, the term "cremation ground" has another meaning. It refers to the Muladhara, the first or root chakra of the kundalini where a different kind of immolation takes place. There, in a chamber at the base of the spiritual spine, retracted semen is burned in the fires of the awakened kundalini. A number of Faustus's experiences in this chapter refer to this internal process, for the yogin he represents is making a second, and this time successful, attempt to raise the raging life force. Faustus's actions are based on an interpretation of a yantra, a diagram of the physio/spiritual structure of the Kundalini and the manner in which it functions. Faustus will be meditating on the symbols in this yantra as he moves to awaken the sleeping goddess.

In his authoritative book on tantric yoga, *The Serpent Power,* Arthur Avalon (Sir John Woodroffe) presents an analysis of seven verses from the *Paduka-Pancaka* (Fivefold Footstool) that are hymns or meditations on the yantra of the *Thousand-Petaled Lotus.*[3] The diagram, as it is described and deciphered, consists of a Lotus, or circle with twelve petals, surrounded by a many-petaled circle, or pericarp. Within the Lotus is an inverted Sakti triangle representing kinetic female energy. Sakti's union with Siva, the static, transcendental male principle (represented by an upright triangle) signifies the integration of polarities sought by Tantra. The Sakti triangle symbolizes a yoni, or vulva, as well as the three components of the Kundalini: Ida, the female lunar energy, Pingali, the male and solar current, and Kundalini, the two united. The angles of the Sakti triangle are Moon, Sun and Fire. The Moon and Sun angles are on the base line, representing the nadis or channels of Ida and Pingali, while the apex, or angle of Fire, signifies sushumna, the central nadi that runs up the invisible spine and attaches to the cranial vault—it is called the "stalk that supports the Lotus."

The triangle's position inside the twelve-petaled Lotus signifies the Kundalini's penetration of the cranial vault, while the pericarp on the outside represents the bliss and enlightenment that attends the piercing of the Lotus. In another sense, the relationship of the triangle to the Lotus is immutable, for Kundalini consciousness is inseparable from the Lotus and its bliss. Inside the triangle sits the Enlightened One, a "Guru on a Jeweled Altar" upon whom drips "crimson nectar" from the downward-facing Lotus, or canopy, overhead. The Guru's placement within the triangle indicates the Kundalini's manifestation as superconscious awareness.

The six verses from the *Paduka-Pancaka* hymn direct the disciple's focus to these aspects of the yantra as he manipulates the processes they represent. The introduction to the hymn calls for the symbolic presence of the guru, and the commentary for the sixth verse echoes its call: "Meditate on your Guru . . . there in the pericarp of the wonderful, everlasting Lotus . . . meditate always on your Guru."[4]

Faustus follows this instruction in his own way. Rather than meditate on a guru, he dreams of Hell and demands that its ruler, Belial, be brought to him. The yogin whose actions Faustus parodies is visualizing the guru as the goddess Sakti, the supreme representation of the yoni, the "manifester and manifestation" of bliss. As he does so, he measures out his breath to steady his mind, direct his focus, and to steady his semen as well; for he will need perfect concentration in order to awaken the Kundalini and then keep it under control.

In place of Belial, a "flying spirit reigning beneath Heaven" named Beelzebub appears to Faustus and seats him on a chair that is "quite enclosed round about" (the Lotus that surrounds the triangle). This is the "Lion's seat," according to the commentary on the *Paduka-Pancaka,* "the seat of the honored one." It is the Hamsa, the union of male (Ham) and female (Sah)[5]—the foundation of liberated thought upon which the Enlightened One sits. It corresponds to the baseline of the yoni triangle—joining the angles of the male (Sun) and female (Moon). Beelzebub carries the chair that Faustus sits in on his back, and—while his posture seems demeaning for a "reigning" spirit—it presents a graphic image of the triangle in this meditation. His horizontal back supports Faustus's enclosed chair just as the baseline supports the apex of the triangle, or the "canopy" over the Guru's head. The commentary on Verse 6 says that the canopy, "with its head downward, is above all," a statement that suggests, in this case, the inferior position of the apex in an inverted triangle.

A version of this chair appears in a ritual that precedes the tantric act of sexual intercourse, which represents the union of universal opposites. In this ritual, say Mookerjee and Khanna, "(The yogin) places two seats on the ground to represent the guru and the sakti, and mentally visualizes that the guru and his sakti have occupied the seats. He then begins the mental worship of the guru."[6] With or without a consort, the symbolic presence of the guru seated on the Hamsa is required when the Kundalini is awakened and the inner marriage is performed.

Faustus falls asleep in the chair, and Beelzebub carries him down to Hell. His descent is accompanied by great heat, flashes of fire or light, percussive sounds, and, deeper down, the sound of sweet instruments playing—all of which can be recognized as perceptions that attend a deepening state of trance. Then "three more devilish dragons (fly) up alongside Beelzebub," representing the triangle Faustus is meditating on. When a flying stag attacks them they repulse him while the fourth one shelters Faustus, just as the pericarp surrounds and shelters the Guru. The flying stag, or deer, signifies *nada,* a subtle sound that issues from the heart chakra and is heard while in a deep trance. It focuses the mind, which merges with it and loses contact with the outside world. "Nada is thus like a snare for catching a deer, for like the hunter, it kills the mind," says Avalon. "It first attracts it, then slays it."[7]

Deep in trance now, the disciple focuses on the sound and, keeping the triangle in his mind's eye, he practices a difficult breathing technique designed to empty the peripheral channels of the Kundalini into the Muladhara, or first chakra. We turn to David White for a description of this process.

> The yogin first draws the subtle breath (prana) in through the left nostril and thereby into the lunar channel. Having retained it for as long a possible in the abdomen, he exhales it, via the solar channel and through the right nostril. He then inhales through the right nostril, retains the breath in the abdomen as before, and releases it, via the lunar channel, out the right nostril. By continuing this process, pumping the outer nadis 'like a Blacksmith's bellows,' the yogin's diaphragm will, at a certain point, remain filled with air, the pressure of which will force open the orifice . . . of the medial channel. The subsequent inrush of air into the medial channel causes the two peripheral channels to empty. Deflated in this way, they are called "swooned."[8]

The control involved in retaining the breath in this exercise is nothing less than heroic and for the moment Faustus displays an iron will. This is evidenced by a flying lion, which suddenly appears and saves him from a "multitude of serpents and snakes." The lion signifies the triumphant will that conquers the serpent of temptation, while the sacrifice of the serpents frees the consciousness (or Kundalini) to rise. Faustus will "rise" in the next chapter when he journeys to the stars, but he is not yet out of danger.

As he falls deeper into the abyss, a "huge, flying, angry bull" comes out of a hole and attacks him. "The winged bull," says Cirlot, "along with other monsters symbolizes the whipping up of desire . . . or improper intentions. . . . On the psychological plane, they allude to the base powers which constitute the deepest strata of spiritual ecology, seething as in a volcano until they erupt in the shape of some monstrous apparition or activity."[9]

Faustus is overcome by this elemental impulse and is thrown from his chair (here called a "pavilion"—a deceptive substitute for "canopy"—which signifies enlightenment) and loses sight of his spirit. Having lost his focus and in danger of losing his semen, he falls deeper and deeper into Hell, "screaming woe and waily," when he is caught by an old ape "who held him up and saved him." This lowly creature has been associated with the Devil or Baselisk but, like Mercury, has a link to the divine. As Nature, he helps "overcome nature" and, in catching Faustus up, he arrests the latter's lust as well as his fall. Here is a tantrist's elliptical version of this remarkable turning:

> The fish which swims in the 'high tide' of a woman's menstrual flow . . . is caught by the enjoyer, the soul who is full of love. This is the tide time of the river, the overflowing of rasa (sexual fluids). He catches the fish and causes it to move in an upward direction.[10]

With a powerful thrust of will that penetrates the biological depths, Faustus, or the disciple, reverses the flow of his semen. To the accompaniment of a storm wind, terrible thunderclaps, earthquakes, and the stench of Sulphur, he is placed by the ape on a coach pulled by two dragons. These creatures represent the life force, or prana, in the peripheral or male and female channels of the Kundalini that is being forced by the pressure of the "storm wind" or "bellows breath" into the chamber where the Kundalini lies.

Common effects of this pressure are trembling, vibrations, involuntary abdominal expansions and contractions (the quaking mountaintops), and deep percussive sounds of the root chakra (thunderclaps so terrible they make Faustus think "that he must faint away and die").

Yogis speak of the emptying of the two nadis as "a death that generates new life," and it does in fact induce a "death-like" trance. Thus, we find Faustus enveloped in "deep darkness . . . for about a quarter of an hour," with "no perception of the dragons or coach," and only the "sensation of movement."

When the fog disappears and "he (can) see his steeds and coach" again, "down the abyss (shoots) such a multitude of lightning and flames upon his head that the boldest man—not to mention Faustus—would have trembled with fear." A quote in the commentary on the third verse of the *Paduka-Pancaka* refers to this lightning: "I meditate on the Jeweled Altar . . . and on Nada and Bindu as within the triangle aforespoken. The pale red glory of the gems in this altar shames the brilliance of the lightning flash."[11]

The brilliance issues from one of the peripheral channels. It is the "reddish-yellow lightning flash" of Pingala as it awakens the Kundalini, which erupts in sulfurous flashes in the Muladhara. White identifies the Muladhara as the "origin of Sulphur," the "flaming mouth" of the Kundalini,[12] which is associated with the consort's vulva. Both are said to erupt volcanically when they are offered semen, which they immolate in a fiery "cremation ground." Little wonder that Faustus trembles with fear.

Now, however, he is submerged in a "body of water" in which he feels "no water at all but great heat and radiance instead." He falls in "deeper and deeper" and "at last (finds) himself upon a high pointed crag." An Indian source says that when wine is "cast into the river Ganges (in) an hour an island called Badava will appear."[13] This is a veiled reference to the Kundalini that rises from the pool of semen that floods the Muladhara when the peripheral channels burst open its gate. The Kundalini ascends in a "column of ambrosial semen,"[14] which has been evaporated by the intense heat fanned by the "bellows breath." This column is called a mountain or island that rises from the sea. The commentary on verse six of the *Paduka-Pancaka* speaks of the guru's feet, which have the "beautiful luster of lotuses growing out of a "lake of nectar." The guru, in the "head of the Great Lotus," is like a "mountain of silver full of eternal bliss."[15] Faustus has raised the Kundalini and experienced bliss in the radiant waters, and now he sits on a mountain peak.

The universal symbol for mountain—a simple upright triangle—also signifies spirit or enlightened consciousness. As Faustus sits on the "high pointed crag," or the apex of the masculine Siva triangle, he assumes the role of the Enlightened One, for his consciousness has risen with the Kundalini. He is visualizing himself as the supreme Siva Guru, the deity who rises from the ashes of Kundalini's fire. Previously, Faustus meditated on an inverted Sakti triangle—the one mimed by Beelzebub—but there he identified with the goddess to awaken the Kundalini.[16]

Now he is torn between returning to the radiant waters and leaping into the fiery abyss and—as he lingers on the mountain top with his head "gazing down"—his posture expresses his dilemma. A dialogue in verse six of the *Paduka-Pancaka* seems to encompass this mime.

> "The head of the Great Lotus of a thousand petals, O Lord, is always downward turned; then say O Deva, how can the Guru constantly dwell there?"
>
> "The head of this Lotus is always turned downwards, but the pericarp is always turned upwards, and united with the Kundalini, is always in the form of a triangle."[17]

Now Faustus leaps into the fiery hole, but before he does he becomes enraged—perhaps at the prospect of returning to the "Hell" of mundane consciousness. The commentary for verse seven of the *Paduka-Pancaka* calls ordinary consciousness the "Wandering" or the "World comprising the Universe from all effects up to Maya."[18] This world of phenomena (maya) is dissolved when the Kundalini rises through the chakras, but when it returns to the Muladhara, or "Hell," it is reconfigured. For the yogin, it is said that true life begins when the Kundalini rises and he "sleeps," and when it descends, he awakens and "dies." Thus Faustus reacts as might be expected.

When he reaches the bottom of Hell he sees a number of its manifestations—emperors, kings, princes, and lords, and many thousands of knights and men-at-arms. All of them are roasting in a fire, and when he tries to grasp one of the "damned souls" it vanishes in thin air. According to Avalon, when the yogin makes the return, he performs a mental ritual that alternates with his visualization of Siva. He meditates on the "black man of sin," imagining him "being burnt and reduced to ashes by the fire" or, like Faustus's "damned soul," "dried up by the air."[19]

Faustus apparently succeeds in eliminating the "man of sin" and visualizing himself as Siva, for Beelzebub reappears and sets him back on the pavilion, the seat of the Enlightened One. He carries him home to his bed, still asleep, and when Faustus wakes up in the morning he writes down all he had seen, a practice the tantric disciple is encouraged to follow after every "dream."

At the end of the comparison we will consider the symbols and actions in this chapter from the Gnostic, Hermetic, and alchemical points of view.

FAUST BOOK

With each passing day Doctor Faustus's end drew closer and he was now come into his eighth year, having been for the most part of the time engaged in inquiry, study, questioning, and *disputationes*.

In these days he again did dream of Hell,

and it caused him to again summon his servant, the spirit Mephistopheles, demanding that he call his own Lord, Belial, unto him.

The spirit agreed to do this, but instead of Belial a devil was sent who called himself Beelzebub, a flying spirit reigning beneath the Heaven.

When he asked what Doctor Faustus desired of him, Faustus asked whether it could not be arranged for a spirit to conduct him into Hell and out again, so that he might mark the nature, fundament, quality, and substance of Hell.

"Yes, answered Beelzebub, I will come at midnight and fetch thee."

Well, when it got pitch dark Beelzebub appeared unto him

bearing on his back a bone chair, which was quite enclosed round about. Here Doctor Faustus took a seat and they flew away.

Now hear how the devil did mystify and gull him, so that he had no other notion than that he really had been in Hell.

FAUST BOOK

He bare him into the air, where Doctor Faustus fell asleep just as if he were lying in a warm bath.

Soon after he came upon a mountain of a great island, high above which sulphur, pitch, and flashes of fire blew and crashed with such a tumult that Dr. Faustus awoke when his devilish dragon swooped down into the abyss.

Although all was violently burning round about him, he sensed neither heat nor fire, but rather little breezes as in May. Then he heard many different instruments whose music was exceeding sweet, but bright as shone the fire, he could see no one playing, nor durst he ask, questions having been strictly forbidden him.

Meanwhile, three more devilish dragons had flown up alongside Beelzebub. They were just like him and they went flying off ahead of him as he penetrated further into the abyss. Now a great flying stag with mighty antlers and many points came at Doctor Faustus and would have dashed him off his chair and into the abyss. It frightened him greatly, but the three dragons flying ahead repulsed the hart. When he was better come down into the *spelunca,* he could see hovering about him a great multitude of serpents and snakes, the latter being unspeakably big.

Flying lions came to his aid this time. They wrestled and struggled with the great snakes until they conquered them, so that he passed through safely and well.

When Doctor Faustus had assumed a greater depth, he saw a huge, flying angry bull come forth out of a hole, which might have been an old gate.

DIALOGUE OF THE SAVIOR

The Savior said to his disciples, "Already the time has come, brothers, for us to abandon our labors and stand at rest. For whoever stands at rest will rest forever.

"And I say to you that are afraid . . . the wrath is fearful. (120:5–15)

"But when I came, I opened the path, and taught them about the passage which they will traverse, the elect and solitary, who have known the Father . . ." (120:25)

FAUST BOOK	DIALOGUE OF THE SAVIOR	PISTIS SOPHIA
Bellowing and raging, he charged Faustus, goring his seat with such force as to overturn the pavilion, dragon and Faustus, who now did fall off from his chair into the abyss, down and down, screaming woe and waily, and thinking: "All is over now." He could no longer see his spirit, but at last an old wrinkled ape caught him up as he fell, held him, and saved him.		The First Mystery again continued and said: "It came to pass that my Father sent me to save Pistis Sophia out of the chaos . . .
But then a thick, dark fog fell upon Hell, so that he could not see anything at all.	"I will teach you. When the time of dissolution arrives, the first power of darkness will come upon you." (122:1–5)	
Until presently a cloud opened up, out of which climbed two big dragons pulling a coach along after them.		"I called down Gabriel and Michael out of the aeons . . . and I gave unto them my Light-stream and let them go down into the chaos to help Pistis Sophia.
	Judas (said,) "Tell me, Lord, how it is that . . . which shakes the earth moves."	
The old ape was setting Faustus up on it	The Lord picked up a stone and held it in his hand, saying . . . "That which supports the earth is that which supports the Heaven.	
when there arose such a storm wind with terrible thunderclaps and stench of sulphur and quaking of the mountain or abyss that Faustus thought he must faint away and die.	"For the earth does not move. Were it to move it would fall. But it neither moves nor falls, in order that the first word might not fail." (132:20, 133:1–10)	

FAUST BOOK	DIALOGUE OF THE SAVIOR	PISTIS SOPHIA
	Matthew said, "Lord, I want to see that place of life where there is no wickedness but rather there is pure light."	
He was indeed enveloped in a deep darkness for about a quarter of an hour, during which time he had no perception of the dragons or the coach,	The Lord said, "Brother Matthew, you cannot see it as long as you are carrying flesh around."	
but he did have a perception of movement.	Matthew said, "Lord, even if I will not be able to see it, let me know it." (132:5–15)	
Again the thick fog disappeared and he could see his steeds and coach.	(And) the Lord said to the disciples, "If one does not stand in the darkness he will not be able to see the light." (133:25)	
Down the abyss shot such a multitude of lightning and flames upon his head that the boldest man—not to mention Faustus—would have trembled for fear. The next thing he perceived was a great turbid body of water. His dragons entered it and submerged. Yet Faustus felt no water at all, but great heat and radiance instead.		"And straightaway, when they had brought down the Light-stream into the chaos, it shone most exceedingly in the whole of the chaos and spread itself over all their regions. And when the emanations of Self-Willed had seen the great Light of that stream, they were terror stricken one with the other." (Ch. 64:129)
The current and waves beat upon him until he again lost both steeds and went falling deeper and deeper into the terror of the water.	(The Lord said to the disciples) "He who knows not the works of perfection knows nothing. If one does not first understand the water he does not know anything. For what is the use for him to receive baptism in it?" (134:5)	

FAUST BOOK	DIALOGUE OF THE SAVIOR
At last he found himself upon a high, pointed crag	"But since you have overcome every word that is upon the earth . . . he will take you up to the mountain. . . .
and here he sat, feeling half dead.	"For the crossing place is fearful before you . . .
He looked about but as he was able to see and hear no one, he began gazing on down into the abyss.	its depth is great and its height is enormous." (124:1)
	Judas said, "Tell us, Lord, what was before the heaven and the earth existed?"
A little breeze arose. All around him there was naught but water.	"There was darkness and water and spirit upon water.
He thought to himself: "What shall I do now, being forsaken even by the spirits of Hell?	"And I say to you, what you seek after and inquire after is within you. . . ." (127:20, 128:1)
Why thou must hurl thyself either into the water or into the abyss."	Judas raised his eyes and saw an exceedingly high place, and he saw the place of the abyss below. Judas said to Matthew, "Brother, who will be able to climb up to such a height or down to the bottom of the abyss? For there is a tremendous fire there and something very fearful."
At this thought he fell into a rage,	
	At that moment a Word came forth from it. . . . And the Son of Man greeted them and said to them,
and in a mad, crazy despair he leapt into a fiery hole,	"A seed from a power was deficient and went down to the abyss of the earth.
calling out as he cast himself in: "Now spirits accept my offering. I have earned it. My soul has caused it."	"And the greatness remembered it and sent the Word to it."
Well, just at the moment when he hurled himself head over heels and went tumbling down, such a frightful loud tumult and banging assailed his ears, and the mountain peak shook so furiously that he thought many big cannons must have been set off.	

FAUST BOOK

But he had only come to the bottom of Hell. Here there were many worthy personages in a fire: emperors, kings, princes, and lords, many thousand knights at arms.

DIALOGUE OF THE SAVIOR

Then his disciples were amazed at all the things that he had said to them and they accepted them on faith.

And they concluded that it is useless to regard wickedness.

FAUST BOOK

A cool stream ran along at the edge of the fire, and some were drinking, refreshing themselves, and bathing,

but some were fleeing from its cold, back into the fire.

Doctor Faustus stepped up, thinking he might seize one of the damned souls, but even when he thought he had one in his hand it would vanish.

On account of the intense heat he knew he could not stay in this vicinity, and he was seeking some way out when his spirit Beelzebub came with the pavilion. Doctor Faustus took a seat and away they soared,

for he could not have endured the thunderclaps, fog, fumes, sulphur, water, cold, and heat, particularly since it was compounded with wailing, weeping, and moaning of woe, anguish, and pain. Now Doctor Faustus had not been at home for a long while. His famulus felt sure that if he had achieved his desire of seeing Hell, he must have seen more than he had bargained for and would never come back.

But even while he was thinking thus, Doctor Faustus, asleep in his pavilion, came flying home in the night and was cast, still asleep, in his bed. When he awoke early the next morning and beheld the light of dawn, he felt exactly as if he had been imprisoned in a dark tower.

At a somewhat later date, he became acquainted only with the fire of Hell, and with the effects of those flames, but now he lay in bed trying to recollect what he had seen in Hell. At first he was firmly convinced that he had been there and had seen it, but then he began to doubt himself, and assumed that the Devil had charmed a vision before his eyes.

And this is true, for he had not seen Hell, else he would not have spent the rest of his life trying to get there. This history and account of what he saw in Hell—or in a vision—was written down by Doctor Faustus himself and afterward found in his own handwriting upon a piece of paper in a locked book.

Faustus's underworld journey, or baptism, mimics the structure of a classic spiritual death and rebirth experience. As he plunges into Hell and out again he follows the circular path of renewal traced by Sophia and the other Light Souls we have encountered. G. R. S. Mead summarizes a Naassene treatise, which interprets Jacob's vision as a baptism: "It is not the mere symbolical washing with physical water, but . . . the descent of the spirit down the ladder of evolution, the Stream of the Logos flowing downward, and then again upward, through the Gate of the Lord." The spirit who descends down the ladder of evolution is represented as the "dead," says Mead, "because it was buried in the tomb and sepulchre of the body. Wherefore the saying, 'Ye are the whitened sepulchres filled within with the bones of the dead . . . for the living man is not in you.'"

Faustus's "bone chair . . . quite enclosed round about" is this tomb or whitened sepulcher. It is filled with the "bones of the dead," that is, with Faustus, who lies sleeping or "dead" inside. In the Naassene treatise, the "living man," or spirit, is not inside the tomb of the body, and in the Faust Book, the spirit is not in Faustus's chair. Beelzebub is on the outside, carrying the chair on his back—burdened, as it were, by the unenlightened state to which he has descended. As the Naassene writer put it, he is "brought down the stream of the Logos from the Heavenly Man above to the plasm of clay." "The spirit is thus made slave to the demiurge of the world," says Mead, "to the fiery, passionate god of creation,"[20] or the god whose presence is signaled in the Faust Book by the flashes of lightening and fire that make Faustus tremble throughout his journey to Hell.

When the bone chair is considered in its context it proves to have alchemical significance as well. Beelzebub, the "flying spirit," appears with the bone chair at night when it is "pitch dark" and Faustus falls asleep in it (that is, dies) "as if he were lying in a warm bath." In the alchemical process, when the metal starts to dissolve it is placed in a sealed vessel and simmered in its own juices. If all goes well, it begins to turn black; as it rots, it deepens with an intensity variously described as "hellish" or "pitchy." The bone chair, then, is the alchemist's retort in which the imperfect, or "dead" metal is decomposing.

The chair is also a locus of magical transformations. The succession of battling monsters that Faustus encounters in the abyss indicates a series of dynamic exchanges that are taking place in the vessel. A flying stag, whose wings suggest that he is a volatile spirit, almost knocks Faustus off of his chair—he must be controlled and fixed by Sulphur. Three dragons who are flying in formation join Faustus's spirit "who is just like them" and together they repulse the stag. This foursome represents the natural order of the elements, or the "fourfold wheel" that the sixteenth-century alchemist Michael Maier says "rules this fiery work." The alchemist is rotating the elements and, by carefully controlling his fire, he captures the volatile spirit and marries it to Sulphur. The winged lions who triumph over the serpents, or chaotic tendencies of the base metal, represent this marriage of Sulphur and Mercury, or Spirit and Soul.

But now they must be sacrificed, for, as Philalethes says in his interpretation of Ripley's vision: "Before the renovation of these natures they must first pass through the eclipse, both of Sun and Moon and the darkness of Purgatory, which is the Gate of Blackness."[21]

When Faustus descends into the spelunca he confronts a "hole that might have been an old gate." This is the gate of the lower mysteries, or the turning point in the spiritual depths where the sinner casts off the body and rises above his carnal nature. Indeed, when the angry bull flies out of the gate, Faustus falls out of his chair—"The dead shall leap forth from their tombs," says the Naassene treatise, "regenerated, spiritual men, not carnal"—and leaves the angry bull down below.

In the alchemist's vessel, spirits are also released. They rise from the corrupted Body in the form of vapors and begin to circulate, just as Faustus did.* Circulation of the vapors and spirits is a relentless process that will slowly dissolve the metal's structure by stimulating its internal fire. Philalethes tells us that these vapors "condensing hourly, and ever and anon running down like little veins in drops, do enter the Body

*In fact, Faustus circulated twice—down to the gate and up to the mountain, then down and up from the fiery abyss. The alchemical process is said to require seven circulations, and seven is the number of flying journeys that Faustus will take.

marvelously . . . [piercing] the very profundity of it . . . till at length it be completely putrefied."

Thus, the metal will receive a deadly baptism, but one that will enable it to assume a newer and nobler form. Faustus is "baptized," too, in the "terror" of mysterious waters, and as he "pierces the profundity" of Hell and falls out of his coach he undergoes his own transformation. An old ape picks him up and saves him. Here, the ape—who has been linked to the dual-natured deities Hermes and Mercurius—demonstrates his transforming capacity. He catches the falling Faustus who is "screaming woe and waily" and sets him in a coach that carries him up and away.

But now a "thick, dark fog" falls upon Hell and Faustus can "no longer see his spirit." The alchemist is having a similar problem, for thick vapors begin to circulate wildly in his vessel. "The spirits," says Philalethes, arising "like Smoak or Wind, sticketh to the concave of the glass" so that "the artist must proceed . . . more by skill and reason, or the eye of the mind than of the body." Now Earth and water are beginning to lose their identities, and when this happens, says Philalethes, "when the Body begins a little to put on the nature of Water, and the Water of the Body, then it is compared to two Dragons."

The coach that Faustus rides in is pulled by two dragons. They enter a turbid body of water and are submerged "in great heat that felt to Faustus like no heat at all." These are spiritual waters, but they also indicate the delicate process that is under way in the alchemist's vessel. The water is drawn out of the Earth and is then returned to it. (Faustus loses his dragons and "falls deeper in the water" then finds himself "at last upon a high, pointed crag.") The alchemist is rotating the elements here, moving from one to another, and skillfully alternating moisture and dryness. Now Faustus must choose between the terror of the water or the fire. A little breeze arises and he leaps into the fiery abyss. Here the heat is carefully controlled in the furnace—"You must govern your fire," says Philalethes, "that your spirits be not so exalted that the Earth want them and they return no more."

When Faustus reaches the bottom of Hell he sees "many worthy personages in a fire" and the rotation continues: "A cool stream ran along at the edge of the fire, and here some were drinking, refreshing themselves and bathing, but some were fleeing from its cold, back into the fire." A passage from Ripley explains: "Sometimes our tree must be burnt by the Sun and then soon after be killed by Water. So that by these means it can be made to rot, now in wet, now again in dry, now in great heat and now in cold shall cause it putrefy."[22] Thus, as Faustus flies away in his second "circulation," putrefaction is proceeding according to the alchemist's plan.

As the chapter closes, the sleeping Faustus flies home in his pavilion and is cast "still asleep in his bed." On awakening in the morning he doubts if he really saw Hell and wonders "if the Devil had charmed a vision before his eyes." Even as he wonders, in the Naassene treatise, Hermes is holding a rod in his hand that is "beautiful, golden, wherewith he spellbinds the eyes of men, whomsoever he would, and wakes them again from sleep."[23]

In chapter 16, the "awakened" Faustus will journey to Heaven with newly acquired visionary powers.

16
How Doctor Faustus Journeyed Up to the Stars

After Faustus's journey down to Hell he reports to a friend, telling him that one night he lay dreaming in bed when he was called by a mysterious voice and carried up to Heaven. His journey to the stars is inspired in part by the Divine Pymander, a Hermetic text whose cosmology envisions an energized bipolar universe that issues from a single, all encompassing, unknowable source—one that is similar to the Gnostic Father. Unlike the Gnostic works, however, the Pymander's attitude toward creation is positive and the human being is an image of God who inspires his love. Evil exists in the universe only from "rust" or the accumulation of waste.

Before his ascent, Faustus lies dreaming in bed when he hears a roaring voice and is taken up to the stars. We assume that his ascent, like other shamanic journeys, is the product of an altered state, and in this we are supported by the report in the Divine Pymander, where a disciple is called by a *nous,* or Mind of God, and receives a revelation while in a state of trance.

> Thought in me on a time concerning the Entities and my meditation having been exceedingly sublimed, and my bodily senses also calmed down like as those oppressed in sleep from satiety, luxury or fatigue of body,

> I supposed someone of very great magnitude, with indefinite dimension, happening to call out my name, and saying to me, "What wishest thou to hear and to contemplate; what, having understood, to learn and to know?"
>
> I say, "I wish to learn the Entities, and to understand the nature of them, and to know the God; this," I said, "I wish to hear."
>
> He said to me again, "Have in mind whatsoever things thou wishest to learn, and I will teach thee."[1]

A similar Call is heard in the Apochryphon of John—shown in the text comparison—where the Savior calls out to a sleeping soul who rises and becomes immortal. These sleeping or altered states, which are part of the baptismal experience, open the disciple to the higher awareness represented by the Call.

The classic version of the Call to a sleeping soul appears in Mani's creation myth where Primal Man lies asleep in the Darkness and is called to remembering by the Living Spirit. While his sleep refers to a state of ignorance, he is nevertheless open to the call and hears it coming to him from the world of Light.

> Then the Living Spirit called with a loud voice, and the voice of the Living Spirit became like unto a sharp sword and laid bare the form of the Primal Man.

The hero savior answered the Call by asking "How is it with our Fathers, the sons of Light in their city?"

> And the Call said unto him: "It is well with them." And Call and Answer joined each other and ascended to the Mother of Life and to the Living Spirit.[2]

As this passage demonstrates, the answer to the Call may come in the form of a question or questions, and Faustus's response to the roaring voice that tells him to get up and see his heart's desire seems to reflect that tradition. "I will follow thee," he says, "but on one condition; that I may ask any question I like."

The Call and Answer is hypostatized in Mani's myth ("the Living Spirit put on the Call, and the Mother of Life put on the Answer, her beloved Son"), and ritualized in the broader tradition. It was elevated to a central position in the Manichaean salvation plan where it may have served as a mystical model of the soul's redemption through communion with God.[3]

Faustus seems to identify himself with Primal Man in his report to his friend. He distinguishes himself from his old companion by reciting the number of subjects they had each studied in the past. Where his friend had studied four, Faustus studied five, having added *theologia* to his list. This addition gives Faustus more or less divine credentials, for his five studies are reminiscent of the five Light souls Primal Man carried with him into battle. Faustus's journey to the stars is an analog of Primal Man's ascension after he received the Living Spirit's Call. Faustus hints at his divinity again when he tells his mortal companion, "But I was not like unto you." This echoes the sentiment of the Pilgrim Savior in the Hymn of the Pearl who carried five burdens of knowledge with him when he entered this world. "I was a stranger," he declared, "to my fellow dwellers in the inn."

In the Pistis Sophia, there is also a "call and answer" between Jesus and the disciples. They question him about the quality of Light in one of the heavenly regions, anticipating the radiance Faustus will encounter on his journey to the stars.

FAUST BOOK

This record was also found among his possessions, having been composed and indicted in his own hand and addressed to one of his close companions, a physic in Leipzig named Jonas Victor. The contents were as followeth.

I yet remember, as ye no doubt do, too, our school days in Wittemberg, where ye at first devoted yourself to *medicina, astronomia, astrologia, geometria,* so that ye are now a *mathematicus* and *physicus.* But I was not like unto you. I, as ye well know, did study *theologia*—although I nevertheless became your equal in the arts ye studied, too.

FAUST BOOK

Now, as to your request that I report some few matters unto you and give you my advice: I neither being accustomed to denying you aught, nor having ever refused to report aught to you, am still your servant, whom ye shall ever find and know to be such.

I do express my gratitude for the honor and praise, which ye accord me.

In your epistle ye make mention of mine ascension unto Heaven among the stars,

for ye have heard about it, and ye write requesting that I might inform you whether it be so or not, sithence such a thing doth seem to you quite impossible. Ye remark in addition that it must have occurred with the aid of the Devil or of sorcery. "Ay, how wilt thou bet, Fritz?" quoth the clown to the emperor when asked if he had sullied his breeches.

Well, whatever means might have been used, it hath finally been accomplished, and of this *figura, actus,* and event I can make you the following report.

One night I could not go to sleep but lay thinking about my almanacs and horoscopes and about the properties and arrangements of the Heavens, how man—or some of the physics—hath measured those ornaments and would interpret them, even though he cannot really visualize such things and must hence base his interpretations quite arbitrarily on books and the tenets in them.

PISTIS SOPHIA

It came to pass . . . that Mary came forward, adored the feet of Jesus and said: "My Lord, be not wroth with me if I question thee. . . . For thou hast said unto us aforetime: 'Seek that ye may find, and knock that it may be opened unto you. For everyone who seeketh shall find, and to everyone who knocketh, it shall be opened.'

"Because thou in the mind hast given us mind of the Light and . . . an exceedingly exalted thought;

for which cause, therefore, no one existeth in the world of men nor anyone in the height of the aeon who can give the decision in the words concerning which we question, save thee alone,

who knoweth the universe, who is perfected in the universe. . . ."

"Because we do not question in the manner in which the men of the world question . . ."

FAUST BOOK	APOCHRYPHON OF JOHN
	And I went into the realm of Darkness and I endured till I entered the middle of the prison.
While in such thoughts, I heard a loud blast of wind go against my house. It threw open my shutters, my chamber door and all else, so that I was not a little astonished.	And the foundations of chaos shook. And I hid myself from them because of their wickedness, and they did not recognize me.
Right afterward I heard a roaring voice saying: "Get thee up! Thy heart's desire, intent and lust shalt thou see."	For a third time I went—I am the Light which exists in the Light, I am the remembrance of the Pronoia—that I might enter into the midst of Darkness and inside of Hades. . . . And I said, "He who hears, let him get up from the deep sleep."
I made answer: "If it be possible for me to see that which hath just been the object of my thoughts and wishes, then I am well content."	And he wept and shed tears. Bitter tears he wiped from himself and said "Who is it that calls my name and from where has this hope come to me while I am in the chains of prison?"
	And I said, "I am the Pronoia of the pure Light; I am the thinking of the virginal Spirit, who raised you up to the honored place.
He did answer again, saying: "Then look out at thy window where thou canst see our carriage."	
That I did, and I saw a coach with two dragons come flying down. The coach was illuminated with the flames of Hell, and inasmuch as the moon shone in the sky that night I could see my steeds as well. These creatures had mottled brown and white wings and the same color back; their bellies, however, were of a greenish hue with yellow and white flecks.	
The voice spake again:	"Arise; and remember that it is you who hearkened,
"Well get thee in and be off!"	and follow your root, which is the merciful one,"

FAUST BOOK	PISTIS SOPHIA	APOCHRYPHON OF JOHN
I answered "I will follow thee, but only on condition that I may ask any question I like."	but because we question in the Gnosis of the Height which thou hast given unto us and we question moreover in the type of excellent questioning which thou hast taught us, that we may question therein."	
"Good," he answered, "be it then in this instance permitted thee."	Jesus . . . answered and said unto her, "Question concerning all with precision, then shall I exult most exceedingly, because ye question . . . in the manner in which it beseemeth to question. Now, therefore, question concerning what thou wouldst question and I will reveal it unto thee with joy." (Ch. 83:182)	
So I climbed up onto my casement		and I raised him up
jumped down into my carriage		and sealed him in the Light of the water with five seals
		in order that death might not have power over him from this time on.
and off I went, the flying dragons drawing me ever upward.		And behold, now I shall go up to the perfect aeon. (31:26)
	It came to pass, then, that when Mary had heard the Savior say these words, she rejoiced in great joy and . . . said unto Jesus: "My Lord and Savior, of what manner are the four and twenty invisibles and	

FAUST BOOK

And it did seem a miracle that the coach really had four wheels that crunched right along as if I were journeying over land. To be sure the wheels did gush forth streams of fire as they whirled around.

The higher I ascended, the darker did the world become, and when I would look down into the world from the Heavens above, it was exactly as if I were gazing into a dark hole from bright daylight.

In the midst of such upward shooting and soaring, my servant and spirit came whirring along

and took a seat beside me in the coach.

I said to him: "My Mephistopheles, what is to become of me now?"

"Let such thoughts neither confuse thee nor impede thee," spake he

and drave on higher upward.

PISTIS SOPHIA

of what type, or rather, of what quality is their light?"

And Jesus answered: "Nothing existeth in this world to which I shall be able to liken them.

"If I lead you into the region of the rulers of the Fate, then will ye see the glory in which they are, and because of their overtowering great glory, ye will deem this world before you as darkness of darknesses." (Ch. 84:184)

THE DIVINE PYMANDER

and a pure fire sprang forth from the moist nature upwards on high. It was light and sharp and drastic also, and the air being light followed the Spirit; it ascending up to the fire from land and water,

so that it seemed to be suspended from it. Earth and water remained mingled in themselves so as not to be distinguished from the water, and they were moved by the onborne Spiritual Word to hearing.

APOCHRYPHON OF JOHN

TRIPARTITE TRACTATE

As for the baptism which exists in the fullest sense into which the Totalities will descend and in which they will be. There is no other baptism apart from this one alone

which is the redemption into God, Father, Son, and Holy Spirit,

when confession is made through faith in those names, which are a single name of the gospel . . .

when they have come to believe what has been said to them, namely that they exist.

From this they have their salvation. (127:31)

Ecstatic ascent experiences that bring the light of universal understanding, as Faustus's journey seems to have done, involve a psychic separation of the kind that normally occurs in dreams. Here, however, the dreamer consciously works to direct the soul's ascent. Evola's description of such an experience accords with Faustus's journeys down to Hell and up to Heaven.

> When a person goes to bed, his consciousness abandons him and goes up. But if every soul leaves the sleeper, not all rise to behold the countenance of the King . . . the Soul passes through numerous regions jumping from place to place. In its journey, it places itself in contact with impure powers that constantly surround the sacred regions. If the Soul is contaminated by impurities, it mixes with them and remains with them during the entire night. Other Souls ascend to the higher regions, and even beyond them to contemplate the glory of the King and visit his palaces. . . .[4]

While Evola's soul-flight results from deep meditation, Faustus's flight follows the ascent of the awakened Kundalini. Here we see the familiar initiating blast of wind, this one more powerful than the last. It "throws open Faustus's shutters, his chamber door and all else" and launches him on his visionary journey. The pressure from retention of the disciple's breath has forced open the Muladhara again and awakened the Kundalini. The roaring voice, the two dragons, and the coach "illuminated with the fires of Hell" represent respectively the sound of the Muladhara, the emptying of the ida and pingala nadis or channels, and the flaming eruption of the Kundalini up the central channel of the sushumna. The whirling chariot wheels that "gush forth streams of fire" signify the spinning energy centers or chakras located along the invisible spine whose heat increases when they are pierced by the Kundalini. As Kundalini rises through the chakras, Faustus will be lifted through the heavenly spheres, gaining supernormal vision and other powers that he desires.

17
Now I Will Tell You What I Did See

Faustus embarks on his second round trip journey in July, in weather "so hot" he might have "burned to a crisp." These conditions are very similar to those in the alchemist's vessel where spirits are being exhaled by the corrupted "Body," which is sweating at a temperature the alchemic philosophers compare to the Sun's heat in July. The fire must be carefully controlled lest the thick, crystal wall of the vessel—referred to by alchemists as the "world" or "world egg"—explode. Faustus refers to the danger the vessel faces in the following way. He observes that the cloud sphere, as "solid and thick as a masonry wall . . . and as clear as crystal," cracks "violently, as if it were about to burst and break the world open."

As Faustus and the vapors circulate, their movements correspond to the circles described in the Divine Pymander:

> The Mind, the God . . . begat by Word another Mind Creator, Who being God of the Fire and Spirit, created some Seven Administrators, encompassing in circles the sensible world; and their administration is called Fate.
>
> But the Creator Mind, along with the Word, that encompassing the circles, and making them revolve with force, turned about

> its own creations and permitted them to be turned about from an indefinite beginning to an interminable end; for they begin ever where they end.[1]

These circular movements also correspond to the revolutions of the Sun and Moon in the Manichaean creation myth. The Father has caused the Heavens to be created, and now, in his latest move to combat the powers of Darkness, he has an emissary fashion the circling "buckets" of the Sun and Moon. Their purpose is to serve as a kind of conveyor belt to transport particles of the scattered Light-soul back to the godhead.

> The parts of the Light (i.e., souls of the dead) mount up by the pillar of dawn to the sphere of the Moon, and the Moon receives them incessantly from the first to the middle of the month, so that it waxes and gets full, and then it guides them to the Sun until the end of the month and this effects its waning in that it is lightened of its burden. And in this manner the ferry is loaded and unloaded again, and the Sun transmits the Light to the Light above in the world of praise, and it goes on in that world until it arrives at the highest and pure Light.[2]

In his journey to the stars, Faustus observes the rolling of the heavens, the circling of the cloud sphere against the movements of the sun and moon, and all beneath the brilliant light of Heaven—a vision that has all the elements of the Father's majestically revolving system of cosmic purification. Hans Jonas observes that in the Manichaean speculation, cyclical movement was the universe's "instrument of salvation." "Thus," he says, "in the sequence of times, of calls and of revolutions, 'all parts of Light ascend incessantly' . . . and the dark parts descend . . . 'until the one are freed from the other and the mixture is nullified.'"[3]

As Faustus rises through the revolving heavens, Hermes in the Divine Pymander speaks of the soul who ascends through the zones of "the Harmony," or levels of awareness. He tells his disciple, Aesclepius, that each of the zones it passes through represents a vice that must be discarded.[4] Mead has referred to this winnowing process as a "way of birth . . . a de-energizing . . . of the body's senses with a corresponding energizing of the One Sense."[5]

Faustus seems to have energized this "One Sense" for he sees a radiance in Heaven, which surpasses even the light of the Sun. It is the light of understanding that Philo, the Hellenized Jewish philosopher, spoke of when he urged the devotee to "transcend the Sun which men perceive and gaze upon the Light beyond, the True Sun or Logos."[6] It is also the light that floods consciousness in deep meditation or when the Kundalini rises up the spiritual spine. One acquires true vision, Hermes says in the Pymander, when the eight zones of the Harmony have been surmounted. This happened to Faustus when he approached the radiant light of Heaven, for he reported acquiring a godlike vision: seeing "all things in the world as they do usually come to pass."

In his discussion of the circling heavens Hermes tells Aesclepius that everything revolves around and is moved by God, a truth which observation of the heavens reveals:

> The One ingenerate is plainly both unimaginable and non apparent.
>
> If, however, thou wishest to see Him, consider the Sun.
>
> Consider the course of the Moon, consider the order of the stars; who is he maintaining this order? For the whole order is determined by number and place. The Sun is the greatest god of the gods in Heaven, to whom all the heavenly gods yield as if to a king and dynasty.
>
> And this, the so vast, greater than Earth and Sea, submits, having above itself stars revolving smaller than itself.
>
> I wish it were possible for thee becoming winged to fly up into the air, and being lifted up in the midst between the Earth and Heaven to behold the solidity of Earth and the fluidity of the Sea, the flowings of rivers, the looseness of the air, the vehemence of fire, the course of stars, the very swift circling of Heaven around these.
>
> O most fortunate spectacle that, child! At one glance to behold all these, the immovable movement, and the invisible apparent.[7]

This sense of God's immanence seems to be a feature of Faustus's revelation as well. He lists the names of numerous countries and continents he sees on his journey even as the Tripartite Tractate reveals the many names of the "baptism that exists," all of which are ultimately names of God.

In the Pistis Sophia, Jesus continues his discourse on the quality of Light in the regions of the Invisibles. As Faustus rises through the heavenly spheres and describes the brilliance of the light he sees, Jesus describes the increasing glories of ascending regions of the Light world.

FAUST BOOK	TRIPARTITE TRACTATE
Departing on a Tuesday, and returning on a Tuesday I was out one week, during which time I neither slept nor did feel any sleep in me.	As for the baptism which exists in the fullest sense. . . .
Incidentally, I remained quite invisible throughout the journey.	This is attaining in an invisible way to the Father, Son, and Holy Spirit in an undoubting faith.
On the first morning, at break of day, I said to my Mephistopheles: "I suppose thou dost know how far we are come."	
	The baptism which we previously mentioned is called "garment of those who do not strip themselves of it," for those who will put it on and those who have received redemption wear it.
(Now as long as I was up there I knew neither hunger nor thirst)	
but I could well observe only by looking back at the world that I was come a good piece this night.	
Mephistopheles said: "In faith, my Fauste, thou art come forty-seven mile up into the sky."	It is also called "the confirmation of the truth which has no fall."
During the remainder of the day I discovered that I could look down upon the world and make out many kingdoms, principalities, and seas. I could discern the worlds of Asia, Africa, and Europe	

FAUST BOOK

and while at this altitude I said unto my servant,

"Now point out to me and instruct me as to the names of these various Lands and Realms."

This he did, saying: "This over here on the left is Hungary. Lo, there is Prussia. Across there is Sicily—Poland—Denmark—Italy—Germany. Now tomorrow shalt thou inspect Asia and Africa and canst see Persia, Tartary, India, and Arabia. But look, right now the wind is changing and we can see Germany again—Hungary—and Austria."

I saw Constantinople before me, and in the Persian and Constantinopolitan Sea, many ships and war troops shuttling busily back and forth.

Constantinople looked so small that there appeared to be no more than three houses there, with people not a span long.

Now I departed in July when it was very hot, and, as I looked now this way and now that, toward the East, South, and North, I observed how it was raining at one place, thundering at another, how the hail did fall here while at another place the weather was fair.

In fine I saw all things in the world as they usually do come to pass,

watching from a distance how the heavens did move and roll around so fast,

for they seemed about to fly asunder into many thousand pieces, the cloud sphere cracking so violently as if it were about to burst and brake the world open.

TRIPARTITE TRACTATE

It is also called "bridal chamber," "the light which does not set and is without flame," "the eternal life."

For what else is there to name it apart from "God?" That is, even if they are given numberless names, they are spoken simply as a reference to it. (129:15)

PISTIS SOPHIA

Jesus continued in the discourse: "And if I lead you into the twelve aeons, then will ye see the glory in which they are;

and because of the great glory the regions of the rulers of the Fate will count for you as the darkness of darknesses

and it will have for you the condition of a speck of dust because of the great distance . . . and because of the great condition it is considerably greater than them." (Ch. 84:185)

FAUST BOOK	PISTIS SOPHIA
The heavens were so bright that I could not perceive anything higher up	"And if I lead you into the region of those of the Midst, then will ye see the glory in which they are." (Ch. 84:185)
and it was so hot I should have burned to a crisp had my servant not charmed a breeze up for me. The cloud sphere, which we see down here in the world, is as solid and thick as a masonry wall, but it is of one piece and as clear as crystal. The rain, which originates there and falls upon the earth, is so clear we could see ourselves reflected in it.	
Now this cloud sphere moveth in the heavens with such a force that it runneth from East to West despite the fact that Sun, Moon, and stars strive against it, so that the momentum of the cloud sphere doth indeed drive Sun, Moon, and stars along with it.	
Down in our world it doth appear—and I thought so too—that the Sun is no bigger than the head of a barrel.	"(And) if I lead you into the region of those who have received the . . . mysteries of the Light, and ye see the glory of the light in which they are, then the Light-land will count for you as the light of the Sun which is in the world of men. And if ye look upon the Light-land, then will it count for you as a speck of dust because of the great distance the Light-land is distant from it." (Ch. 85:188)
But it is much bigger than the whole world; for I could discover no end to it at all.	"The light of the Sun in its shape in truth is not in this world, for its light pierceth through many veils and regions.
At night when the Sun goeth down, the Moon must take on the Sun's light, this being why the Moon shineth so bright at night. And directly beneath Heaven there is so much light that even at night it is daytime in Heaven—this even though the earth remains quite dark.	"But the light of the Sun in its shape in truth, which is in the region of the Virgin of Light, shineth ten thousand times more than the four and twenty invisibles and the great invisible forefather and also the great triple-powered god . . ." (Ch. 84:184)
Thus I saw more than I had desired. One of the stars, for example, was larger than half the world. A planet is as large as the world.	

FAUST BOOK

And in the airy sphere, I beheld the airy spirits, which dwell beneath Heaven. While descending I did look down upon the world again, and it was no bigger than the yolk of an egg. Why to me the world seemed scarcely a span long, but the oceans looked to be twice that size.

Thus on the evening of the seventh day did I arrive home again, and I slept for three days on a row. I have disposed my almanacs and horoscopes in accordance with my observations

and I did not wish to withhold this fact from you.

Now inspect your books and see whether the matter is not in accordance with my vision.

And accept my cordial greetings.

Dr. Faustus
The Astroseer

Faustus's descent into Hell referred to the physiological processes and techniques involved in raising the Kundalini but, now, as Faustus journeys to the stars, focus shifts for the most part to the psychological and spiritual perceptions involved in an ecstatic ascent experience. Omar Garrison describes deepening levels of a trance state known as the Four Blisses or Lights of Sleep that resemble things Faustus sees in his travels around the heavens.[8]

Leaving behind the world of transient forms, the yogin enters a world of graduated light, and, according to Garrison, the first thing he experiences is the "Light of Revelation"—an inner glow that resembles "effulgent, moth white moonlight in a cloudless sky." "One night," wrote Faustus, "I lay thinking about the arrangements and properties of the Heavens." It was a night "when the moon shone in the sky."

"As the admixture of residual sense impressions and discriminating thoughts begin to subside," says Garrison, "the second illumination, known as the Light of Augmentation, dawns. It appears to the Jiva usually as a brilliant clear sunlight." Faustus saw a brilliant light as well—a coach which was " illuminated with the flames of Hell."

"Only advanced yogis are able to proceed beyond this stage. . . . For those who can, however, the sunlight fades into total darkness, like an eclipse." "The higher I ascended," Faustus goes on, "the darker did the world become, and when I would look down into the world from the heavens above, it was exactly as if I were gazing into a dark hole from bright sunlight."

Then the yogin perceives a dim glow "which dissolves as [he] plunges deeper into profound slumber. It merges into the ultimate Void, or Innate Light, described as the primal radiance of all reality. From it comes the light and heat of the Sun, and the reflected brilliance of the Moon." Faustus observes the Sun's reflected brightness on the Moon and describes the remarkable light in Heaven—so primal in its radiance that "even at night it is daytime in Heaven."

Garrison says that the dreamer, "having subdued by sleep all that belongs to the body, not asleep himself looks down upon the sleeping senses."[9] "I neither slept nor felt any sleep in me," Faustus reported, and he became "quite invisible," as if he, too, had separated from bodily awareness. Indeed, he reports on his journey as if he were a detached observer.

According to Geshe Kelsang, the power of invisibility comes through "subtle Mantra recitation,"[10] perhaps indicated by Faustus's recitation of the many countries he saw, which parallels the Tripartite Tractate's reference to the "names of God." With the sense of invisibility comes an overarching vision such as Faustus has acquired. According to Mead, as the disciple's "spiritual senses" are being born, "already he is losing touch with the physical (and) no longer sees himself."

> But this is not enough; he must not only be able to lose consciousness of his physical body, and see and hear as though with the mind alone, but he must invert himself, pass right through himself, and no longer see things as though without him, but all things as within him.

Faustus has acquired what Mead calls a "cosmic Body," one that "embraces the cosmos within it."[11] His superawareness here is compatible with activation of the fifth, or throat chakra as Oscar Marcel Hinze describes it in *Tantra Vidya:* "The yogin is able to view together the past, the present and the future and perceive the being as well the creation."[12] Faustus's experience is not the fulfillment he seeks, however, for as Hermes tells Tat in *Thrice Greatest Hermes,* "this revelation merely (affords) to us the first beginning of (God's) being known" and Mead explains its limitation.

> They who receive the baptism of the Mind are made "perfect men," not Perfect. . . . Those who have received this Baptism know why they have come into being . . . they become consciously immortal . . . they know the real constitution of the cosmos . . . that is to say . . . as far as Nirvanic state of consciousness. Not yet have they reached Nirvana . . . become one with the Logos. They have seen the sight or vision but not yet entered the promised land.[13]

Faustus has not yet pierced the Lotus that will bring him immortality.

Certain features in Faustus's ascent accord with the yogin's physical perceptions during the Kundalini's awakening. According to Hinze, "When the Kundalini awakes and begins to course through the Citrini-Nadi, thereby piercing the six chakras, the Yogin has a threefold experience."

1. He feels a glowing heat at the lower end of the abdomen. [Faustus embarks on his upward journey in the heat of July.]
2. He hears a sound. [A roaring voice calls out to Faustus.]
3. During the ascent through the chakras, these make a rotating movement. [They recall the whirling chariot wheels whose likeness to the spinning chakras we noted in the last chapter.][14]

As Faustus rises through the spheres, he observes that night is subsumed into the radiance of Heaven: "there is so much light that even at night it is daytime there." His remark refers to the nadis, pingala, and ida, which are called the "paths of day and night." When the energy in them rushes downward into the central channel "day and night come together," says Hinze, "a necessary step on the way to the Divine being where there is no day or night, no past nor future, in short, there is no time."[15]

18
Doctor Faustus's Third Journey

In this chapter Faustus performs an "extraction" like that of the alchemist who extracts the volatile spirits from the sweating "Body" in the vessel. Faustus journeys to the corrupt palace of the pope in Rome and steals dishes and goblets made of silver. Silver is also matched in the text comparison with the creative Spirit, or Light of revelation. Then Faustus flies off to Turkey, and—as the spirits rise and fall in the vessel, piercing and penetrating the Body—he "rises and falls" in the emperor's harem, that is, fornicates with the emperor's whores and wives. While this may be a reference to the disciple's continuing practice of raising and lowering the Kundalini, it seems to be a more general reference to the drawing out and exchanging of sexual fluids as an act of personal and universal salvation.

David White points to a "striking" resemblance between Tibetan alchemy's "extraction of the innate, divine essence from the gross, corporeal body" and a Hindu practice of Kundalini yoga in which the power of flight is attained by "extracting the quintessence of [the] five bodily elements."[1] Elsewhere he says that extracting this essence—sexual fluids or their sumbolic correlates—is the concrete ground of tantric experience.

> The cosmic force that activates and acutalizes every facet of tantric practice . . . is ultimately nothing other than a stream of sexual fluid in tantric initiation and worship rituals. . . . If, then, the pres-

> ervation of the universe depends upon—indeed, is nothing other than—the endless cosmic orgasm of the divine, and if the bliss of orgasm is that human experience which is closest to the very being of godhead—then the stuff of orgasm—male semen and female sexual emission and uterine blood—will of necessity play a vital role in the tantric quest for divine autonomy, immortality and power . . . and for controlling a universe that is understood as a body, the body of the divine consort, of Siva, the body of one's own consort, and the feminine in one's own body.[2]

The procreative nature of Faustus's act also signals the reforming and fecundating of the alchemist's metal, a process that is beginning as the newly freed spirits return to penetrate the corrupted earth and induce a chemical transformation. It is one of several facetious metaphors for events that are obviously serious matters in the Gnostic works. It reflects a passage in the Paraphrase of Shem, included in this chapter, in which Derdekias tells Shem how—using bizarre sexual ploys—he fertilizes the Womb, or Nature, to produce the heavens, the earth, and its various forms of life.

Faustus's indelicate behavior is a parody of events in the Pistis Sophia as well. There, the angels Gabriel and Michael retrieve Sophia's stolen Light and pour it back into the body of the goddess whom, we may recall, was referred to as "the whore" in her fallen state. Use of sexual imagery to illustrate the creative acts that formed the cosmos is not confined to these texts. In the Mani myth, a bizarre sexual seduction designed to free the Father's Light accidentally produces the earth's vegetation. An androgynous emanation of the Father reveals his male and female forms to the male and female children of Darkness.

> And at the sight of the Messenger, who was beautiful in his forms, all the Archons became excited with lust for him, the male ones for his female appearance, and the female ones for his male appearance. And in their concupiscence they began to release the Light of the Five Luminous Gods which they had devoured.[1]

They released an equal amount of Dark matter, however, and the Messenger was forced to separate it from the Light. The purer parts ascended with the Sun and Moon but the residue that was mixed fell below, forming the flora that covers the earth.

In the Valentinian Light-physics system described by Mead, as each new sphere or realm is created, a veil or mist appears; in the Faust Book a fog descends on the Turkish Emperor's palace as Faustus performs the sexual act that signals creation of the Heavens and Earth.

When the alchemist's Earth or Body is bathed and penetrated, it begins to be redeemed, and redemption is the focus of most of the passages underlying this chapter. The Sophia of Jesus Christ, a revelation myth from the Nag Hammadi collection, features Sophia Ennoia in the role of a cocreator who facilitates the redemption of her errant creation. She sends down drops of Light to the visible world to reveal the form of the Savior, who brings with him the searing Light of Truth.

> From the aeons above the emanations of Light . . . a drop from Light and Spirit came down to the lower regions of Almighty in chaos, that their molded forms might appear from that drop, for it is a judgment on Arch-Begetter, who is called Yaltabaoth.
>
> That drop revealed their molded forms through the breath as a living soul. It was withered and it slumbered in the ignorance of the soul.
>
> When it became hot from the breath of the Great Light and of the Male, and it took thought, then names were received by all who were in the world of chaos and all things that are in it through that Immortal One. . . . when the breath blew into him, but when this came about by the will of Mother Sophia—
>
> Man might piece together the garments there for a judgment on the robbers he then welcomed the blowing of that breath. (118:5–121:5)

Christ performs a similar act in the highlights from the Tripartite Tractate. Both complement the mission Gabriel and Michael undertake to enlighten and redeem the fallen Sophia.

FAUST BOOK	PISTIS SOPHIA	TRIPARTITE TRACTATE
It was in his sixteenth year that Doctor Faustus undertook a pilgrimage	The First Mystery . . . said: "It came to pass . . . that the power which had come out of the Height . . . which did go from me,	
instructing his servant that he should conduct and convey him withersoever he would go.	and the soul which I had received from Sabaoth the Good—they drew toward one another and become a single Light-stream,	
He journeyed invisible down to Rome		About the [One] who appeared in flesh, they believed without any doubt that he is the Son of an unknown God who was not previously spoken of and who could not be seen.
and went unseen into the Pope's Palace		They abandoned their gods whom they had previously worshipped and the lords who are in heaven and earth. (133:15–25)
and beheld all the servants and courtiers and the many sorts of dishes that were being served.		They first desired their numerous services and wonders, which were in the temple on their behalf, to be performed continuously . . . (134:5)
"For shame!" he remarked to his spirit. "Why did not the Devil make a Pope of me?"		but they granted to Christ . . . a place of gods and lords whom they served, worshipped and ministered to

FAUST BOOK	PISTIS SOPHIA	TRIPARTITE TRACTATE
Yes, Doctor Faustus found all there to be his ilk in arrogance, pride, much insolence, transgression, gluttony, drunkenness, whoring, adultery and other fine blessings of the Pope and his rabble.		
"Methought I was the Devil's own swine,		in the names which they had received on loan.
but he will let me fatten for long while yet. These swine in Rome are already fatted and ready to roast and boil."		They were given to the one who is designated by them properly.
Since he had heard much of Rome, he remained for three days and nights in the Pope's Palace.		They gave them their kingdoms;
Now hear ye the adventures and the art which he used in the Pope's Palace. The good Lord Faustus, having little good meat and drink for some time, came and stood invisible before the Pope's board		they rose from their thrones,
even as he was about to eat. The Pope crossed himself before taking meat, and at that moment, Doctor Faustus did blow into his face. Every time the Pope crossed himself before taking meat, and at that moment Doctor Faustus did blow into his face again.		they were kept from their crowns. (134:15–30)

FAUST BOOK	PISTIS SOPHIA	TRIPARTITE TRACTATE
	(The Light-stream Jesus gave unto Gabriel and Michael "shone most exceedingly in the whole of the chaos")	
Once he laughed aloud so that it was audible in the whole hall,	"and spread itself over all the regions,	
again he did weep most convincingly. The servants knew not what this might be.	"and when the emanations of Self-Willed had seen the great Light of that stream, they were terror stricken one with the other.	
But the Pope told his people it was a damned soul of which he had exacted penance and was now begging for absolution.		
Doctor Faustus enjoyed this very much, for such mystifications well pleased him, too.		
When the last course finally arrived and was set before the Pope, Doctor Faustus, feeling his own hunger, raised up his hands, and instantly all the courses and fine dishes together with their platters flew right into them.	"And that stream drew forth out of them all the Light-powers which they had taken from Pistis Sophia,	Thus they were entrusted with the services which benefit the elect
Together with his spirit he then rushed away to a mountain in Rome called the Capitolineum, there to dine with great relish.		bringing their iniquity up to heaven.

FAUST BOOK	PISTIS SOPHIA	TRIPARTITE TRACTATE
Later, he sent his spirit back with an order to fetch the daintiest wines from the Pope's table together with the finest goblets and flagons.		They tested them eternally, for the lack of humility . . . while their bodies remain on earth. (135:5–15)
When the Pope found out how many things had been stolen from him, he caused all the bells to be rung throughout the entire night and had mass and petition held for the departed souls.	and the emanations of Self-Willed could not dare to lay hold of that Light-stream in the dark chaos; nor could they lay hold of it with all the art of Self-Willed who ruleth over the emanations." (Ch. 64:129)	
In anger toward one departed soul, however, he formally condemned it to purgatory with bell, book, and candle.	"And Michael and Gabriel will give them the mysteries of the Light,	
As for Doctor Faustus, he accepted the Pope's meat and drink as an especial dispensation.	it is they to whom the Light-stream was entrusted, which I have given unto them and brought into the chaos.	
The silver was found in his house after his death.	"And Michael and Gabriel have taken no Light for themselves from the Lights of Sophia, which they had taken from the emanations of Self-Willed."	
At midnight, when he was sated with his victuals	"It came to pass then, when the Light-stream had ingathered into Pistis Sophia all her Light-powers, which it had taken from the emanations of Self-Willed . . .	
he bestrode a horse	they took unto themselves a Light-power	

FAUST BOOK	PISTIS SOPHIA	PARAPHRASE OF SHEM
	and became again as they were before. . . ." (64:130) [Then] Peter came forward and said: "My Lord, concerning the solution of the words which thou hast spoken . . ." (65:131)	
and flew off to Constantinople.	"The Light-stream hath spread itself out in the chaos over all the regions of the emanations of Self-Willed. . . .	
Here Doctor Faustus viewed the Turkish Emperor's might, brilliance, and court entourage for a few days.	"It tore away all to itself and led it over the temple.	
One evening when the emperor sat at table	"They who were in the dry sand drank." (65:132)	
Doctor Faustus performed for him an apish play and spectacle.		And the exalted, infinite Light appeared for he was very joyful. He wished to reveal himself to the Spirit.
Great tongues of fire burst up in the hall, and when everyone was hastening to quench it, it commenced to thunder and to lighten. Such a spell was cast upon the Turkish Emperor that he could not arise, nor could he be carried out of there. The hall became as bright as the very homeland of the Sun,		and the likeness of the exalted light appeared to the unbegotten spirit. I appeared. I am the son of the incorruptible, infinite Light.

FAUST BOOK	PISTIS SOPHIA	PARAPHRASE OF SHEM
and Faustus's spirit, in the figure, ornaments, and trappings of a Pope, stepped before the Emperor		I appeared in the likeness of the spirit
saying: "Hail, Emperor, so full of grace that I, Mahomet, do appear unto thee!"		
Saying nothing more, he disappeared.	"Michael and Gabriel, who have ministered, have brought the Light-stream into the chaos and also led it forth again. . . ."	And his appearance to me was in order that the mind of Darkness might not remain in Hades. (3:31–4:10)
This hoax caused the Emperor to fall down upon his knees, calling unto Mahomet and praising him that he had been so gracious as to appear before him.	"They have refreshed parched lips. . . . They have raised up limbs which were fallen. (65:133)	
The next morning, Doctor Faustus went into the Emperor's castle, wherethe Turk has his wives and whores, and where no one is permitted except gelded boys who wait upon the women. He charmed this castle with such a thick fog that naught could be seen. Now Doctor Faustus transformed himself as had his spirit before, but posed as Mahomet himself, and he did reside for awhile in this castle, the mist remaining throughout his stay, and the Turk during this same period admonishing his people to perform many rites.		

FAUST BOOK	PISTIS SOPHIA	PARAPHRASE OF SHEM
But Doctor Faustus drank and was full of good cheer, taking his pleasure and dalliance there.	"When the Light-stream had taken all the Light-powers of Pistis Sophia and had spoiled them from the emanations of Self-Willed, it poured them into Pistis Sophia	And I appeared in the cloud of the hymen without my holy garment . . . (16:36)
When he was through, he used the same art as before and ascended into the sky in papish raiment and ornament.		For I am the ray of the universal Light.
Now when Faustus was gone and the fog disappeared,		The Darkness which was (the earth's) garment was cast into the harmful waters. The middle region was cleansed from the Darkness.
The Turk came to his castle, summoned his wives and asked who had been there while the castle was for so long surrounded with fog.		But the Womb grieved because of what had happened. She perceived in her parts what was water like a mirror. When she perceived it she wondered how it had come into being.
They informed him how it was the god Mahomet who at night had called this one and that one to him, lain with them		For because of the grace of the majesty, I came forth to her from the water for a second time. For my face pleased her. Her face also was glad.
and said that from his seed would rise up a great nation and valiant heroes.		And I said to her, "May seed and power come forth from you upon the earth."
The Turk accepted it as a great benefit that Mahomet had lain with his wives.		And she obeyed the will of the Spirit that she might be brought to naught.
But he wondered if it had been accomplished according to the manner of mortals.		And when her forms returned, they rubbed their tongues with each other; they copulated; they begot winds and demons and the power which is the fire and the Darkness and the Spirit . . . (21:11–30)

FAUST BOOK	PISTIS SOPHIA	PARAPHRASE OF SHEM
He had called them, embraced them,	and came over thee, thou who art the temple.”	And in order that the demons might also become free from the power which they possessed through the impure intercourse, a womb was with the winds resembling water.
and was well-fitted out—they would fain be served in such sort every day. He had lain with them naked and was certainly a man in all parts.		And an unclean penis was with the demons in accordance with the example of the Darkness, and in the way he rubbed the womb from the beginning.
Except that they had not been able to understand his tongue.		And after the forms of nature had been together they separated from each other.
The priests instructed the Turk that he ought not believe it were Mahomet, but a phantom.		They cast off the power, being astonished about the deceit which had happened to them.
The wives on the other hand said, be it Ghost or man, he had been very kind to them and had served them masterfully, once or six times—nay even more often—in a night;		They grieved with an eternal grief. . . .
all of which caused the Turk much contemplation.		And when I had put them to shame, I arose with my garment . . . in order that I might make Nature desolate. (21:34–22:21) And I gave him a likeness of fire, light, and attentiveness, and a share of guileless word.

19
Concerning the Stars

In the Faust Book it is nighttime, and Faustus and a friend gaze calmly at the heavens and contemplate the stars. Star imagery is appropriate to this stage of the alchemical process, for the black surface of the metal will soon begin to show tiny specks of white, which alchemists liken to stars in a nighttime sky. Ripley, for example, calls the metal at this stage "our sterry stone." Star symbolism, because of its complexity, also encompasses the several themes that underlie these chapters, as this definition in the *Dictionary of Symbols* indicates.

> As a light shining in the darkness, the star is a symbol of the spirit . . . it nearly always alludes to multiplicity. In which case it stands for the forces of the spirit struggling against the forces of darkness. . . . As far back as the days of Egyptian hieroglyphics (the five pointed star) signified "rising upwards towards the point of origin," and formed part of such words as "to educate," "the teacher," etc. . . . Being nocturnal, (the) symbolism (of stars) is associated with that of night; they are also linked with the idea of multiplicity (or with disintegration) because they appear in clusters . . .[1]

"Multiplicity" suggests the proliferating creation, which is bringing forth the earth and star-filled skies. "Night" and "disintegration" implies the blackness of the decomposed metal in the alchemist's vessel, which is slowly reviving and assuming new form. George Ripley describes its progress in the Sixth Gate of his "Compound of Alchemy."

In the tyme of thys seed processe naturall,
While the Sperme conceyved is growyng,
The substance is nurryshed with hys own menstruall;
Which Water only out of the Earth did bring,
Whose color ys Greene in the first showing.
And for that tyme the Son hydeth his lyght,
Taking his course throw owte the North by nyght.[2]

This is a time of waiting as the blackened Body reabsorbs its own "blood" and transforms internally. In the text comparison the telling of the creation myth is suspended and time seems to stop as the quality of this moment is captured. The tiny stars that will soon appear on the resurrected surface of the corrupted metal signify a revelation of its "Spirit" or essence. The teacher, or educator, is, of course, represented by Faustus who instructs his friend concerning the stars.

For the tantric disciple who has emerged from a difficult testing period, this is a time of reintegration and rebirth. According to Mookerjee and Khanna, he begins to understand his relationship to "the totality of which he is a centre," a totality represented in these chapters by the heavens whose mysteries Faustus is pondering. The disciple's new understanding creates a sense of "balance" and "equanimity," say the authors, "a state of . . . emptiness, of mental tranquility, serenity, imperturbability (and) self-restraint."[3] Faustus's calm perusal of the heavens while waiting for his supper seems to be a case in point. As he gazes serenely out the window, his mood is like that of the disciple in Allogenes after he is told by the luminaries he meets that he may not experience the invisible Spirit directly, but rather through stillness and withdrawal.

> O Allogenes, behold your blessedness, how it silently abides, by which you know your proper self, and seeing yourself, withdraw to the Vitality that you will see moving.

> And although it is impossible for you to stand, fear nothing; but if you wish to stand, withdraw to the Existence, and you will find it standing and at rest after the likeness of the One who is truly at rest and embraces all these silently and inactively.
>
> And when you receive a revelation of him by means of a primary revelation of the Unknown One . . . withdraw to the rear and still yourself. . . .
>
> Now I was listening to these things as those ones spoke them. There was within me a stillness of silence, and I heard the Blessedness whereby I knew my proper self. (59:10–60, 15)

According to Guenther and Trungpa, when a disciple demonstrates this new understanding, the guru changes his tactics. Where before he was evasive and challenging, now he is open and cooperative. Again the authors use Naropa's experience with his guru as an example.

> When Naropa had shown that he was a person worthy of receiving instruction, the whole pattern we have been describing changed. Tilopa then showed himself to be the kindest person that could be imagined. He withheld nothing that Naropa wished of him. . . . He gave everything that he had to his disciple.
>
> This is the manner of continuing the teacher-disciple relationship. At a certain point the teacher transmits the entirety of his understanding to a disciple. But the disciple must show himself worthy and be brought to a state of complete receptivity.[4]

Faustus plays the role of the guru here, willingly answering the many questions put to him by his doctor friend, whose worthiness is demonstrated by his prominence as a scholar, a "doctor of physic," and a "good astrologus."

In keeping with the revelatory symbolism of stars, revelations of one sort or another are the subject of the highlights in this and the next three chapters. In the Gospel of Truth the Father brings forth his Son to impart a revelation about things that are "secret," such as the final resting place, which is the Father, and in the Pistis Sophia, Jesus has much to say about the relative sizes and brightness of the planets and the increasing brilliance of ascending regions of the Light world. His revelations are elicited by questions from Mary Magdalene, just as Faustus's information about the stars is prompted by questions from Dr. N. V. W.

FAUST BOOK

A prominent scholar in Halberstadt, Doctor N.V.W.,

invited Doctor Faustus to his table.

Before supper was ready, Faustus stood for awhile gazing out the window at the heavens, it being harvest time and the sky filled with stars.

Now his host, being also a doctor of Physic and a good *astrologus*

had brought Doctor Faustus here for the purpose of learning divers transformations in the planets and stars.

Therefore he now leaned upon the window beside Doctor Faustus

and looked also upon the brilliance of the heavens, the multitude of stars,

some of which were shooting through the sky and falling to the earth; in all humility he made request that Doctor Faustus might tell him the condition and quality of this thing.

GOSPEL OF TRUTH

When, therefore, it pleased him that his name which is loved should be his Son, and he gave the name to him,

that is, him who came forth from the depth, he spoke about his secret things, knowing that the Father is a being without evil.

For that very reason he brought him forth in order to speak about . . . his resting place from which he had come forth, and to glorify the pleroma. . . . (40:25–35)

PISTIS SOPHIA

Mary Magdalene came forward and said . . . "Be not wroth with me if I question thee, because I trouble repeatedly. . . . (Ch. 88:199)

"My Lord, by how much greatness then is the second Helper greater than the first Helper? By how much distance is he distant from him, or rather, how many times more does he shine than the latter?"

FAUST BOOK

Doctor Faustus began in this wise: "My most dear Lord and brother, this condition doth presuppose certain other matters which ye must understand first.

"The smallest star in Heaven, although beheld from below it seems to our thinking scarcely so big as our large wax candles, is really larger than a principality. Oh yes, this is certain. I have seen that the length and breadth of the heavens is many times greater than the surface of the earth.

"From Heaven, ye cannot even see earth. Many a star is broader than this land, and most are at least as large as this city. See, over there is one fully as large as the dominion of the Roman Empire. This one right up here is as large as Turkey. And up higher there, where the planets are, ye may find one as big as the world."

PISTIS SOPHIA

Jesus answered and said unto Mary . . . "Amen, amen, I say unto you: 'The second Helper is distant from the first Helper in great immeasurable distance in regard to the height above and the depth below and the length and the breadth. . . . (Ch. 89:200)

"'And he shineth more than the latter in an utterly immeasurable measure, there being no measure for the Light in which he is . . . In like manner, also the third Helper and fourth and fifth Helper, one is greater than the other . . . and shineth more than the latter and is distant from him in a great immeasurable distance through the angels and archangels and the gods and all the invisibles, as I have already said unto you at another time . . .'" (Ch. 89:201)

20
A Question on This Topic

In this chapter Faustus continues his discourse with his companion, speaking of "vexing spirits" who come down to earth to escape the Sun and frighten people with nightmares, howling, spooks, and strange fantasies. These spirits are the equivalent of the hellish entity in the Pistis Sophia called the "dragon of outer darkness," which seems to represent abysmal ignorance and to embody the fears that afflict human beings.

The dragon of outer darkness is described with relish elsewhere in the Pistis Sophia as containing twelve chastisement dungeons whose rulers have animal faces and mete out punishments. The dragon spews out ice, hail, disease, and violent fire; it is the ultimate Hell where sinners are consigned who have never repented and whose torment never ends. The Pistis Sophia says it would destroy the world were it not for the Light of the Sun.

The Sun represents the Father's pleroma in the text comparison—the revelation that is the subject of these chapters—and not even good people can endure its Light. Such people are equated with the vexing spirits who rise up beneath the cloud sphere but can go no higher because they "cannot suffer the aspect of the Sun." The spirits' upward movements mimic the good people's thoughts, which reach up to the heights. Although their thoughts may ascend, they themselves are not exalted and must keep the places assigned to them, which are their own pleromas. Faustus's spirits are also free to descend but not to rise above the cloud sphere, that is, the good person's level of attainment. The Gospel of Truth tells us that the people who return to their spiritual roots and send their thoughts up to the Father do possess something of the Father's greatness and are immune to the fears that afflict others.

FAUST BOOK	GOSPEL OF TRUTH	PISTIS SOPHIA
"I know that to be true" saith this doctor. "But, my Lord Faustus, how is it with the spirits who vex men and thwart their works (as some people say) by day and by night as well?"		Mary continued . . . and said: "My Lord, doth the dragon of the outer darkness come into this world or doth he not come?"
Doctor Faustus answered: "We ought not to begin with this topic, but with the ordinances and creation of God,	About the place each one came from (the Son) will speak,	
it being in accordance with these that the Sun doth at break of day turn again toward the world with his radiance	and to the region where he received his establishment he will hasten to return again	The Savior answered and said . . . : "When the Light of the Sun is outside
(it being also nearer in summer than in winter)		
	and to take from that place . . . receiving nourishment, receiving growth.	
and that the spirits then move beneath the cloud sphere		he covereth the darkness of the dragon
	And his own resting place is his pleroma. Therefore all the emanations of the Father are pleromas. (41:5–15)	
where God hath committed them	He assigned them their destinies,	

FAUST BOOK	GOSPEL OF TRUTH	PISTIS SOPHIA
that they may discover all his portents.	each one then is manifest. . . .	
"As the day progresses, they rise upward beneath the cloud sphere;	For the place to which they send their thought, that place, their root, is what takes them up in all the heights to the Father. They possess his head, which is rest for them, and they are supported approaching him,	
for they are granted no affinity with the Sun;	as though to say that they have participated in his face by means of kisses. (41:20–35)	
the brighter it shines the higher they do seek to dwell. In this context we might speak of forbidden days, for God hath not granted them light nor allowed them such a property.	But they do not become manifest in this way for they were not themselves exalted;	
"But by night, then they are among us, for the brightness of the Sun—even though it is not shining here—is in the first heaven so intense that it is as day light there	yet neither did they lack the glory of the Father, nor did they think of him as small nor that he is harsh nor that he is wrathful but that he is a being without evil, imperturbable, sweet . . . (42:1–9)	
(this being why, in the blackness of night, even when stars do not shine, men still perceive Heaven).	This is the manner of those who possess something from above of the immeasurable greatness. (42:11)	

FAUST BOOK	GOSPEL OF TRUTH	PISTIS SOPHIA
"It followeth therefore that the spirits, not being able to endure or to suffer the aspect of the Sun, which hath now ascended upwards, must come near to us on earth and dwell with men, frightening them with nightmares, howling, and spooks.	And they do not go down to Hades	"but if the Sun is below the world, then the darkness of the dragon abideth as veiling of the Sun and the breath of the darkness cometh into the world in the form of a smoke in the night,
"Now what will ye wager and bet: when ye go abroad in the night if ye dare do such a thing—a great fear will seize you. Furthermore, if ye are alone by night ye are possessed by strange phantasies,		"that is, if the Sun withdraweth into himself his rays, then indeed the world is not able to endure the darkness of the dragon in its true form;
although the day bringeth no such things.		"otherwise it would be dissolved and go to ruin withal." (Ch. 131:355)
"At night some will start up in their sleep, another thinks there will be a spirit near him, or that he be groping out for him or that he walk round in the house, or in his sleep, etc.	nor have they envy nor groaning nor death within them, but they rest in him who is at rest,	
"There are many such trials, because the spirits are near to vex and plague men with their multitudinous delusions."	not striving nor being twisted around the truth. (42:19–25)	

21
The Second Question

In the previous chapter, the spirits Faustus described rose and fell through the heavens, while the dragon of outer darkness in the Pistis Sophia waxed and waned with the rising and setting of the Sun. Now Faustus discusses the alternation that occurs between daytime and night as the Sun makes its "God ordained" rounds.

These oscillations relate to an elemental rotation that is beginning in the alchemist's vessel. We learn from a further reading of Ripley's Sixth Gate that the Body has been fed its own juices and has calcified, and now it must be dissolved and coagulated again. "When thou hast made seven times imbibition," says Ripley,

> *Again then thou must turn thy wheel,*
> *And purify all that matter without addition,*
> *First Blackness abiding if thou do will do well,*
> *Then into Whiteness congeal it up each deal*
> *And by Redness into the South ascend,*
> *Then hast thou brought thy base to an end.*[1]

"By easy decoction," says Ripley, the blackened Body will display the white or silvery flecks that resemble stars in a nighttime sky. Faustus seems to signal this event when he speaks of the "right of the stars to shine" when the Sun withdraws its light.

In the Pistis Sophia, Jesus continues his revelations about the inner mysteries and Mary Magdalene interprets his words. Speaking about a shift in spiritual status that occurs between the powerful who repent and the humble who receive the inner mysteries, she quotes Jesus and, like Faustus, evokes the oscillations of an alchemical rotation, "The first shall be last and the last shall be first." The "last," she explains, are "the whole race of men which will enter the Light kingdom sooner than all those of the region of the height, who are the 'first.'"

FAUST BOOK	PISTIS SOPHIA
"I thank you very much," spake the doctor, "my dear Lord Faustus, for your brief account. I shall remember it and ponder upon it all my life long. But if I may trouble you further, would ye not instruct me once more as concerns the brilliance of the stars and their appearance by night?"	Mary . . . said: "I have heard thee say: 'If I lead you into the region of those who have received the mysteries of the Light, then will the region of the Light-land count for you as a speck of dust because of the great Light which it is . . .'
	"Will, therefore, my Lord, the men who have received the mysteries be superior to the Light-land and superior to those in the Kingdom of the Light?" (Ch. 85:188)
"Yea, very briefly," answered Doctor Faustus.	and Jesus answered and said:
"Now it is certain that as soon as the sun doth ascend into the third heaven (if it should move down into the first heaven it would ignite the earth—	"Hearken, Mary, that I may speak with thee about the consummation of the aeon and the ascension of the universe.
but the time for that is not come yet,	"It will not yet take place. . . ." (Ch. 86:189)
and the earth must still proceed along her God-ordained course).	"Before the consummation everyone will be in his own region into which he hath been set from the beginning, until the numbering of the ingathering of the perfect souls is completed." (Ch. 86:195)
"When the Sun doth so far withdraw itself, I say,	"But I have said unto you: 'If I lead you into the region of the inheritances of those who shall receive the mystery of the Light,

FAUST BOOK	PISTIS SOPHIA
then doth it become the right of the stars to shine for as long as God hath ordained. The first and second heavens, which contain these stars, are then brighter than two of our summer days	then will the Treasury of the Light, the region of the emanations, count for you as a speck of dust only and as the Light of the sun by day.'"
	"I have said: 'This will take place at the time of the consummation and of the ascension of the universe. . . .
and offer an excellent refuge for the birds by night.	the emanations of the seven Voices and the twelve Trees, they will be with me in . . . my kingdom.'" (Ch. 86:189)
	"My Lord," (said Mary) "my indweller of Light hath ears and I comprehend every word which thou sayest.
"Night, therefore, observed from Heaven, is nothing else than day	"Now, therefore, my Lord, on account of the word which thou hast spoken: 'All the souls of men who shall receive the mysteries of the Light will go into the Inheritance of the Light before all the rulers who will repent, and before those of the whole region of the Right and before the whole region of the Treasury of the Light . . .' On account of this, my Lord, thou hast said unto us aforetime:
or, as one might aver, the day is half the night. For ye must understand that when the Sun ascends, leaving us here in night, the day is just beginning in such places as India and Africa.	"'The first will be last and the last will be first,'—
"And when our Sun shineth, their day waneth and they have night."	that is, the 'last' are the whole race of men which will enter into the Light-Kingdom sooner than all those of the region of the Height, who are in the 'first.'" (CH. 87:197)

22
The Third Question

Now Faustus and his friend discuss falling stars. While there is no apparent text comparison for this chapter, it reflects the alchemical event we have been anticipating. The Nigredo phase of the process (in which base metal is dissolved and reduced to its essential components) has come to an end, and now, says renowned scholar and alchemist Stanislas Klossowski de Rola, comes "the appearance on the (metal's) surface of a starry aspect, which is likened to the night sky . . . And so the first work, the first degree of perfection, nears completion when, from the mutual destruction of conjoint opposites, there appears the metallic, volatile humidity which is the Mercury of the wise."[1]

When Mercury in its starry aspect appears on the blackened Body, it is said by alchemists that a "messenger" has appeared who will reunite Heaven and Earth. The falling stars are clearly a reference to Mercury's role as mediator between the two realms, notwithstanding Faustus's dismissal of them as "a fancy of mankind."

Faustus also mentions "hard, black and greenish" shooting stars, a reference, perhaps, to the chemical element antimony, a silvery substance that assumes a star-shaped pattern when crystallized and, when dissolved, turns brilliantly black. In its dual aspect, it calls to mind the star-flecked blackened stone, but antimony is to Mercury as falling slag is to the immutable stars.

FAUST BOOK

But I still do not understand," spake the Doctor from Halberstadt, "the action of the stars, how they glitter, and how they fall down to earth."

Doctor Faustus answered: "This is nothing out of the ordinary, but an everyday happening. It is indeed true that the stars, like the Firmament and other Elementa, were created and disposed in the heavens in such a fashion that they are immutable. But they do have their changes in color and in other external circumstances. The stars are undergoing superficial changes of this sort when they give off sparks or little flames, for these are bits of match falling from the stars—or as we call them, shooting stars. They are hard, black, and greenish.

"But that a star itself might fall—why this is nothing more than a fancy of mankind. When by night a great streak of light is seen to shoot downward, these are not falling stars, although we do call them that, but only slaggy pieces from the stars. They are big things, to be sure, and, as is true of the stars themselves, some are bigger than others. But it is my opinion that no star itself falleth except as a scourge of God. Then such falling stars bring a murkiness of the Heavens with them and cause great devastation of lives and land."

PART THREE

Here Followeth the Third Part

Doctor Faustus, His Adventures, the Things He Performed and Worked with His Nigromantia at the Courts of Great Potentates

In part three Faustus experiences a dramatic transformation. In his journey to the stars he transcended the bounds of ordinary reality and became omniscient, and now he begins to exhibit extraordinary powers. He teleports himself and others on four more "circulations" or journeys, summons objects out of the air, conjures up historical figures, and performs magical healings and transformations—all of which signify stages of the ongoing spiritual process.

As part three opens, a new alchemical phase begins. It is a time of greening as the metal revives and takes on new form. The volatile Mercurial spirits that appeared on its surface rise in the vessel "receiving . . . celestial and purifying influences above," as de Rola reports, then fall again to reenter the Body and induce a chemical transmutation. The reforming of the Stone corresponds to the creation of Adam in the underlying myth. He represents the "new Earth" that must be "mined" to produce the Gold. As Adam's story begins and we move to the microcosmic phase of the myth, the divine souls' stories end. In chapters 24–27 the scriptural passages are devoted to a Gnostic version of Adam's birth, his temptation in paradise and the soteriological issues arising from the contradictions in his nature. The Apochryphon of John turns the Genesis account on its head, reversing good and evil by portraying the God of the Bible, in the person of false god, Yaltabaoth, as Adam's seducer. In this account, Yaltabaoth competes with the Father for possession of Adam's soul, and it is the Father who urges Eve to eat from the tree of knowledge (Epinoia of the light)—not to debase her, but to remind her of her heavenly origin. The Epinoia (also a female emanation of the Light) watches over Adam and protects him from the false god's temptations.

As the struggle between the gods goes back and forth, the oscillations in the alchemist's vessel are bringing the metal closer to balance and a stable conjunction. The alchemist rotates it on the "fiery wheel" of elements, transmuting it from fire (warm and dry) to earth (cold and dry) to air (hot and moist) to water (cold and moist) in order to alter its elemental structure, reduce inherent oppositions of the elements and bring unity to the chaotic mixture. Then he slowly intensifies his fire, drying the Body and "feeding" it solids and liquids, although not so much of the latter that it would prevent the desired congelation. The metal begins to display a succession of vibrant colors called Peacock's Tail. They demonstrate the varying strengths of the different qualities of the mixture and herald the appearance of the Queen, the glorious Stone whose whiteness encompasses every color of the visible spectrum. The alchemist keeps strict control of his fire and the feeding of the Stone, maintaining sufficient moisture in the vessel so that it "grows," says Ripley, "and waxes full of courage."

In Faustus's final "circulation" he charms up silver bowls with exotic fruits for a hungry pregnant countess to eat. Silver signifies the essence of the Stone that is now revealed, the Prima Materia—or ground of being from which all forms arise—whose purity reflects the ineffable light of Spirit. The hungry countess's consumption of the white, red, and green fruits is a reference to the White Stone's having absorbed the colors of the Peacock's Tail; her condition reflects the state of the resurrected Stone which is pregnant with all earthly potential. Its glorious appearance completes the lesser half of the alchemical process and represents the triumph of the feminine principle, which is signified by the Moon.

Faustus' "circulations" also suggest that the disciple is continuing to raise and lower the Kundalini. As it rises and pierces each whirling energy center along the invisible spine, it burns out impurities or emotional knots, just as the revolving Sun and Moon in the Mani myth extract and purify the Father's Light. As part three ends Faustus will sign a second pact with the Devil and embark on another soul separation to purge his remaining gross matter and ready himself for a final assault on the "Gates of Heaven."

23
A History of the Emperor Charles V and Doctor Faustus

In this chapter the events of Faustus's visit to Emperor Charles the Fifth in Innsbruck signify the beginning of the expansive Jupiter phase of the alchemical process. As the metal in the vessel transmutes and begins to reveal a series of beautiful colors, the feminine principle begins to assert itself. The glyph for Jupiter, ♃, symbolizes the resurgence of the feminine, for there the lunar crescent is above, although still attached to, the cross of matter. In the glyph for Saturn, which ruled the previous phase, the Moon is set beneath the cross, ♄, signifying the universal, feminine life force imprisoned in matter.

In the Faust Book this transition is demonstrated by the courtly interactions between Emperor Charles the Fifth and conjured images of Alexander the Great and his spouse. Charles is presented here as Alexander's descendant who cannot equal him in power and organizational ability. His relative weakness vis-à-vis Alexander illustrates the waning influence of the cross at this stage of the alchemical process. Just as earth limits and restrains the life force, Alexander limited or imposed his will on the lands he conquered. He appears before the Emperor clad in "full harness," suggesting authoritarian control or the "measures and moments" of the material realm that bind the universal spirit. The emperor's relative weakness is confirmed when he attempts to rise to greet the legendary Emperor (a gesture unworthy of a monarch) and is further confirmed when Faustus prevents him from rising to Alexander's height. Alexander is associated in the text comparison with the lion-faced basilisk in the Pistis Sophia, a creature linked to infernal things and to the earth, or imperfect matter. As Jesus subdues the basilisk, Alexander's image in the Faust Book bows and disappears.

When Alexander exits his spouse becomes the focus of attention. Her colorful appearance corresponds to the changing colors of the Stone as it turns on the alchemist's "wheel." She was "clothed all in blue velvet, embroidered with gold pieces and pearls and her cheeks were rosy like unto milk and blood mixed." Her complexion suggests Ripley's prescription for the Body when it has been sufficiently dried. Feed it "mylke and mete," he says, and not too much of the former, lest "watry humors not overgrow the blood."[1]

In the Faust Book, the emperor's amusing discovery of a wen hidden beneath the spouse's clothing signifies Yaltabaoth's discovery in the Apochryphon of John of the Mother-Father's image illuminated beneath the waters overhead. This sight will inspire the inferior god to create the first man.

FAUST BOOK

Our Emperor Charles the Fifth of that name was come with his court entourage to Innsbruck,

Whither Doctor Faustus had also resorted.

Well acquainted with his arts and skills were divers knights and counts, particularly those whom he had relieved of sundry pains and diseases, so that he was invited, summoned, and accompanied to meat at court.

Here the Emperor espied him and wondered who he might be.

When someone remarked that it was Doctor Faustus, the Emperor noted it well, but held his peace until after meat (this being in the summer and after St. Philip and St. James).

Then the Emperor summoned Faustus into his privy chamber and, disclosing to him that he deemed him adept in nigromantia, did therefore desire to be shown a proof in something, which he would like to know.

He vowed unto Faustus by his Imperial Crown that no ill should befall him, and Doctor Faustus did obediently acquiesce to oblige his Imperial Majesty.

"Now hear me then," quoth the Emperor. "In my camp I once did stand a-thinking, how my ancestors before me did rise to such high degree and sovereignty as would scarcely be attainable for me and my successors, especially how Alexander the Great, of all monarchs the most mighty, was a light and an ornament among all Emperors.

"Ah, it is well known what great riches, how many kingdoms and territories he did possess and acquire, the which to conquer and organize again will fall most difficult for me and my succession, such territories being now divided into separate kingdoms.

"It is my constant wish that I had been acquainted with this man and had been able to behold him and his spouse in the figure, form, mien, and bearing of life. I understand that thou be an adept master in thine art, able to realize all things according to matter and complexion, and my most gracious desire is that thou give me some answer now in that regard."

"Most gracious Lord," quoth Faustus, "I will, in so far as I with my spirit am able, comply with your Imperial Majesty's desire as concerns the personages of Alexander and his spouse, their aspect and figure, and cause them to appear here. But your Majesty shall know that their mortal bodies cannot be present, risen up from the dead, for such is impossible.

"Rather it will be after this wise: the spirits are experienced, most wise and ancient spirits, able to assume the bodies of such people, so transforming themselves that your Imperial Majesty will in this manner behold the veritable Alexander."

Faustus then left the Emperor's chamber to take counsel with his spirit. Being afterward come in again to the Emperor's chamber, he indicated to him that he was about to be obliged, but upon the one condition that he would pose no questions, nor speak at all, which the Emperor agreed to.

FAUST BOOK	PISTIS SOPHIA
Doctor Faustus opened the door. Presently Emperor Alexander entered	And Jesus continued: "And Self-Willed sent out of the height . . . another great Light power.
in the form which he had born in life—	"It came down into the chaos as a flying arrow, that he might help his emanations so that they might take away the Lights from Pistis Sophia anew.
namely: a well-proportioned, stout little man with a red beard, ruddy cheeks, and a countenance as austere as had he the eyes of the Basilisk.	"One of them changed itself into the form of a great serpent; another again changed itself also into the form of a seven-headed basilisk. . . ." (Ch. 66:136)

FAUST BOOK	PISTIS SOPHIA
He stepped forward in full harness and, going up to Emperor Charles, made a low and reverent curtsey before him.	"I myself went down into the chaos, shining most exceedingly, and approached the lion-faced power, which shone most exceedingly. . . .
Doctor Faustus restrained the Emperor of Christendom from rising up to receive him.	"And took its whole Light in it . . . and I took away the power of all the emanations of Self-Willed and they all fell down in the chaos powerless." (Ch. 66:139–140)
Shortly thereafter, Alexander having again bowed and gone out the door, his spouse now approached the Emperor, she, too, making a curtsey.	"And Pistis Sophia continued and sang praises unto me, saying: 'Thou hast led me down out of the higher aeon which is above, and hast led me up to the regions which are below. . . . And thou hast smitten the basilisk with the seven heads and cast it out with thy hands and hast set me above its matter. . . .'" (Ch.70:154)
She was clothed all in blue velvet, embroidered with gold pieces and pearls. She too was excellent fair and rosy cheeked, like unto milk and blood mixed, tall and slender and with a round face.	**APOCHRYPHON OF JOHN**
Emperor Charles was thinking the while: "Now I have seen two personages whom I have long desired to know,	And a voice came from the exalted aeon heaven: "The Man exists and the Son of Man."
and certainly it cannot be otherwise but that the spirit hath indeed changed himself into these forms, and he doth deceive me.	And the chief archon, Yaltabaoth, heard it and thought that the voice had come from his mother. And he did not know from where it came.
"It being even as with the woman who raised the prophet Samuel for Saul." But desiring to be the more certain of the matter, the Emperor thought to himself:	
"I have often heard tell that she had a great wen on her back. If it is to be found upon this image also, then I would believe it all the better."	And he taught them, the holy and perfect Mother-Father, the complete foreknowledge, the image of the invisible one who is the Father of the all and through whom everything came into being, the first Man. For he revealed his likeness in a human form.

FAUST BOOK

So, stepping up to her

he did lift her skirt, and found the wen.

APOCHRYPHON OF JOHN

And the whole aeon of the chief archon trembled, and the foundations of the abyss shook.

And of the waters which are above matter, the underside was illuminated by the appearance of his image which had been revealed. And when all the authorities and the chief archon looked, they saw the whole region of the underside, which was illuminated. And through the Light they saw the form of the image in the water. (14:14–35)

24
Concerning the Antlers of a Hart

In this chapter Faustus "charms a pair of hart's horns upon [a] knight's head" and traps him in a window where he sleeps. The horns, like tombs, sepulchers and other death-associated objects, signify matter in which the spirit is imprisoned or lies undiscovered. An account of Sophia's enlightenment in the Pistis Sophia uses similar imagery. She praises her Savior for restoring "the activity of life" to her "dead bones."

These accounts surround the creation of Adam in the Apochryphon of John. The false god enlists a host of angels and authorities to create the first man, but in their ignorance, they omit the spark of Light that gives life. As a result, Adam, like Faustus's sleeping knight, does not move. He "lies inactive and motionless" or "asleep." Although they do not all appear in the text comparison, the Apochryphon of John lists each angel and authority by name together with the body part he creates. The list is long and the names, such as Dearko, Boabel, Belual, and Abenlenarchei, evoke a sense of ceremonial magic. The rulers in the false god's hierarchy create the pattern for the first man and fashion the body-soul while certain angels make the body and others devise the workings of the mind and senses. The mother of matter oversees demons who create the evil impulses that are native to the flesh. Sophia moves to correct their oversight and makes a hidden intervention. It enables the unwitting Yaltabaoth to revive the lifeless Adam and, as he does, Faustus awakens the sleeping knight.

FAUST BOOK	APOCHRYPHON OF JOHN	PISTIS SOPHIA
	And (the chief) Archon said to the authorities which attend him: "Come, let us create a man according to the image of God and according to our likeness. . . ."	
	And they created by means of their respective powers in correspondence with the characteristics, which were given.	
Upon a time, soon after Dr. Faustus had accomplished the Emperor's will, as was reported above, he, hearing the signal for meat in the evening, did lean over the battlements to watch domestics go out and in.	And each authority supplied a characteristic in the form of the image, which he had seen in its natural form.	
There he espied one who was fallen asleep while lying in the window of the great Knights' Hall across the court (it being very hot).	He created a being according to the likeness of the first, perfect Man.	
I would not name the person for it was a knight and a gentleman by birth.	And they said, "Let us call him Adam, that his name may become a power of Light for us."	
Now with the aid of his spirit Mephistopheles, Faustus did charm a pair of hart's horns upon the knight's head.	And the powers began: the first one, goodness, created a bone soul. . . .	"Thou hast taken dead bones and hast clothed them with a body . . .

FAUST BOOK	APOCHRYPHON OF JOHN	PISTIS SOPHIA
	This is the number of the angels: together they are 365. They all worked on it until, limb for limb, the natural and the material body was completed by them. . . . (19:3–6) And their product was completely inactive for a long time. (19:15)	
	The Mother-Father sent . . . the five Lights down upon the place of the angels of the chief archon. (And they said) to Yaltabaoth: "Blow into his face something of your spirit and the body will arise. . . ." And the power of the Mother went out of Yaltabaoth into the natural body.	
The good lord's head nodded on the window sill.	The body moved and gained strength,	"And to them who stirred not hast thou given the activity of life,
He awoke and perceived the prank.	and it was luminous. (19:17–35)	"and thou hast taken all my powers in which was no Light, and hast bestowed on them within purified Light.
	And his intelligence was superior to all those who had made him. (20:5)	
Who could have been more distressed!	When (the powers) looked up they saw that his thinking was superior. . . . (20:34) And they brought Adam into the shadow of death in order that they might form him again from earth and water and fire and the spirit, which originates in matter, which is the ignorance of darkness and desire.	

FAUST BOOK	APOCHRYPHON OF JOHN	PISTIS SOPHIA
For the windows being closed, he could go neither forward nor backward with his antlers, nor could he force the horns from off his head.	This is the tomb of the newly formed body, with which the robbers had clothed the man, the bond of forgetfulness;	
The Emperor, observing his plight, laughed and was well-pleased withal.	and he became a mortal man.	
Until Faustus at last released the poor knight from the spell.	But the Epinoia of the Light, which was in him, she is the one who was to awaken his thinking. (21:4–160)	"And unto all my limbs in which no Light stirred, thou hast given life-Light out of thy Height." (Ch. 70:159)

25
Concerning Three Lords Who Were Rapidly Transported to a Royal Wedding in Munich

The birth of the divided Adam shifts the focus to human rather than divine salvation, and the stories of the divine transgressors now come to an end. Sophia and the Logos are redeemed and the pleroma is restored to its original unity. The three young lords who attend a royal wedding in this chapter represent the three soul-types mentioned in the Tripartite Tractate—the spiritual, psychic, and material—who descended through Adam from the fallen and trifurcated Logos. They become separated in the story and their subsequent reunion corresponds to the Logos's reunification, while the wedding they attend signifies the restoration of the pleroma resulting from his return.

Sophia will continue to appear as Ennoia, her enlightened self,[1] however, to bring the Father's Light to the world. In keeping with her role as an exemplar, highlights from her hymns and her return to the pleroma will appear later on when Faustus receives his final revelation.

In the Faust Book, the three lords are given specific instructions by Faustus before attending the wedding. Their different responses to the instructions reflect the responses of the different soul-types. One of them speaks when he has been told not to and is thrown into prison. He is the hesitant psychic soul who the Tripartite Tractate says "through a voice must be instructed."

The young lords fly through the air with Faustus, from Wittemberg and back again, signifying that another alchemical circulation is taking place. The metal has been fed with "mylke and mete," and now it is being sublimed. A temperate heat sustained over a long period putrefies the mixture once again, whereupon the "Soul" emerges and circulates gently, returning to spiritualize the Body. The disobedient lord's imprisonment in the dungeon signifies the metal's putrefaction, while his release reflects the freeing of the "metal's Soul" from the corrupted Body.[2] The royal wedding represents the conjunction being formed by this process in which the Body will be spiritualized and the Spirit embodied. When this occurs, says Ripley, a change is seen in the color of the metal.

> *When they thus together purified be,*
> *They will sublime up whiter than the snow,*
> *(Which) sight will greatly comfort thee.*[3]

The conjunction will take place in the following chapter and, soon thereafter, the glorious White Stone or "White Swan" will appear.

FAUST BOOK	TRIPARTITE TRACTATE
Three sons of noble lords (whom I dare not call by name)	Mankind came to be in three essential types, the spiritual, the psychic and the material, conforming to the triple disposition of the Logos. (118:15)
	The election shares body and essence with the Savior
were students in Wittemberg.	since it is like a bridal chamber
They met together on a time	because of its unity and agreement with him.
and, talking of the magnificent pomp which would attend the wedding of the son of the Duke of Bavaria	The calling, however, has the place of those who rejoice at the bridal chamber and who are glad and happy at the union of the bridegroom and bride.
in Munich,	The place, which the calling will have, is the aeon of the images, where the Logos has not yet joined with the pleroma.

FAUST BOOK	TRIPARTITE TRACTATE	PISTIS SOPHIA
did heartily wish that they might go there, if only for a half hour.	And since the man of the Church was happy and glad at this, as he was hoping for it, he separated spirit, soul, and body . . .	
Such talk caused one of them to take thought of Doctor Faustus,	though within him is the man who is the Totality—and he is all of them. (22:15–35)	
and he said to the other two lords: "Cousins, if ye will follow me, hush and keep it to yourselves, then will I give you good counsel, how we can see the wedding	When the redemption was proclaimed, the perfect man received knowledge immediately,	
and then be back to Wittemberg again in the self-same night.	so as to return in haste to the place from which he came, to return there joyfully, to the place from which he flowed forth.	
Here is what I have in mind; if we send for Doctor Faustus		(And Jesus said) "It came to pass then, when they pursued after Pistis Sophia,
tell him what we desire, and explain our plans to him, giving him a bit of money besides, then he surely will not deny us his aid."		"that she cried out again and sang praises to the Light
Having deliberated and agreed upon the matter, they called on Doctor Faustus, who, touched by their present and also well pleased with a banquet which they were clever enough to give in his honor, did consent to grant them his services.		"since I had said to her: 'If thou shalt be constrained and singest praises unto me, I will come quickly and help thee.' It came to pass, then . . . that she sang praises to the Light . . ." (Ch. 77:171)

FAUST BOOK	TRIPARTITE TRACTATE	PISTIS SOPHIA
The day arrived when the Bavarian Duke's son was to be celebrated, and Doctor Faustus sent word to the young lords that they should come to his house	His members, however, needed a place of instruction	
arrayed in the very finest clothing they possessed.	which is in the places which are adorned, so that they might receive from them resemblance to the images and archetypes, like a mirror	
He then took a broad cloak, spread it out in his garden (which lay right beside his house) seated the lords upon it, himself in their midst,	until all the members of the body of the Church are in a single place, and receive the restoration at one time, when they have been manifested as the whole body—the restoration of the pleroma.	
and at last gave strict command that none should speak a word so long as they be abroad even though they should be in the Bavarian Duke's palace and someone should speak to them, they should give no answer—the which they did all pledge to obey.	It has a preliminary concord with a mutual agreement, which is the concord which belongs to the Father,	
The matter being settled, Doctor Faustus sat down and commenced his *conjurationes.*		It came to pass, then, when Jesus had finished telling his disciples all the adventures which had befallen Pistis Sophia . . . that (he) continued . . .

FAUST BOOK	TRIPARTITE TRACTATE	PISTIS SOPHIA
Presently there arose a great wind, which lifted the cloak and transported them through the air with such speed that they arrived betimes at the Duke's court in Munich.		"It came to pass, then, after all this time, that I took Pistis Sophia and led her into the thirteenth aeon. . . .
They had traveled invisible, so that no one noticed them	until the Totalities receive a countenance in accordance with him.	"I entered the region of the four and twenty invisibles, shining most exceedingly.
until they entered the Bavarian Palace and came into the hall where the marshall, espying them, indicated to the Duke of Bavaria how, although the princes, lords, and gentlemen were already seated at table, there were still standing three more gentlemen without who had just arrived with a servant, and who also ought to be received.	The restoration is at the end, after the Totality reveals what it is, the Son . . . and after the Totalities reveal themselves in that one, in the proper way,	"And they fell into great commotion; they looked and saw Sophia, who was with me.
The old Duke of Bavaria arose to do this, but when he approached and spake to them, none would utter a word.	who is the inconceivable one, and the ineffable one, (123:4–30)	"Her they knew, but me they knew not who I was. "It came to pass then, when Pistis Sophia saw her fellows, the invisibles, that she rejoiced . . . and desired to proclaim the wonders I had wrought on her below in the earth of mankind. . . .
		"And in their midst she sang praises unto me, saying:
This occurred in the evening, just before meat, they having hitherto observed all day the		

FAUST BOOK	TRIPARTITE TRACTATE	PISTIS SOPHIA
pomp of the wedding, without any hindrance,		"'And when I was come out of the Height, I wandered in regions in which is no Light.
for Faustus's art had kept them invisible.	and the invisible one,	
As was reported above, Doctor Faustus had sternly forbidden them to speak this day.	and the incomprehensible one,	
He had further instructed them that so soon as he should call out: "Up and away!" all were to seize upon the cloak at once and they would fly away again in the twinkling of an eye.	so that it receives redemption.	"'And the Light saved me in all my afflictions. "'It guided me in the creation of the aeons to lead me up into the thirteenth aeon, my dwelling place.
Now when the Duke of Bavaria spoke to them and they gave no answer, hand water was proffered them anyhow.		"'When I failed of my power, thou hast given me power, and when I failed of my Light, thou didst fill me with purified Light.
It was then that Doctor Faustus, hearing one of the lords forget himself and violate his command,		"'For I have provoked the commandment of the Light and have transgressed
did cry aloud: "Up and away!" Faustus and the two lords who held to the cloak were instantly flown away	It was not only release from the domination of the left ones, nor was it only escape from the power of those of the right . . .	
but the third, who had been negligent, was taken captive and cast into a cell.	from whom none escapes without quickly becoming theirs again. (124:1–2)	and I have made wroth the commandment of the Light.'" (Ch. 81:176) Philip . . . said: "The prophet David hath prophesied the solution to (Sophia's) song:

FAUST BOOK	TRIPARTITE TRACTATE	PISTIS SOPHIA
The other two lords did upon arrival at midnight in Wittemberg behave so glumly on account of their kinsman that Doctor Faustus sought to console them, and he promised that the young man would be released by morning.	Among the men who are in the flesh redemption began to be given, his first born, and his love, the Son . . . (125:15)	"'Let them give thanks unto the Lord for his graciousness and his wondrous works unto the children of men.
	he is called "the Redemption of the angels of the Father," he who comforted those who were laboring under the Totality for his knowledge, because he was given the grace before anyone else. (125:20)	
The captive lord, being thus forsaken, in locked custody besides, and constrained by guards was sore afraid.		"'Them who sat in darkness and the shadow of death, who were fettered in misery and iron.
	Just as reception of knowledge of him is a manifestation of his lack of envy and the abundance of his sweetness . . .	
To make matters worse, he was questioned as to what manner of vision he had been part of, and as to the other three who were now vanished away.	so, too, he has been found to be a cause of ignorance, although he is also a begetter of knowledge.	
He thought: "If I betray them, then the ending will be bad." He therefore gave no answer to those who were sent to him,	In a hidden and incomprehensible wisdom he kept the knowledge to the end	
and when they saw that nothing was to be got out of him this day,	until the Totalities became weary while searching for God the Father, whom no one found through his own wisdom or power.	

FAUST BOOK	TRIPARTITE TRACTATE	PISTIS SOPHIA
they finally informed him that on the morrow he would be brought down to the dungeon, tortured and compelled to speak.		"'Their hearts were humbled in their miseries; they became weak and no one helped them.
The lord thought to himself: "So my ordeal is appointed for the morrow. If Doctor Faustus should not release me today, should I be tortured and racked, well then I must needs speak."	He gives himself so that they might receive knowledge of the abundant thought about his great glory . . . he who reveals himself eternally to those who have been worthy of the Father. (126:1–24)	
But he still had the consolation that his friends would entreat Doctor Faustus for his release, and that is the way it turned out.		"'They cried unto the Lord in their affliction; he saved them out of their necessities.
Before daybreak Doctor Faustus was in the cell, having cast such a spell on the watch that they fell into a heavy sleep. Faustus used his art to open all doors and locks.		"'And he led them out of the darkness and the shadow of death and brake their bonds asunder. "'For he hath shattered the gates of brass and burst the bolts of iron asunder.
And he brought the lord punctually to Wittemberg, where a sumptuous honorarium was presented him as a reward.		"'He hath taken them unto himself out of the way of their iniquity.'" (82:180)

26
Concerning an Adventure with a Jew

This adventure of Faust and a moneylender seems to be a reworked version of a tale written around the time the Faust Book appeared. The author, one Christof Rosshirt from Nuremberg, wrote four stories thought to have been based on the life of the legendary sorcerer, George Faust. As Rosshirt's story goes, Faustus borrows money from a Jew and, when the latter comes to collect it, he pretends to be asleep. The Jew tugs on Faustus's leg to wake him up, but the leg comes off and flies away. When the terrified man flees, thinking he will be accused of murder, Faustus retrieves his leg and keeps the borrowed money. In the Faust Book, Faustus pulls off his own leg and gives it to a Jewish money lender as pawn for a loan. He also regains his leg and keeps the money.

Like the Faust Book version, Rosshirt's tale may have a Gnostic origin, for it adapts itself to a revelation by Jesus in the Pistis Sophia concerning the expansion of the universe. There Jesus tells the disciples that the Ineffable has "rent itself asunder" and assures them that souls who have understood this mystery of emanation must pass through the "retributive receivers" but, like Faustus's elusive leg and money, they "cannot be grasped." As Faustus and the Jew argue over money, in the Apocryphon of John, we find the Father and Yaltabaoth battling for Adam's soul, or the Light that is hidden inside him. The false god and his archons have refashioned Adam out of material substance to make him a mortal man and, as the Apochryphon puts it, "clothed (him) in the bond of forgetfulness." Now the Epinoia of the Light, a reflection of the Mother/Father, hides inside of Adam, and as the archons plot to tempt and corrupt him, she reveals herself to remind him of his divine nature and to help him resist the archons' seduction.

The chief archon tries to capture the Epinoia by pulling her out of Adam's rib, and when that fails he creates a false image of her in order to seduce the divided man. This is Eve, the first woman, who, the author reminds us, did not come out of Adam's rib as the Bible reports but was fashioned from a portion of the false god's power. As the chief archon tries to pull the Epinoia out of Adam's rib, Faustus pulls off his leg. "Money" and "leg" are thus equated in the comparison with the Epinoia's revelation.

The imagery in Rosshirt's version most certainly has roots in the alchemical tradition, as demonstrated by Nicholas Flamel in fourteenth-century frescoes based on an old (date unknown) manuscript by Abraham the Jew. There, Saturn wields a scythe and is about to cut off the legs of Mercurius. In two manuscripts in the Bibliothéque de l'Arsenal entitled *Les Figures d'Abraham le Juif* (nos. 2518 and 3047) this has been interpreted as the capture or fixation of Mercury by Sulphur.[1] Indeed, this imagery appears in the Faust Book to inform us that the conjunction anticipated in the last chapter has occurred. The Royal Wedding has taken place and the purified Stone will soon reveal its essence: the Prima Materia or Philosophical Tree with its marvelous fruits that signify all earthly potential. This crowns the first or feminine half of the Work; in the glyph for this lunar phase the Moon stands alone, ☽, freed from the cross of matter.

FAUST BOOK	APOCHRYPHON OF JOHN	PISTIS SOPHIA
It is said that the fiend and the sorcerer will not wax three penny richer in a year, and even so did it come to pass with Doctor Faustus.		Then Mary Magdalene came forward . . . wept aloud and said: "Have mercy on me, my Lord, for my brethren have heard and let go of the words which thou saidst unto them. . . .
Much had been promised by his spirit,		"But I have heard thee say unto me: 'From now on I will begin to discourse with you concerning the total gnosis of the mystery of the Ineffable. . . .'
but much had been lies, for the Devil is the spirit of lies.	"And the archons took (Adam) and placed him in paradise. And they said to him, 'Eat . . .' for their luxury is bitter and their beauty is depraved. And their luxury is deception and their trees are godlessness and their fruit is deadly poison and their promise is death. "And the tree of their life they had placed in the midst of paradise.	"'For this cause, therefore, my brothers have . . . ceased to sense in what manner thou discoursest with them. . . . If the gnosis of all this is in that mystery, where is the man . . . in this world who hath the ability to understand that mystery with all its gnosis and the type of all these words which thou hast spoken concerning it?" (Ch. 94:217)
Mephistopheles at once reproached Doctor Faustus,		When Jesus . . . knew that the disciples had heard (these words) and had begun to let go, . . . he encouraged them
saying: "With the skill wherewith I have endowed thee thou shouldst acquire thine own wealth. "Such arts as mine can scarcely lose thee money.	"And I shall teach you what is the mystery of their life, which is the plan which they made together, which is the likeness of their spirit.	and said: . . . "Grieve no more, my disciples, concerning the mystery of the Ineffable, thinking that ye will not understand it. . . .

FAUST BOOK	APOCHRYPHON OF JOHN	PISTIS SOPHIA
"Thy years are not yet over. Only four years are past since my promise to thee that thou wouldst want neither for gold nor for goods.	"The root of this tree is bitter and its branches are death . . . and desire is its seed,	"That mystery is yours and everyone's who will renounce the whole world and the whole matter therein." (Ch. 95:217)
"Why thy meat and drink hath been brought thee from the courts of all the great potentates, all by mine art."	and it sprouts in darkness." (21:19–36)	"Now, therefore hearken . . . that I may urge you on to the gnosis of the mystery of the Ineffable concerning which I discourse with you . . ." (Ch. 95:218)
(What the spirit states, we did already report above.)		"He, then, who shall receive the one and only word of that mystery, which I have told you. . . .
Doctor Faustus, who did not know how to disagree with these things, began to wonder just how apt he might be in obtaining money.	"But what they call the tree of knowledge of good and evil, which is the Epinoia of the Light, they stayed in front of it in order that Adam might not look up to his fullness and recognize the nakedness of his shamefulness.	
Not long after the spirit had told him those things, Faustus went banqueting with some good fellows.	"But it was I who brought about that they ate . . . The serpent taught them to eat from wickedness of begetting, lust, and destruction, that Adam might be useful to him.	
		"If he cometh forth out of the body of the matter of the rulers,
		when, therefore, the retributive receivers free the soul which hath received this one and only mystery of the Ineffable . . .

FAUST BOOK	APOCHRYPHON OF JOHN	PISTIS SOPHIA
And finding himself without money		then will it straightaway, if it be set free from the body of matter,
went and raised some in the Jewish quarter,		become a great Light-stream in the midst of those receivers
accepting sixty Talers for a month's time. The money lender, when the loan fell due, was ready to take his capital together with the usury, but Doctor Faustus was not of the opinion that he ought to pay anything.	"And Adam knew that he was disobedient to him (the chief archon) due to the Light of the Epinoia which is in him, which made him more correct in his thinking than the chief archon.	and the receivers will not be able to seize it." (Ch. 96:227)
The fellow appeared at Faustus' house with his demand	"And (the latter) wanted to bring about the power which he himself had given him.	"But it will pass through all the regions of the rulers . . .
and received this answer:		and it will not give answers to any region,
"Jew, I have no money. I can raise no money.	"And he brought a forgetfulness over Adam." (22:5–20)	nor giveth it apologies nor giveth it any tokens. . . .
"But this I will do. From my body I will amputate a member, be it arm or leg, and give it thee in pawn,	"Then the Epinoia of the Light hid herself in Adam. And the chief archon wanted to bring her out of his rib.	
but it must be returned so soon as I am in money again."	"But the Epinoia of the Light cannot be grasped.	
The Jew (for Jews are enemies of us Christians anyhow) pondered the matter and concluded that it must be a right reckless man who would place his limbs in pawn. But still he accepted it.		"And that mystery knoweth wherefore the Incomprehensibles, which pertain to the second space of the Ineffable, have rent themselves asunder and come forth from the Fatherless." (Ch. 95:220)

FAUST BOOK	APOCHRYPHON OF JOHN	PISTIS SOPHIA
Doctor Faustus took a saw and, cutting off his leg withal, committed it unto the Jew		"And that mystery knoweth itself, wherefore it hath rent itself asunder to come forth from the Ineffable.
(but it was only a hoax)	"Although Darkness pursued her, it did not catch her.	
		"Of these, then, will I speak unto you . . . those who will arise and those who . . . emanate, and those who come forth . . .
upon the condition that it must be returned so soon as he be in money again and would pay his debt for he would fain put the member back on.		and those who are implanted in them . . ." (Ch. 96:225)
The Jew went away with the leg,	"And he brought a part of his power out of him.	
	"And he made another creature in the form of a woman according to the likeness of the Epinoia . . . (22:30–37) And he brought the part which he had taken from the power of the man into the female creature, and not as Moses said, 'his rib bone.'	
well satisfied at first with his contract and agreement.	"And he (Adam) saw the woman beside him.	
But very soon he became vexed and tired of the leg, for he thought, "What good to me is a knave's leg? If I carry it home it will begin to stink.	"And in that moment the luminous Epinoia appeared, and she lifted the veil which lay over his mind.	

FAUST BOOK	APOCHRYPHON OF JOHN	PISTIS SOPHIA
"I doubt that he will be able to put it on again whole, and besides this pledge is a parlous thing for me, for no higher pawn can a man give than his own limb. But what profit will I have of it?"	"And he became sober from the drunkenness of Darkness."	
		"But all of the regions of the rulers and all of the emanations of the Light—every one singeth unto (the soul) praises in their regions
Thinking these and such like things as he crossed over a bridge, the Jew did cast the leg into the water.	**TRIPARTITE TRACTATE**	in fear of the Light of the stream which envelopeth that soul,
Doctor Faustus knew all about this of course,	"And he recognized his counter image,	
and three days later he summoned the Jew in order to settle his account. The Jew appeared		until it goeth to the region of the inheritance of the mystery which it hath received
and explained his considerations, saying he had thrown the leg away because it was of no use to anyone. Doctor Faustus immediately demanded that his pledge be returned or that some other settlement be made. The Jew was eager to be free of Faustus and he finally had to pay him sixty Guilders more (Doctor Faustus still having his leg as before).	and he said, 'This is indeed bone of my bones and flesh of my flesh.'" (23:1–12)	and until it becometh one with its Limbs." (Ch. 96:228)

27
An Adventure at the Court of Count Anhalt

Food and fruit play a special role in this chapter, in which Faustus satisfies a hungry pregnant countess by charming up exotic fruits for her to eat. At the same time, in the Apochryphon of John, Adam and Eve eat from the tree of the knowledge of good and evil. This is the Father's tree and its fruit is the Epinoia of the Light who has come to awaken them and to "rectify the deficiency" Sophia had created.

The Pistis Sophia refers back to Sophia's own rectification—the model for all human redemption—by returning to her hymns. Philip interprets her final song of praise to Jesus for having cleansed her of error and returned her to the pleroma. As in the Apochryphon of John, he uses a gustatory metaphor for spiritual enlightenment, quoting from David's 106th Psalm, which praises the Lord "who hath satisfied a hungering soul with good things."

A second passage from the Pistis Sophia refers to the nature of this spiritual "food." It consists of secrets that comprise the First Mystery of the Ineffable. Jesus tells the disciples that those who receive the First Mystery will understand why the earth, the heavenly regions, and the varieties of natural phenomena were formed, and why the wide range of human behavior arose. The list is long and continues in the chapter that follows.

There is much alchemical symbolism in this chapter. The countess's hunger, or the image of eating, represents the White Stone's absorption of the colors of the Peacock's Tail—a sign of its new purity or unity. Her pregnancy reflects the generative qualities of the White Stone, of which more will be said at the end of the comparison.

The Apochryphon of John picks up where we left it in the last chapter and the Pistis Sophia opens with random stanzas from David's psalm—the ones Philip chose when he interpreted Sophia's hymn.

FAUST BOOK	APOCHRYPHON OF JOHN	PISTIS SOPHIA
	The savior said,	Philip came forward (and gave) the solution of the song which Pistis Sophia hath uttered, saying:
Doctor Faustus came upon a time to the Count of Anhalt	"And our sister Sophia . . . came down in innocence in order to rectify her deficiency.	
where he was received with all kindness and graciousness.		"Give ye thanks to the Lord, for he is good, his grace is eternal.
Now this was in January, and at table he perceived that the Countess was great with child.	"Therefore she was called Life, which is the mother of the living. . . .	
When the evening meat had been carried away		"Their heart abhorred all manner of meat and they were near unto the gates of death.
and the collation of sweets was being served	"And through her they have tasted the perfect Knowledge.	
Doctor Faustus said unto the Countess: "Gracious lady, I have always heard that the great bellied women long for diverse things to eat. I beg your Grace not to conceal from me what you might want."	"I appeared in the form of an eagle on the tree of knowledge, which is the Epinoia from the foreknowledge of the pure Light, that I might teach them and awaken them out of the depth of sleep.	

FAUST BOOK	APOCHRYPHON OF JOHN	PISTIS SOPHIA
	"For they were both in a fallen state and they recognized their nakedness.	
She answered him: "Truly, my Lord, I will not conceal from you my present wish that it were harvest time and I were able to eat my fill of fresh grapes and other fruit."		"Hungry and thirsty their soul fainted in them. "They cried unto the Lord
Hereupon, Doctor Faustus said: "Gracious Lady, this is easy for me to provide. In an hour your Grace's will shall be accomplished."	"The Epinoia appeared to them . . . and she awakened their thinking. "And when Yaltabaoth noticed that they withdrew from him, he cursed his earth. (23:21–38) He found the woman as she was preparing herself for her husband.	and he hearkened unto them in their affliction.
Doctor Faustus now took two silver bowls and set them out before the window. When the hour was expired he reached out and drew in one bowl with white and red grapes which were fresh from the vine, and the other bowl full of green apples and pears, but all of a strange and exotic sort.	"He was Lord over her though he did not know the mystery which had come to pass through the holy decree.	
	"And they were afraid to blame him. . . . And he cast them out of Paradise and he clothed them in gloomy darkness.	"They wandered round in the desert, in a waterless country; they found not the way to the city of their dwelling place.
Placing them before the Countess he said to her: "Your Grace need have no fear to eat,		"He led them on a straight way

FAUST BOOK	APOCHRYPHON OF JOHN	PISTIS SOPHIA
for I tell you truly that they are from a foreign land where summer is about to end, although our year is, to be sure, just beginning here."		that they might go to the region of their dwelling place.
While the Countess did eat of all the fruit with great pleasure and wonderment	"And the chief archon saw the virgin who stood by Adam, and that the luminous Epinoia of life had appeared to her.	"For he hath satisfied a hungering soul; he hath filled a hungering soul with good things." (Ch. 82:180)
the Count of Anhalt could not withhold to ask for particulars concerning the grapes and other fruit.	"And Yaltabaoth was full of ignorance." (24:1–12)	
Doctor Faustus answered: "Gracious Lord, may it please your grace to know that the year is divided into two circles in the world, so that it is summer in Orient and Occident when it is winter here, for the heavens are round. Now, from where we dwell the Sun hath now withdrawn to the highest point, so that we are having winter here, but at the same time it is descending on Orient and Occident as in Sheba, India, and the East proper.		And Jesus said unto John: "He who will receive that mystery of the Ineffable . . . "That mystery knoweth why the west hath arisen and why the east hath arisen. "And that mystery knoweth why the south hath arisen and why the north hath arisen.
"The meaning is that they are having summer now.		
"They enjoy fruits and vegetables twice a year there.		"And that mystery knoweth why famine hath arisen and why superfluity hath arisen." (Ch. 92:212)

FAUST BOOK	PISTIS SOPHIA
"Furthermore, gracious Lord, when it is night here, day is just dawning there. The Sun hath even now betaken himself beneath the earth, and it is night: but in the same instant the Sun doth run above the earth there, and they shall have day	"And that mystery knoweth why the darkness hath arisen and why the Light of Lights hath arisen." (Ch. 91:206)
(in likeness thereof the sea runneth higher than the world, and if it were not obedient to God, it would inundate the world in a moment).	"And that mystery knoweth why the seas and the waters have arisen." (Ch. 92:211)
"In consideration of such knowledge, gracious Lord, I sent my spirit to that nation upon the circumference of the sea, where the sun now riseth, although it setteth here. He is a flying spirit and swift, able to transform himself in the twinkling of an eye.	"And he who hath received the master mystery of the First Mystery all together. . . hath power to pass through all the orders of the spaces and the three Thrice-spirituals and the three spaces of the First Mystery and all their orders, and hath power to pass through all the orders of the inheritances of the Light, to pass through them from within without and from below and from below/above . . . in a word, he hath the power to pass through all the regions of the inheritances of the Light. . . ." (Ch. 91:206)
"He hath procured those grapes and fruit for us."	"And that mystery knoweth why herbs, that is the vegetables have arisen." (Ch. 92:210)
The Count did attend these revelations with great wonderment.	"And that mystery knoweth why appreciation hath arisen . . ." (Ch. 91:209)

The silver bowls that Faustus fills with conjured fruit represent the purified ground of being, or the snowy white residue that has just been sublimed in the alchemist's vessel. This is the coveted White Stone, which alchemists represent as a winter landscape that is "cold, white, still and silver under the illumination of the Moon."[1] As we saw, Faustus placed the silver bowls in the countess's window when it was winter or the month of January.

The snowy ash in the vessel is "the first embodiment or projection of the Spirit,"[2] says Julius Evola—the generative "tree" upon which grow "the fruits of Sun (gold) and Moon (silver), the red and white tinctures of the Stone."[3] The bowl with red and white grapes signifies the "tree" with its "fruit" while the bowl with green apples and pears refers to the Stone's potential for growth or transformation. "Green," says the *Dictionary of Alchemical Imagery*, "is the color of fertility, of springtime growth, of new life associated with the alchemical generation which occurs after the chemical wedding of the two seeds of metals, male Sulphur and female Argent Vive."[4]

This growth cannot be accomplished, however, unless the Stone is broken down again, for as Ripley advises in his Ninth Gate,

> *Looke how thou didst with thy imperfect body*
> *And do so with thy perfect bodys in every degree*
> *That is to say, first thou them putrefy*
> *Her primary qualities destroying utterly.*[5]

A rambling discourse by Faustus in this chapter seems to indicate that the process has begun. He tells the count that the fruit he charmed up for the countess grows in another hemisphere and then mentions alternating seasons and movements of the Sun from one part of the earth to another. These all suggest the oscillations of an alchemical rotation:

1. When it is summer in Orient and Occident, he says, it is winter here.
2. When the Sun withdraws to its highest point, the Sun descends there.
3. When it is winter here, it is summer there.
4. When it is nighttime here, day is dawning there.
5. When the Sun is beneath the earth here, the Sun rises above the earth there.
6. When it is nighttime here, the Sun is setting there.
7. When the Sun rises there, the Sun sets here.

This also seems to be a reference to the symbolic number of seven alchemical rotations and to the separation of the masculine gold (hot and solar, or summer and day) from the feminine silver (cold and lunar or winter and night). Night suggests the metal's "death" or putrefaction and daytime the reforming of the earth. The appearance and disappearance of the Sun may indicate that a copper-colored residue alchemists look for at this stage is beginning to appear, for the red-colored copper that contains the seed of gold is also represented by the Sun. To achieve its potential, the seed must be nourished and gestated, suggested by the pregnant countess and the green fruit in the second silver bowl. Green is also associated with copper because of the greenish patina that forms on its surface.

Titus Burckhardt speaks of the "rhythm of . . . successive 'rollings and unrollings' of Nature," relating these alternating forces to the movements of a serpent or dragon "which winds itself round the axis of the tree of the world." He associates them with the rhythms of alchemy and uses the same solsticial imagery as Faustus does: "the two forces represented as serpents or dragons are Sulphur and Quicksilver. Their macrocosmic prototype is the two phases—increasing and decreasing—of the sun's annual course, separated from one another by the winter and summer solstices." Burckhardt adds that this imagery is associated with "certain traditions of the East," especially tantrism.

> The connection between the tantric and Alchemical symbolisms is obvious; of the two forces, Pingala and Ida, which wind themselves round the Merudanda, the first is described as being hot and dry, characterized by the color red and, like alchemical Sulphur, compared with the sun. The second force, Ida, is regarded as being cold and humid, and in its silvery pallor is associated with the moon.[6]

Activation of these forces brings into play "wider and higher states of consciousness," just as Faustus' seasonal changes produce the exotic fruit.

It was mentioned earlier that the countess's hunger represents the absorption of the color spectrum into white, which signifies the metal's return to a state of primal unity. It also represents a hatha yogic practice in which substrates of sound on which the body rests are absorbed into the essential, all encompassing vibration, OM. According to David White,

> When the yogin raises the inner Kundalini, he is in effect telescoping these phonemes back into their higher emanates, causing the last and "lowest" phonemes, the final letters of the alphabet, to be absorbed into ever more subtle phonemes, culminating in the vowels and the phonemes Ha and Ksa . . . located on the two petals of the sixth chakra.

These phonemes still fall in the audible range, but beyond the Ajna center "exist a number of levels of increasingly subtle substrates of sound, through which manifest sound is made to shade into nonmanifest sound."[7]

Even as the alchemist's metal absorbs the colors of the Peacock's Tail and uncovers the pure white ground of the Soul, the yogin uncovers the vibratory ground of being through the absorption of manifest sound. We will return to this subject in a later chapter where Faustus chants a mantra and prepares to break through to unified consciousness.

28
The Manner in Which Doctor Faustus as Bacchus Kept Shrovetide

Faustus and his companions sneak into a nobleman's wine cellar and immerse themselves in a "luminous cloud" of inebriation, reflecting the Gnostic version of the flood story. After Adam and Eve were expelled from Paradise, the chief archon seduced Eve and the cycle of generation began. He also seduced Sophia, bringing such bitter fate upon the world that he brought forth a flood to dispel it. Here again, the story in the Apochryphon of John "is not as Moses said," for the Holy Spirit asserts that Noah and his chosen companions hid themselves in a luminous cloud and not in the ark as the Bible would have us believe.

The two seductions in the Apochryphon are appropriate to this phase of the alchemical process, for it is ruled by Venus, the goddess of love. As we enter the second, or Greater, half of the Work, the Stone has been putrefied again and now it is being fermented. The darkness of the cellar visited by Faust implies the putrefaction of the metal, while the wines being drunk there are, of course, fermented.

Copper or "impure gold" is being extracted from the mix and the solar or masculine principle begins to assert itself. "In the sign for Venus or copper," says Titus Burckhardt, "the 'sun' of the spirit appears above the 'tree' of the elemental tendencies. The color of gold appears, but it is not yet purified."[1]

The Sun is elevated above the cross of matter but is still attached to and limited by it, ♀, as a bizarre event that occurs in this chapter demonstrates. A butler who discovers the illicit revelry taking place in the nobleman's cellar is seized by Faustus, dragged by his hair and deposited on the top of a high fir tree which, like the cross in Venus's sign, has "no branches except at the very top." He represents the Sun or Spirit, which is "crucified" or bound to the cross of matter. In terms of the alchemical event taking place, the Butler's elevation above the drunken revelers represents the Spirit's release from the still unstable Body.

Copper contains a large proportion of Mercury and possesses some of its ability to transform. In this it resembles the dual-natured Venus who symbolizes matter in its initial chaotic state, but also bears the seed of the Philosophical Child. Venus presides over the "marriage bed" or union of opposites that produces the gold; her ability to rise from the depths to become the "chaste bride" is illustrated in the Faust Book by the lowly butler's lofty ascent by the hairs of his head.

Esoterically, hairs of the head are held to be spiritual strands that connect us to the divine. One of the forgotten logoi—oracular utterances attributed to the Lord—that contributed to the canonical sayings uses this imagery: "My Mother the Holy Spirit even now took me by one of the hairs of my head and carried me to the Great Mountain Tabor."[2] A twelfth-century engraving does the same. It shows a man being pulled by his hair out of the circle of the elements into the celestial spheres, while above him others are ascending to the enthroned Christ at the top of the twenty-fourth sphere.[3] The notion that the lowliest may rise to the heights is reflected in the Pistis Sophia where Jesus tells the disciples that he who receives the Mystery of the Ineffable "is a man in the world, but he towereth above all the angels and will tower still more above them all." In the Faust Book, the lowly butler "towers" above the countryside as he hangs from the top of the tree.

His fate in this chapter also recalls that of Jesus patibilis in the Mani myth—the Christ who "hangs from every tree." As a lower emanation of the Living Spirit who created the world, he embodies the portion of the Father's Light that was left behind in the Darkness. As such, he brings illumination and healing to the suffering, but he also presides over the death and renewal of life. He is the "power of the fruit, vegetables and seeds" whose forms are created daily by his ritual rounds of sacrifice. According to the Kephalaia, a collection of Coptic Manichaean texts, he "is slain, oppressed and murdered . . . plucked and cut down [to] give nourishment to the worlds of the flesh."[4] Faustus reflects the creative aspect of Jesus patibilis here, for we learn that in addition to the marvelous fruits he procured for the countess, he has created "all sorts of four-footed beasts as well as winged and feathered fowl, too."

In Jesus patibilis's capacity as the "Luminous Jesus," he delivers the call that awakens Adam in the third part of the Manichaean drama and he prefigures the old man in the Faust Book who will deliver the word of God to Faustus in chapter 32. The destruction of Faustus's material form is based on Jesus patibilis's sacrifice and provides the Faust Book with the bloody ending it requires, but rebirth is implicit in his never-ending cycles of return. As the comparison opens, Jesus in the Pistis Sophia continues to list the mysteries that will be revealed to those who are initiated into the full Gnosis.

FAUST BOOK	APOCHRYPHON OF JOHN	PISTIS SOPHIA
	(The chief archon) made a plan with his authorities . . . and they committed together adultery with Sophia, and bitter fate was begotten through them, which is the last of the changeable bonds. . . . And it is harder and stronger than she with whom the gods united . . . until this day.	
The greatest effort skill and art produced by Doctor Faustus was that		

FAUST BOOK	APOCHRYPHON OF JOHN	PISTIS SOPHIA
which he demonstrated to the Count of Anhalt, for with the aid of his spirit he accomplished not merely the things I told about, but he created all sorts of four-footed beasts as well as winged and feathered fowl, too.		"And that mystery knoweth why the wild beasts have arisen and why they will be destroyed. "And that mystery knoweth why the cattle have arisen and why the birds have arisen." (Ch. 92:210)
Now after he had taken leave of the Count and was returned to Wittemberg, Shrovetide approached. Doctor Faustus himself played the role of Bacchus, entertaining several learned students, whom he persuaded (after they had been well fed and sated by Faustus, had crowned him Bacchus, and were in the act of celebrating him)	For from that fate came forth every sin and injustice and blasphemy and the chain of forgetfulness and ignorance and every severe command and serious sins and great fears. And thus the whole creation was made blind in order that they may not know God who is above all of them.	"And that mystery knoweth why insolence and boasting have arisen, and why humbleness and meekness have arisen." (Ch. 91:209)
to go into a cellar with him	And because of the chain of forgetfulness their sins were hidden. . . . (28:12–30)	
and to try the magnificent drinks which he would there offer and provide them,		"And that mystery knoweth why knavery hath arisen and why deceit hath arisen." (Ch. 91:207)
	And the chief archon repented for everything which had come into being through him. (28:34) This time he planned to bring a flood upon the work of man. But the greatness of the Light of the fore-knowledge informed Noah, and he proclaimed it to all the offspring which are the sons of men.	

FAUST BOOK	APOCRYPHON OF JOHN	PISTIS SOPHIA
a thing to which they readily assented.	But those who were strangers to him did not listen to him. . . . (29:1–6)	
Doctor Faustus then laid out a ladder in his garden, seated a man on each rung,	for they are bound in measures and times and moments. . . . (28:31)	
coming by night into the cellar of the Bishop of Saltzberg.	It is not as Moses said, they hid themselves in an ark, but they hid themselves in a place, not only Noah but also many other people from the immovable race.	
Here they tasted all sorts of wine, for this Bishop hath a glorious grape culture, but when the good gentlemen were just in a fine temper.	They went into a place and hid themselves in a luminous cloud.	"And that mystery knoweth why love of the belly hath arisen and why satiety hath arisen.
The Bishop's butler by chance did come downstairs and, seeing them	And Noah recognized his authority	"And that mystery knoweth why the great Self-Willed hath arisen and why his faithful hath arisen.
(for Doctor Faustus had brought along a flint so that they might better inspect all the casks)	and she who belongs to the Light was with him, having shone on them because he had brought darkness upon the whole earth. (29:7–16)	"And that mystery knoweth why the Light-givers have arisen and why the sparks have arisen." (Ch. 93:214)
did charge them as thieves who had broken in.		"And that mystery knoweth why the chastisements and judgments have arisen." (Ch. 91:207)
This offended Doctor Faustus, who, warning his fellows to prepare to leave, seized the butler by the hair and rode away with him		"And that mystery knoweth why motion of the body hath arisen and why its utility hath arisen." (Ch. 91:209)

FAUST BOOK	PISTIS SOPHIA
until he saw a great high fir tree, in the top of which he deposited the frightened man.	"And why all the emanations of the Light hath arisen." (Ch. 91:207)
Being returned home again, he and his Shrovetide guests celebrated a valete with the wine, which he had brought along in a big bottle from the Bishop's cellar.	"Now, therefore I say unto you: 'Every man who will receive that mystery of the Ineffable and accomplish it in all its types and all its figures,
The poor butler had to hold fast all night to the tree, lest he fall out,	he is a man in the world, but he towereth above all angels and will tower still more above them all.'" (Ch. 96:228)
and he almost froze to death.	"And that mystery knoweth why the hoar frost hath arisen and why the healthful dew hath arisen." (Ch. 93:212)
When day brake and he perceived the great height of the fir as well as the impossibility of climbing down (for it had no branches except in the very top)	"He is a man in the world but he is not one of the world." (Ch. 96:230)
he had to call out to some peasants, whom he saw arrive by, and tell them what had happened to him.	"The men who shall know (the word of the Ineffable) will know the gnosis of the words which I have spoken unto you, both those of the depths and those of the height. . . .
The peasants did marvel at all this and, coming into Saltzberg, reported it at court.	and they will know in what manner the world is established, and they will know in what type all those of the height are established,
This brought out a great crowd, who with much exertion and effort with ropes did bring the butler down.	and they will know out of what ground the universe hath arisen . . ." (Ch. 96:232)
	"Everyone who shall receive a mystery of the Light-Kingdom, will go and inherit up to the region up to which he hath received mysteries.
But he never knew who those were whom he had found in the cellar, nor who he was who had put him in the tree top.	"But he will not know the gnosis of the universe unless he knoweth the one and only word of the Ineffable." (Ch. 97:233)

29
Concerning Helen Charmed Out of Greece

Now Venus appears in full glory, in the guise of the legendary Helen of Greece. The text comparison equates her with the Mysteries of the Ineffable and the spirit of life who comes to souls who have drunk the evil archons' "water of forgetfulness." In the Faust Book, Faustus conjures Helen's tantalizing figure for his bibulous students after they have all gotten drunk on his wine.

One of them makes a remark that points to Helen's true identity. "She must have been very beautiful," he says, "for she had been stolen away from her husband and a great deal of strife had arisen on her accord." He echoes the words of Simon Magus, who declared Helen to be a representation of the goddess Sophia. Speaking of Sophia's suffering he wrote: "Since all the powers contended for her possession, strife and warfare raged among the nations whenever she appeared. Thus, she was also that Helen about whom the Trojan War was fought." Through the image of Helen, he added, "the Greeks and barbarians beheld a phantasm of the truth."[1] Faustus's students must have beheld the truth behind Helen's phantasmic figure, too, for they recognized her "to be a spirit" and so were able to control the passion she aroused in them.

They were so taken with her image, however, that they had copies made of it, presumably to maintain a sense of her numinous presence. In the Pistis Sophia these "copies," or iconic representations, prove to be various "types" and "figures" of different aspects of the First Mystery. According to the Christian father, Hippolytus, they are projected by Sophia and fashioned by the ignorant Workman, a power projected from the psychic substance, or Sophia's ignorant son.

In the Apochryphon of John another copy appears. Here she is called the Mother of life, a name that also attaches to Sophia, and she is sent by the Mother/Father to awaken Adam and Eve. As we saw in an earlier chapter, Adam was copied by the false god from an image of the Mother/Father who is also a reflection of the Light. As these texts suggest, the unknowable God cannot be perceived directly and neither can its immediate image. In the Faust Book, the students' copies of Helen's figure are made from a portrait of her spirit, not from her spirit itself. The Gospel of Philip, a third-century Christian-Gnostic catechistic text not included in the comparison, explains this need for indirection. "Truth did not come into the world naked," it asserts, "but it came in types and figures. The world will not receive Truth in any other way. There is a rebirth and an image of rebirth. It is certainly necessary to be born again through the image. Which one? Resurrection. The image must rise again through the image."[2]

The concept of a hidden God that could be known only through a representation or image was entertained in Platonic and Hermetic circles during the Renaissance. Cusanus's "face of faces veiled in all faces and hidden in a riddle,"[3] could be evoked, it was held, by images of surpassing beauty. Statues or paintings of Venus, both sensuous and sublime, were adored for their capacity to call forth the splendor of the Ineffable. Edgar Wind, summarizing the words of Pico della Mirandola—a fifteenth-century Hermetic scholar who contemplated Venus's numinous qualities and the link between carnal and spiritual desire—wrote: "The human lover will recognize that the Venus who appears clothed in an earthly garment is an image of the celestial."

The Faust Book author seems to have had a similar understanding of the Helen/Venus figure and to have fully appreciated its complexity. Venus's dual nature (which Pico said "did not designate two opposite kinds of love . . . but two noble loves," of which the sensuous was "but the humbler image" of the chaste)[4] is revealed by Helen's "wanton mien," which arouses passion in the students, and by the power of her spiritual essence, which enables them to "control their passion without difficulty."

While Helen's spirit in the Faust Book represents the classical goddess of love, she also signifies the alchemical Venus. Her colors range from purple to gold to red to black to pink and her neck is "like a white swan." These are colors alchemists associate with Venus or the still unstable Gold that has been extracted from the White Stone or White Swan. The Stone is not perfect yet, as the touch of black in Helen's eyes reveals, but she is dazzling in her promise of perfection.

In the students' love for Helen's ravishing but ephemeral "figure and form," we are reminded of Faustus's earlier yearning after similar female phantasma. At that time, however, he was at the mercy of his undisciplined ego and he indulged himself in lechery and dissipation. As we have seen, his degraded condition corresponded to the stage in the alchemical process governed by Saturn, in which the metal is dissolved, blackened, and corrupted. By contrast, in this later stage—where Venus's sensuous rule is giving way to the controlled aggression of Mars—we see the students plumb the depths again and test the limits of their senses, but approach the experience with a measure of discipline that Faustus was unable to muster. The spiral of transformation, having gone full circle, begins again on a higher level of development.

FAUST BOOK	APOCHRYPHON OF JOHN	PISTIS SOPHIA
	"Now up to the present day sexual intercourse continued due to the chief archon. And he planted sexual desire in her who belongs to Adam. And he produced through intercourse the copies of the bodies, and he inspired them with his counterfeit spirit. . . . (24:27–34)	"All men who shall receive the mysteries of the Ineffable (will) be fellow-kings with me. . . .

FAUST BOOK	APOCHRYPHON OF JOHN	PISTIS SOPHIA
On Whitsunday the students came unannounced to Doctor Faustus's residence for dinner	"Likewise the mother also sent down her spirit which is in her likeness and a copy of those who are in the pleroma,	"And Amen, I say unto you: 'Those men are I, and I am they . . .'" (Ch. 96:230)
but as they brought ample meat and drink along, they were welcome guests.	for she will prepare a dwelling place for the aeons which will come down.	"Ye will sit on your thrones on my right and on my left in my kingdom and will rule with me. On this account . . . I have not hesitated nor have I been ashamed to call you my brethren and my companions.
The wine was soon going around at table	"And he made them drink water of forgetfulness, from the chief archon, in order that they might not know from where they came.	
	"Thus the seed remained for awhile assisting him in order that when the Spirit comes forth from the holy aeons, he may raise up and heal him from the deficiency, that the whole pleroma may again become holy and faultless.	
and they fell to talking about beautiful women, one of the students asserting that there was no woman whom he would rather see than fair Helen from Greece, for whose sake the worthy city of Troy had perished.	"And I said to the savior: 'Lord, will all souls then be brought safely into the pure Light?'	

FAUST BOOK	APOCHRYPHON OF JOHN	PISTIS SOPHIA
"She must have been beautiful," he said, "for she had been stolen away from her husband, and a great deal of strife had arisen on her account."	"He answered and said to me, 'Great things have arisen in your mind,	
Doctor Faustus said: "Inasmuch as ye are so eager to behold the beautiful figure of Queen Helen, I have provided for her awakening and will now conduct her hither so that ye may see her spirit for yourselves, just as she appeared in life		"This, therefore I say unto you, knowing that I will give you the mystery of the Ineffable;
(in the same way, after all, that I granted Charles V his wish to see the person of Alexander the Great and his spouse)."	for it is difficult to explain them to others, except to those who are from the immovable race.	
		that is: 'That mystery is I, and I am that mystery.' Now, therefore, not only will ye reign with me, but all men who receive the mystery of the Ineffable will be fellow kings with me in my kingdom. And I am they and they are I.
Forbidding that any should speak or arise from the table to receive her,		"But my throne will tower over them. . . ." (96:21)
Faustus went out of the parlor and, coming in again, was followed at the heel by Queen Helen,	"'Those on whom the spirit of life will descend,	"And all men who will find the word of the Ineffable—

FAUST BOOK	APOCHRYPHON OF JOHN	PISTIS SOPHIA
who was so wondrously beautiful that the students did not know whether they were still in their right minds, so confused and impassioned were they become.	they will be . . . purified in that place from all wickedness and the involvements in evil. Then they have no other care than the incorruption alone, to which they direct their attention from here on, without anger or envy or jealousy or desire and greed of anything.	Amen, I say unto you: 'The men who shall know that word will know the gnosis of all those words I have spoken unto you. . . .
For she appeared in a precious deep purple robe, her hair, which shone golden and quite beautifully glorious, hanging down to her knees. She had coal black eyes, a sweet countenance on a round little head. Her lips were red as the red cherries, her mouth small, and her neck like a white swan's. She had cheeks pink like a rose, an exceeding fair and smooth complexion and a rather slim, tall and erect bearing. In summa, there was not a flaw about her to be criticized.		"'It is the one and only word of the Ineffable.'" (96:231)
Helen looked all around her in the parlor with a right wanton mien, so that the students were violently inflamed with love for her,	"'They are not affected by anything except the state of being in the flesh alone. . . .'" (25:4–35)	
but since they took her to be a spirit they controlled their passion without difficulty, and she left the room again with Doctor Faustus.	"'For they endure everything and bear up under everything that they may finish the good fight and inherit eternal life. . . .'"	

FAUST BOOK	PISTIS SOPHIA
After the vision had passed away, the young men begged Faustus to be so good as to have the image appear just once more, for they would fain send a painter to his house the next day to make a counterfeit of her.	
This Doctor Faustus refused to do, saying that he could not make her spirit appear at just any time, but that he would procure such a portrait for them.	"And I will tell you the expansion of all mysteries and the types of every one of them and the manner of their completion in all their figures.
Later he did indeed produce one, and all the students had it copied by sending painters to his house, for it was a fair and glorious figure of a woman.	"And I will tell you the mystery of the One and Only, the Ineffable, and all its types, all its figures and the whole economy.
Now it is unknown to this day who got this painting away from Doctor Faustus.	"Wherefore it hath come forth from the last limb of the Ineffable. For that mystery is the setting up of them all." (Ch. 96:226)
As concerns the students, when they came to bed, they could not sleep for thinking of the figure and form which had appeared visibly before them	"The second mystery of the First Mystery, on the other hand, if thou accomplishest it finely in all its figures,
and from this we may learn how the Devil doth blind men with love—	(if he) who shall accomplish its mystery . . . speaketh that mystery over the head of any man who . . . hath received no mysteries. . . . That man will be judged in no . . . region at all,
oh it doth often happen that a man goeth a-whoring for so long that at last he can no longer be saved from it.	nor will the fire touch him, because of the great mystery of the Ineffable which is with him." (Ch. 98:238)

For the tantric disciple, the appearance of a divinity has its own significance and requires its own response. The erotic images he has encountered in his dreams have coalesced into the single figure of a goddess, and now he calls to her and asks her to appear, just as the students asked for a vision of Helen. Before entering the waking dream state he repeats again and again: "O my Sakti, come to me, come to me."

According to Garrison, when the yogin perceives this representation of the Siva-Sakti he moves to stabilize the image. "Upon awakening," and "with eyes still closed [he] continues to visualize the key image and return to the dream." In other words, says Garrison, "he seeks to repeat the entire dream, but to carry it into his waking consciousness, with the latter's lucidity and control."[5] Similarly, in the Faust Book, the students lay in bed and "could not sleep for thinking of the figure and form which had appeared visibly before them."

In previous chapters we saw the disciple employ various techniques to induce deeper states of awareness and awaken the Kundalini. Now he focuses on a goddess figure to achieve these ends, a figure whose colors are remarkably vivid. Tantrists, like Hermeticists, venerate the Sun and seek the divine reality behind it. One of the ways they do this is by utilizing the seven rays of the color spectrum, of which sunlight is the source. Meditating on different color frequencies to stimulate and clear the energy centers along the invisible spine, they enable the Kundalini to rise without obstruction to the cranial vault and induce a blissful experience. The Indian philosophical texts known as the Upanishads call this "piercing the Sun."

Mookerjee and Khanna speak of "saturated color fields," which tantric artists paint in the course of meditation "where all images are totally effaced in a patternless visual field." The purpose of this meditation is to reduce all forms to an essence or to "energy as a reference of the Absolute."[6] Helen's form was, if not totally effaced, overwhelmed by her striking colors and, indeed, what form she had—a "round little head" on a "slim, tall," and "erect" body—suggests the "stalk that supports the Lotus," or the stiffened Kundalini attached to the cranial vault. It would seem, then, that the essence the students' vision of Helen represents to the tantrist is the inner lover, or the goddess Kundalini, and the blissful revelation her awakening brings.

Some of the colors of the Helen/Venus image in the Faust Book are in the long-wave or red spectrum of the visible color field. Red is a stimulant to the lower chakras, which resonate with its vibration and govern the sexual organs. The students' response to it was as might be expected, "so confused and inflamed were they become." On the other hand, and in keeping with Venus's dual nature as both "whore" and "chaste bride," the gold of her hair and her purple robe resonate with the middle and upper chakras. Stimulation of these centers, two of whose qualities are detachment and spiritual vision, may have enabled the students to perceive her as spirit and "control their passion without difficulty."

The copies of Helen which the students had painted may also refer to actual women—partners with whom they practice sacred intercourse while visualizing them as a goddess. More will be said of this later when Helen reappears to Faustus and they consummate a union. At that time he will have another portrait of the goddess's "figure" painted.

30
Concerning a Gesticulation Involving Four Wheels

In the Faust Book, a surly peasant, or churl, refuses to allow Faustus into his wagon. He is the still imperfect Body, the "common thing" or impenetrable Earth that must be made transparent to receive the Spirit. We have clearly entered the phase ruled by Mars in which the metal is dissolved, putrefied, and then etherealized in preparation for the lasting union of Spirit and Soul. The Spirit has been submerged in matter as the glyph for Mars indicates (♁) and the Sun, or consciousness, has plunged into the depths once more. The metal is not as unstable as it was in the first half of the Work and its increased stability was demonstrated in the previous chapter when the students controlled their passions for Helen, "without difficulty." Another aspect of Mars' nature was revealed when the students visualized Helen in their sleep, for the Martian plunge into the depths is associated with the exercise of active imagination.[1]

As the process continues, the components of the metal are refined and, as the title of this chapter suggests, the wheel of the elements is turning. The Body is being reduced to its "First Matter," the "state of pure, undifferentiated power, or ether,"[2] as Julius Evola puts it. This is the form-giving, organizing principle symbolized by Saturn. In its "sleeping" state it delimits and imprisons the life force, but, when arisen as etherealized Body, it receives the Spirit in an immutable fixation, steadying it and manifesting as gold.

Here Faustus initiates the peasant's development by causing the wheels of his wagon to fly off and land outside the four gates of the town. These gates represent the four directions, each of which is associated with a particular elemental transmutation, or spinning of the wheel, and a corresponding transformation of consciousness. In his Tenth Gate, Ripley speaks of wheels, gates, and directions when he describes an alchemical rotation taking place at this stage of the process.

> *Thy wheel is now turned nigh about,*
> *Into Air turn Earth which is the proper nest,*
> *Of other elements there is no doubt,*
> *For Earth in Fire is, which in Air taketh rest,*
> *This circulation thou begin must in the West:*
> *Then forth into the South till they exhaled be,*
> *Proceed duly, as in the figure I have taught thee.*
> *Tenth Gate: 9*[3]

Elsewhere he says,

> *Altitude, Latitude, Profundity,*
> *By which gates we must turn our Wheel,*
> *Knowing thy entrance in the West shall be;*
> *Thy passage forth into the North if thou do well,*
> *Second Gate: 11*[4]

In the text comparison Brunswick is equated with the Kingdom of Light to which all deserving souls are heading. The city with four gates whose "wheels" are turning without may be seen as the raw Earth or Soul in process of transformation, while the wagon, its four wheels having been rotated and returned, may signify the newly receptive vessel that is ready to receive the Spirit. The square wagon with its four "elemental" wheels, suggests the image of a certain liturgical cross described by Titus Burckhardt. The circles on the arms of the cross represent the four elements; at the center of its reverse or passive side the virgin is enthroned. She "symbolically assumes the role of ether," he observes, "which from a certain Hermetical point of view is to be identified with materia prima, or the virgin ground of the soul."[5] Faustus initiates the churl's transformation by "spinning his wheels" and reveals his receptive soul (the empty wagon) by forcing a bitter self-examination on him, a visit to the "interior of the Earth," as Basil Valentinus put it, "where the hidden stone is found."

Faustus's role here, as physician who travels on foot whenever he is called to heal the sick, is another reference to Jesus patibilis from the Mani myth.[6] He appears here as the Light Jesus who was said to walk on many roads to bring enlightenment to men and was called the "physician of the wounded." "You have come with salvation, our beneficent Father and true hope," says a hymn of Mani's which was dedicated to him, "You have come like a Father, our beneficent physician. . . . Come quickly beneficent Father, put our souls in order."[7]

In the Pistis Sophia, Jesus tells the disciples that he brought the Mysteries of the Light to the race of humans who are material refuse and have "need of the physician." His mission, like that of the Light Jesus, is to purify men so that they may "inherit the Kingdom of the Light." In the Apochryphon of John, the Holy Spirit tells the disciple that those on whom the "power and Spirit" descends are invincible, while others, dragged down by the counterfeit spirit, will be drawn to the works of evil. The churlish peasant in the Faust Book has been awakened by the "power and Spirit," and henceforth his heretofore unwelcoming wagon will be a more receptive vessel.

The comparison includes a brief passage from the Tripartite Tractate that speaks of a unitary end of times when conflicts such as these will be overcome and "angels and men will receive the Kingdom."

FAUST BOOK	PISTIS SOPHIA	TRIPARTITE TRACTATE
		The end will receive a unitary existence, just as the beginning is unitary where there is no male nor female, nor slave and free . . . but Christ is in all. (32:20–29)
Doctor Faustus was summoned and commanded to come to the town of Brunswick to cure a marshall there who had consumption.		Even if some are exalted because of the organization, since they have been appointed as causes of the things which have come into being,
Now he used to ride neither horseback or by coach, but was of a mind to walk		since they are more active as natural forces
wherever he was invited as a guest or summoned as a physician.		and since they are desired because of these things,
When he was about half a quarter from Brunswick and could see the town before him	Andrew . . . said: "My Lord, I am astonished . . . how the men who are in the . . . body of this matter . . . will enter (all the regions of the emanations of the Light) and inherit the Light-kingdom." (Ch. 100:247)	angels and men will receive the kingdom and the confirmation and the salvation. (133:9–15)
		APOCHRYPHON OF JOHN
a peasant with four horses and an empty wagon came clattering along.		I said to him, "Lord, the souls of those who did not do these works,
Doctor Faustus addressed the clown in all kindness,	The Spirit of the Savior was roused in him; he cried out and said: "How long am I to endure you? How long am I to bear with you? Have ye not then even yet understood and are ye ignorant?"	but on whom the power and Spirit descended,

FAUST BOOK	PISTIS SOPHIA	APOCHRYPHON OF JOHN
requesting that he be allowed to climb on and be driven the rest of the way up to the town gate	"Know ye . . . that ye all . . . are out of the same paste and the . . . same substance, and that ye all are out of the same Mixture.	will they be rejected?" (26:9–11)
		He answered and said to me, ". . . when the Spirit of life increases and the power comes and strengthens that soul, no one can lead it astray with works of evil.
but the bumpkin refused to do this and turned Faustus away,	"And at the commandment of the First Mystery, the mixture was constrained	"But those on whom the counterfeit spirit descends are drawn by him and they go astray."
		And I said, "Lord, those who did not know to whom they belong, where will their souls be?" (26:34)
saying he would have enough to haul on his return trip.		And he said to me, "(The counterfeit spirit) burdens the soul
Doctor Faustus had not been serious in his request, wanting only to prove the peasant, whether there were any love to be found in him	until all the great emanations of the Light . . . purified themselves and until they purified themselves from the mixture.	
but now he repaid the clown's churlishness (such as is, after all, commonly found among peasants)	"And they have not purified themselves of themselves but they have purified themselves by necessity	
in like coin	according to the economy of the One and Only. . . ."	

FAUST BOOK	PISTIS SOPHIA	APOCHRYPHON OF JOHN
speaking to him thus: "Thou bumpkin and worthless ass, since thou hast demonstrated such churlishness unto me,	"Ye, then, in particular are the refuse of the region of the Light and ye are the refuse of the region of those of the Midst, and ye are the refuse of all the invisibles and of all the rulers; in a word, ye are the refuse of all these.	
and since thou wilt certainly use others the same and probably already hast done so,		and draws it to the works of evil." (26:35–27:2)
thou shalt this time be paid for thy trouble.	"And ye are in great suffering and great afflictions in your being poured from one another of different kinds of bodies of the world." (Ch. 100:248)	
Thy four wheels shalt thou find one at each gate of Brunswick town."	"For this cause have I said unto you aforetime: 'Seek that ye may find. . . .' Ye are to seek after the mysteries of the Light which purify the body of matter and make it into refined Light exceedingly purified."	
Immediately the wagon wheels sprang away, floating along in the air so that each one came to a different gate, without being noticed by anyone.	"Amen, I say unto you: 'For the sake of the race of men, because it is material, I have torn myself asunder	
The peasant's horses also fell down as if they had suddenly died and lay there quite still.	and brought into them all the mysteries of the Light,	

FAUST BOOK	PISTIS SOPHIA
At this the poor clown was sore affright, measuring it as a special scourge of God for his misanthropy.	that I may purify them,
All troubled and weeping with outstretched hands and upon his knees, he did beg Faustus for forgiveness, confessing himself indeed well worthy of such punishment,	for they are the refuse of the whole matter of their matter;
but vowing that the next time this would serve as a remembrance to him, so that he would never use such misanthropy again.	
Doctor Faustus took pity upon the clown's humility and answered him, saying that he must treat no one else in this hard manner, these being nothing more than the qualities of churlishness and misanthropy—and the wicked pride which accompanieth them.	else would no soul of the total race of men have been saved, and they would not be able to inherit the kingdom of the Light,
Now the man should but take up some earth and throw it upon the team, which would rise up and live out its days. So it came to pass,	if I had not brought unto them the purifying mysteries. . . .'
Faustus saying as he departed from the peasant:	"For this cause, therefore, have I said unto you aforetime: (Ch. 100:249) "'The healthy have no need of the physician but the sick—that is: Those of the Light have no need of the mysteries, for they are purified Lights;
"Thy churlishness cannot go altogether unpunished, but must be repaid in equal measure,	but it is the race of men which hath need of them, for they are material refuse.'
inasmuch as thou hast deemed it such a great effort to take a tired man into an empty wagon. Lo, thy wheels are without the town at four different gates. There wilt thou find all four of them."	"For this cause, therefore, herald to the whole race of men, saying: 'Cease not to seek day and night until ye find the purifying mysteries;'

FAUST BOOK

The peasant went along and found them as Doctor Faustus had said, but with great effort, travail and neglect of the trade and business which he had intended to accomplish.

And thus will churlishness ever punish its owners.

PISTIS SOPHIA

"and say unto the race of men: 'Renounce the whole world and the whole matter therein. For he who buyeth and selleth in the world and he who eateth and drinketh of its matter and who liveth in all its cares and all its associations

ammasseth other additional matters to the rest of his matter.'" (Ch. 100:250)

31
Concerning Four Sorcerers Who Cut Off One Another's Heads and Put Them On Again, Wherein Doctor Faustus, Attending Their Performance, Doth Play the Major Role

In this chapter Faustus watches as a carnival sorcerer beheads three of his fellows, one after the other. Before each beheading the sorcerer charms a lily, which he calls the Root of Life, into a cruse of distilled water. After each severed head is trimmed he returns it to its body, whereupon the lily disappears and the man is "made whole" again. When the chief sorcerer is beheaded, Faustus cuts the stem of his lily and he dies.

This repetitious process, together with certain symbolic words appearing in this chapter, suggests that spirits are circulating in the alchemist's vessel again. Distilled water, for example, is the alchemist's "Aqua Vitae," the corrosive spirit that both corrupts and transforms the Stone.[1] "Beheading" refers to the separation of the volatile Spirit, or Soul of the metal, from the Body that has been corrupted, while "head" is a symbol for the Spirit itself.[2] The sorcerers' heads that are severed from their bodies in the Faust Book are these volatile, circulating Spirits, and their return to the bodies from which they were separated signifies that the metal, like the sorcerers themselves, has been fixed or "made whole again." These are components of an alchemical circulation in which the dissevered Body is transformed by circulating Spirits and then fixed in a higher form.

In terms of the tantric process this represents, the Spirits' departure from the Body corresponds to a difficult and complex separation of psychophysical consciousness brought on by the raising and lowering of the Kundalini. The yogin is engaged in a final attempt to pierce the lotus chakra and in this context, the sorcerers' heads take on a different meaning. "Head" in general refers to the vessel in which the Work takes place, but here it is the vessel that is being worked on, or consciousness in the process of being transformed.[3]

This final transformation is a risky process—riskier than Faustus's journeys to Heaven and Hell, which also involved a strenuous separation for, as we recall, Faustus "slept" throughout his journeys. "In the first trial," says Julius Evola, referring to the suspension of ordinary consciousness that occurs in the first part of the work, "the separation of the vital principle from the denser body combination that kept it immobilized did not affect the combination itself, which went on existing and kept the seals of individuality. But now these seals have been broken and we pass beyond the absolutely undifferentiated point."[4]

During this challenging operation the Body must maintain a connection with the separated Soul, for as Petrus Bonus warns, "when the Anima Candida is perfectly risen," it must be joined "at the same moment with its body, for the Anima without its body cannot be held."[5] The yogin must maintain a degree of conscious control within the hypnogogic state. This joining is represented in the Faust Book by the mysterious appearance of the lily before each beheading. The symbol of the lily refers to the soul as enlightened mind. Here it floats on "distilled waters," signifying Mercury, the "swift messenger" who the *Dictionary of Alchemical Imagery* tells us "opens up a path of Light, a line of communication between the greater self and the limited personality of every day."[6] During the time the sorcerers' bodies and heads are separated, the lily's presence in the "mercurial" waters symbolizes the continuing union of Body and Soul. The lily as a symbol of illumination disappears each time the head is returned and the man is "made whole" again—presumably restored to an ordinary, albeit higher, level of awareness. This water, or Aqua Vitae, also feeds the gestating Stone, or developing consciousness, whose potential for growth and transformation is indicated by the lily's waxing green in the Faust Book.

In the text comparison, the Pistis Sophia continues with Jesus's instruction to the disciples concerning the godlike attributes that will be acquired by a person who has learned the mysteries of the first, second, and third spaces of the Ineffable. The comparison supports the notion of beheading as a heightening of consciousness, for—in the manner of a Greek chorus—it matches each beheading and each appearance of the lily with a line from the Pistis Sophia that praises "the man who hath found the words of the mysteries (in) divine truth."

The lily with its root intact signifies the connection of Soul and Spirit inasmuch as "root" is associated in certain Gnostic, Hermetic, and Manichaean writings with Spirit. In one of Mani's teachings in the Kephalaia he uses "root" in this way and demonstrates the need to maintain this vital link:

> The first man dispersed himself in the limbs of the Living Soul. . . . After the fashion of this fleshly body; as the root of all the limbs hang upon the head, so that should one of the person's limbs be cut off while the head exists he has hope . . . but if his head should be cut off, the entire body will die and, he is lost.[7]

Thus, the sorcerer in the Faust Book perishes when Faustus snips the lily's stem and separates it from its spiritual "root," referred to there as the "Root of Life."

It should be added that in Mani's speculation there are also roots of evil, the Five Dark Natures or elements that had become commingled with the Five Light Natures. According to the Kephalaia, Primal Man descended into the depth of the abyss and cut out the roots of the five trees and "the root of the evil tree . . . so that from this time it cannot bear evil fruit."[8] This is not incompatible with the psychophysical separation whose goal is to triumph over the infernal forces of the body.

FAUST BOOK	PISTIS SOPHIA
	(Jesus continued:) "And those who are worthy of the mysteries which abide in the Ineffable, which are those which have not gone forth,
Doctor Faustus came to the Carnival at Frankfurt	
where his spirit Mephistopheles did inform him that there were four Sorcerers at an Inn in Jew's Alley	these exist before the First Mystery . . . they are as the Limbs of the Ineffable.
who were attracting a great audience by chopping off one another's heads and sending them to the barber to be trimmed.	"And everyone existeth according to the dignity of its glory: the head according to the dignity of the head. . . .
Now that vexed Faustus who liked to think that he were the only cock in the Devil's basket.	"There is a multitude of Limbs but one only body. . . . And all the Limbs which are in it . . . I am their treasury, beside whom there is no other treasury, who hath not his like in the world;
When he went to behold the thing, he found the sorcerers just getting ready to chop off their heads, and with them was a barber who was going to trim and wash them. Upon a table they had a glass cruse with distilled water in it. One among them, the chief sorcerer and also their executioner, laid his hands upon the first of his fellows and charmed a lily into this cruse.	but there are still words and mysteries and other regions.
It waxed green and he called it the Root of Life.	"Now, therefore, blessed is he who hath found the words of the mysteries of the first space which is from without;
Now he beheaded that first fellow, let the barber dress the head, then set it upon the man's shoulders again. In one and the same instant the lily disappeared and the man was whole again.	and he is a god who hath found these words of the mysteries of the second space, which is in the midst;
This was done with the second and third sorcerer in like manner. A lily was charmed for each in the water, they were executed, their heads were then dressed and put back on again.	and he is a savior and an uncontainable who hath found the words of the mysteries of the third space. . . ." (Ch. 101:253)

FAUST BOOK	PISTIS SOPHIA
At last it was the turn of the chief sorcerer and executioner. His Root of Life was blooming away in the water and waxing green,	"He on the other hand who hath found the words of the mysteries which I have described unto you . . .
now his head was smitten off also	"That man who hath found the words of these mysteries in divine truth is the first in truth and like unto the First." (Ch. 101:254)
	Jesus continued again in the discourse and said unto his disciples: "When I shall have gone into the Light, then herald it unto the whole world and say unto them: (Ch. 102:255)
and they set to washing and dressing it in Faustus's presence, which sorcery did sorely vex him, the arrogance of this *Magicus Princes,* how he let his head be chopped off so insolently	"'Renounce magic potions that ye may be worthy of the mysteries of the Light and be saved from the great cold and the hail of the outer darkness.
with blasphemy and laughter in his mouth.	"'Renounce blasphemy that ye may be worthy of the mysteries of the Light and be saved from the great dragon of the outer darkness.'" (Ch. 102:258)
Doctor Faustus went up to the table where the cruse and the flowering lily stood, took out his knife, and snipped the flower, severing the stem. No one was aware of this at the time, but when the sorcerers sought to set the head on again their medium was gone, and the evil fellow had to perish with his sins upon his severed head.	"Say unto those who teach the doctrines of error . . . 'Ye will go into the chastisements of the great dragon and of the outer darkness . . . and never will ye be cast up into the world, but will be non-existent until the end.'" (Ch. 102:258)
Afterwards they did find the stem cut but were not able to discover how this came to pass. This is the way the Devil at last rewards all his servants, absolving them thus, the manner in which Doctor Faustus dealt with this man being entirely consonant with the shameful absolution which he did himself receive when he was repaid for his own sins.	"Say unto those who abandon the doctrines of truth of the First Mystery: 'Woe unto you, for your chastisement is sad compared with that of all men.'" (Ch. 102:259)

Repeated cutting off of the head refers to the "deaths" and "rebirths" that attend the piercing of the six chakras in kundalini yoga. It suggests that the disciple has mastered this technique and is raising and lowering the Kundalini at will. David Gordon White describes a tantric hatha yoga practice analogous to alchemical circulations that features a series of hypnogogic descents in which the yogin goes in and out of consciousness while the Kundalini rises and falls. His aim is to reduce the components of his being ("the five sense-capacities, action-capacities, and subtle and gross elements") to their "ethereal essences," just as the alchemist rotates his Stone through the elements and reduces it to its first matter.

Here is White's description of the elemental "rotation" that takes place in the yogin's body as the Kundalini rises through the energy centers along the invisible spine:

> The element earth, predominant in the lowest chakra . . . becomes absorbed into the element water at the level of the second chakra. . . . Water is absorbed back into fire at the third chakra . . . fire into air at the fourth . . . air into ether at the fifth. . . . All are telescoped, swallowed back, into the mind which, identified with the sixth chakra . . . will, in the final phases of this process, itself be absorbed into its source and essence, the pure Siva-consciousness located in the thousand petaled lotus of the cranial vault.[9]

Having become adept at raising and lowering the Kundalini, the disciple is preparing now for the most difficult feat of all—to pierce the seventh chakra and achieve a final breakthrough to the realm of undifferentiated Light.

32
Concerning an Old Man Who Would Have Converted Doctor Faustus from His Godless Life

As the alchemist strives to rid his metal of impurities in order to reveal its inner gold, a pious old man implores Faustus to abandon sin and emulate the olden grace of the apostles and evangelists. In the text comparison, the Tripartite Tractate speaks of the incarnate Savior who heals both spiritual and psychic souls. His compassionate mission is reflected in the old man's effort to redeem both Faustus and his students. The Gospel of Truth praises virtuous deeds, warns against the others, and tells us that the awareness of Christ causes ignorant souls to turn back and acknowledge the Father.

The old man's sermon—contrasting the examples of the Church fathers with Faustus's evil deeds—is patterned on the Call delivered by the Luminous Jesus to the sleeping Adam in the Mani myth. Here is a version from Bar Konai, an eighth-century Christian writer who summarized some of Mani's works.

> Jesus the Luminous approached Adam the Innocent and woke him from the sleep of death in order that he may be delivered from the two great spirits. And just as a man who is righteous and finds a man

> possessed of a mighty demon and quiets him by his art, like this was also Adam because that Beloved One (Jesus) found him sunk in the great sleep. And he woke him and took hold of him and shook him. . . . Then Adam examined himself and recognized what he was. And he (Jesus) showed him the Fathers in the Height, and his own self thrown into the teeth of the leopards and into the teeth of elephants and swallowed by the voracious and eaten by dogs, and mixed and imprisoned in all that exists and bound in the pollution of Darkness.
>
> And Jesus raised him and made him taste of the Tree of Life.[1]

In the Faust Book, the old man delivers his sermon "at table" and offers Faustus the "Tree of Life" in the form of "small victuals" that "our sweet Lord provideth."

The old man represents the "beheaded" or separated soul discussed in the last chapter, the higher consciousness that plunges into the depths now to cleanse the body of its remaining impurities. Until now, the old man has been observing and judging Faustus as if from an elevated position, but now he approaches him or descends to his level.

In order for the Soul (Mercury) to achieve its purpose, it must contact the "sleeping" life force that resides in the depths, the fiery, creative power (Saturn) that informs Earth. Julius Evola summarizes the words of a contemporary alchemist, Narayana-Swami, who speaks of this Saturnian force as "the power of life . . . [it] lies at the base of every function and pattern of the organism, once its complete development has been reached. The goal of Hindu alchemy was to introduce consciousness into this vital force, causing it to become part of it; then to reawaken and retrace all the phases of the organization, reaching thereby an actual and creative rapport with the completed form of one's own body, which could then, literally, be called regenerated."[2] According to Evola, when the two principles meet and merge, both are transformed and the "'black Earth' produces precious stones." The spiritual old man and the spirit who binds Faustus anew to the Devil are working together to achieve this end. In doing so, they mimic the Mercurial spirits who, having taken on corporeal form, elevate themselves "as divine or sulfurous mysteries—as celestial bodies . . . and (then redescend) to the darker depths of the infernal."

Faustus continues the descent with the aid of his spirit. He plunges into the infernal darkness, that is, succumbs to the spirit's demand that he reaffirm his bondage to the Devil. The spirit's imperious demand is in keeping with Evola's characterization of this darkness as the "organic correspondence of the will principle." Faustus's craven submission represents the ego's merging with this overwhelming force, "of which," says Evola, "the body expresses the . . . mute state of dark slavery."

Even as he surrenders to this willful power, however, he must seize its hidden gold without being overwhelmed by it, and that will require what Evola calls "the primordial act of control."[3]

FAUST BOOK	TRIPARTITE TRACTATE
A Christian, pious, god-fearing physician, a person zealous of the honor of God	He it is who was our Savior in willing compassion. . . .
was also a neighbor of Doctor Faustus,	For it was for their sake that he became manifest in an involuntary suffering.
and, seeing that many students frequented Faustus's house, he considered such a den as bad as a brothel,	They became flesh and soul . . . which things hold them, and with corruptible things they die. . . . (114:31–40)
for he did compare Faustus to all the Jews, who, so soon as they fell from God, also became his declared enemies, dedicating themselves unto sorcery for the sake of prophecy and deceit,	Not only did he take upon himself the death of those whom he thought to save, but he also accepted their smallness to which they had descended when they were born in body and soul. (115:5–9)
	Among all the others who shared in them and those who fell and who received the Light, he came being exalted, because he had let himself be conceived without sin, stain, and defilement. He was begotten in life, being in life,
but seeking not only the bodily harm of many a pious child whose parents have devoted much effort to his Christian rearing, but also causing him to forget the Lord's Prayer.	because the former and the latter are in passion and changing opinion from the Logos who moved. . . . (115:12–21)

FAUST BOOK	TRIPARTITE TRACTATE	GOSPEL OF TRUTH
This old neighbor of Doctor Faustus had observed his rascality in such a life for long years	He came into being from the glorious vision and the unchanging thought of the Logos who returned to himself, after his movement, from the organization, just as those who came with him took body and soul	
and no longer doubted the devilish nature of his mischief,	and a confirmation and stability and judgment of things. . . .	
	When they thought of the Savior they came . . . they also came more exalted . . . than those who had been brought forth from a defect. (115:26–40) These others were . . . of the spiritual substance. . . .	
but he also knew that the time was not yet ripe for the civil authorities to establish these facts.	The organization is different. This is one thing, that is another.	
Considering thus above all the weal of the young men, he did in Christian zeal summon Faustus as a guest into his own lodging.		Speak of the truth with those who search for it and of knowledge to those who have committed sin in their error. (32:24) Make firm the feet of those who have stumbled and stretch out your hand to those who are ill,
Faustus came, and at table, his old god-fearing patron addressed him thus: "My sweet Lord, as a friend and as a Christian I ask you not to receive my discourse in rancor and in ill will, nor to despise		

FAUST BOOK	TRIPARTITE TRACTATE	GOSPEL OF TRUTH
these small victuals, but charitably to take and be content with what our sweet Lord provideth us."		feed those who are hungry . . . (32:1–50)
Doctor Faustus requested him to declare his purpose,		For you are the understanding that is drawn forth.
saying he would attend him obediently.	Some come forth from passion and division, needing healing.	If strength acts thus it becomes even stronger.
His patron then commenced: "My sweet Lord and Neighbor, ye know your own actions, that ye have defied God and all the saints, that ye have given yourself up unto the devil, whereby ye are now come into God's greatest wrath and are changed from a Christian into a very heretic and Devil. O why do ye deprive your soul? Ye must not heed the body, but your sweet soul, lest ye reside in the eternal punishment and displeasure of God.		Be concerned with yourselves; do not be concerned with other things which you have rejected from yourselves. Do not return to what you have vomited to eat it. Do not be moths. Do not be worms for you have already cast it off. Do not become a dwelling place for the Devil, for you have already destroyed him. (33:9–22)
"Look to it, my Lord, ye are not yet lost if ye will but turn from your evil way,		**PISTIS SOPHIA** (And Jesus continued): "Renounce evil doing, that ye may be saved from all the demons of Yaltabaoth and all his judgments." (Ch. 102:257)
beseech God for Grace and pardon,	Others are from prayer,	
as ye may see in the example in Acts VIII concerning Simon in Samaria, who had also traduced many. They		

FAUST BOOK	TRIPARTITE TRACTATE	PISTIS SOPHIA
thought him to be a god, calling him Simon Deus Sanctus. But he was converted when he heard a sermon of St. Philip, was baptized and did believe on our Lord Jesus Christ.	so that they heal the sick when they have been appointed to treat those who have fallen.	(And Jesus continued): "Renounce evil doing, that ye may be saved from all the demons of Yaltabaoth and all his judgments." (Ch. 102:257)
"It is particularly noted and praised in Acts how he did afterward much consort with Philip. "Thus, my Lord, allow my sermon also to appeal to you. O let it be a heartfelt Christian admonition! To sin no more is the penance wherewith ye must seek Grace and pardon, as ye may learn from the fine examples of the thief on the cross, as well as from St. Peter, St. Matthew, and Magdalena.	These are the apostles and the evangelists.	
"Yea, Christ our Lord speaketh unto all sinners: 'Come unto me all that labor and are heavy laden and I will give you rest.'	They are the disciples of the Savior, and teachers who need instruction.	
"Or, in the prophet Ezekiel: 'I have no pleasure in the death of the wicked; but that the wicked should turn from his way and live, for his hand is not withered, that he were no longer useful.'		
"I beg you, my Lord, take my plea to your heart, ask God for pardon for Christ's sake, and abjure at the same time your		"Say unto them: 'Renounce all, that ye may receive the mysteries of the Light and go on high into the Light Kingdom.'" (Ch. 102:250)

FAUST BOOK	TRIPARTITE TRACTATE	GOSPEL OF TRUTH
evil practices, for sorcery is against God and his Commandment, inasmuch as he doth sorely forbid it in both the Old and the New Testaments.		
"He speaketh: 'Ye shall not allow them to live, ye shall not seek after them nor hold counsel with them, for it is an abomination unto God. Thus St. Paul called Bar-Jesus, or Elymas the Sorcerer, a child of the Devil and an enemy of all righteousness, saying that such should have no share in the Kingdom of God.'"		Do not strengthen those who are obstacles to you who are collapsing, as though you were a support for them. For the lawless one is someone to treat ill rather than the just one. (33.22–25)
Doctor Faustus attended him and said that the speech had well pleased him. He expressed his gratitude to the old man for his good will and took his leave, promising to comply in so far as he was able. When he arrived home he took the old man's counsel to heart,		Error . . . is a thing that falls, it is a thing that easily stands upright again in the discovery of him who has come to him. . . .
considering how he had indeed depraved his soul by yielding himself up to the accursed Devil	Why, then, did they, too, share in the passions in which those who have been brought forth from passion share, if indeed they are bodily productions in accordance with the organization and the Savior who did not share in the passions?	

FAUST BOOK	TRIPARTITE TRACTATE	GOSPEL OF TRUTH
and at last Faustus felt a desire to do penance and to revoke his promise to the Devil.		For the bringing back is called repentance.
While he was occupied in such thoughts, his spirit appeared to him,	The Savior was an image of the unitary one, he who is the Totality in bodily form.	For this reason incorruptibility breathed forth:
groping after him as if to twist his head off his shoulders.		It pursued the one who had sinned in order that he might rest.
		For forgiveness is what remains for the Light in the deficiency,
The spirit then spake, rebuking him: "What is thy purpose with thyself?"		the word of the pleroma. . . . (35:16–30)
He reminded him of his motives in first consigning himself to the Devil.	Therefore he preserved the form of indivisibility. . . .	When that which was diminished was received, he revealed what he lacked,
Having promised enmity toward God and all mankind, he was not now fulfilling that pledge but was following after this old reprobate,		
feeling charity toward a man and hence toward God—	They, however, are images of each thing which became manifest.	
now, when it was already too late and when he was clearly the property of the Devil.	Therefore they assume division (116:6–36) [and] share in the evil which exists. . . .	that is the discovery of the Light of Truth which rose upon him because it is immutable.
"The Devil hath the power" (he spake)		That is why Christ was spoken of in their midst,
"to fetch thee away. I am in fact now come with the command to dispose of thee—or to obtain the		

FAUST BOOK	TRIPARTITE TRACTATE	GOSPEL OF TRUTH
promise that thou wilt never more allow thyself to be seduced, and that thou wilt consign thyself anew with thy blood.	For he will hold the Totality under sin,	
"Thou must declare immediately what thou wouldst do or I am to slay thee."	so that by that will he might have mercy on that Totality and they might be saved. (117:1–6)	so that those who were disturbed might receive a bringing back. (36:9–16)
	The men and angels who are not from the good disposition of the right ones but from the mixture . . . first chose for themselves honor,	
Sore affright, Doctor Faustus consented, sat down and with his blood did write as followeth (this document being found after his death).	though it was only a temporary wish and desire. (121:20–25)	

In this chapter, Faustus is confronted with a stark choice between good and evil. Indeed, the entire chapter is a dialectic between these opposing values as the old man's shining virtue is pitted against the dark powers of the Devil for possession of Faustus's soul. In the text comparison, the old man's sermon, which contrasts good and evil deeds, is matched by highlights from the Gospel of Truth and the Pistis Sophia. Both texts condemn certain lapses into error and approve the righteous deeds that lead to salvation.

In the context from which the Pistis Sophia highlights were taken, Jesus denounces a lengthy list of misdeeds and opposes them with a number of virtuous acts that, he tells the disciples, will ensure them entry into the Kingdom of Light. These opposing admonitions—forty-one in all—are couched in liturgical sentences that are almost trance inducing when read aloud. Here are but a few.

Say unto them: "Renounce litigiousness that ye may be worthy of the mysteries of the Light and be saved from the chastisements of Aries."

Say unto them: "Renounce false slander, that ye may be worthy of the mysteries of the Light and be saved from the fire-rivers of the dog-faced one."

Say unto them: "Renounce craftiness, that ye may be worthy of the mysteries of the Light and be saved from the chastisements which are in Amente."

Say unto them: "Renounce avarice that ye may be worthy of the mysteries of the Light and be saved from the fire-rivers of the dog-faced one."

Say unto them: "Renounce wrath, that ye may be worthy of the mysteries of the Light and be saved from the fire-rivers of the dragon-faced one."

Say unto them: "Renounce slandering, that ye may be worthy of the mysteries of the Light and be saved from the fire-rivers of the lion-faced one."

Say unto them: "Be ye gentle, that ye may receive the mysteries of the Light and go on high into the Light Kingdom."

Say unto them: "Be ye peaceful, that ye may receive the mysteries of the Light and go on high into the Light Kingdom."

Say unto them: "Be ye merciful, that ye may receive the mysteries of the Light and go on high into the Light Kingdom."

Say unto them: "Be ye righteous, that ye may receive the mysteries of the Light and go on high into the Light Kingdom."

The rhythmic alternation of do's and don'ts, of threats and promises, invites a comparison to a Sakta-tantra meditative technique described by Guy Beck, in which sounds or letters rather than sentences embodying opposing principles are chanted ceaselessly to arouse the inner fire and induce an ecstatic encounter with the divine.[4] The key to this practice is the guru's passing to a disciple the "pure light or fire," a spiritual essence that awakens the dormant Kundalini. We saw this happen in chapter 5 when Mephistopheles sounded his transforming name for Faustus. The guru offers the "fire" to his pupil in the form of a protective "carrier" or mantra lest he be burned by it. By this is meant that whatever irrational tendencies the pupil may harbor might be exaggerated by a direct spiritual infusion, which could overwhelm his ego and produce dire consequences.

In this mantra, the sounds repeated are the phonems *r* and *m.* The fire resides in the letter *r,* which is perceived to be the concrete representation of the fire god, Agni, while the letter *m* encases the soothing Soma, the god of nectar. The opposing qualities of the gods are set in mutual tension when their letters are sounded alternately.

According to Bengali scholar Govinda Gopal Mukhopadhyaya, whom Beck quotes, the letters congealing the "flowing sounds of the gods" must be "melted" in order to contact the power they contain. To this end, they are repeated or muttered incessantly. The sounding of the *r* "with its expansion and elongation," results in "the heating effect," while the *m,* with its "gradual compression and diminishing of the tone produces a soothing effect." This recitation has an "inner dialectical motion," which assumes a movement of its own, blending the letters into a unity. As they "melt" and the heat is released, the disciple's inner fire is aroused and his consciousness is swept into a "continuous flow of sound" that merges with the Absolute or original cosmic Sound.[5]

In the Faust Book, the old man, in a role similar to the guru's, offered Faustus the "pure light or fire" in the form of "humble victuals" and then proceeded to deliver a lengthy list of do's and don'ts. The evil deeds (litigiousness, slander, craftiness, pillage, murder, avarice, for example) have the character of the fiery *r;* the qualities of expansion and elongation, and the righteous deeds (be good, be calm, be merciful, be peaceful, be gentle, and so on) have the somatic qualities of compression and diminution encased in the *m*. As with the mantra "dialectic," the resolution of the tension between these hypnotically repetitious and opposing moral commands is a union with the divine.

An observation by Geshe Kelsang supports the notion that the old man's quoting of scripture refers to the chanting of a mantra. He asserts that mantra itself is scripture—the letters and phonemes being audible expressions of profound or universal consciousness[6]—and Garrison identifies profound consciousness as Kundalini, the "manifest sound of God."[7] The tantric disciple muttering his mantra and the old man who quotes from the Bible are both reciting scripture: sacred letters, syllables, and words that arise from consciousness itself or, according to a Vedic text, "from God's own mind."

33
Pact

Now Faustus renews his allegiance to the Devil by signing a second pact, or "will," thus identifying with the dark Saturnian power. His mission is to extract the gold that lies hidden in the infernal womb or "crude masses of (the) 'Earth.'"[1] Attaining this goal requires an exercise of will, for the aspirant must will the awesome power he has aroused into submission. The "Evil Fiend" who threatens the old man's life is this elemental force that threatens to overwhelm the disciple's consciousness.

As Faustus signs his "will," the Gospel of Truth discusses the will of the Father, without which, it says, "nothing happens." It is the equivalent of his Word—the creative vibration that underlies the form-giving power of Saturn. Faustus must release this power without becoming imprisoned in its "unawakened" darkness.

He seems to be failing, however, for, as soon as he signs the Devil's pact, he turns against the good old man. Indeed, he wants to kill his would-be savior who, shielded by prayer, threatens to redeem the Devil's darkness.[2] Support for the old man's efforts comes from the Tripartite Tractate, which celebrates the redemption that brings "release from the servile nature." Indeed, the old man's prayers restrain Mephistopheles, who complains that he couldn't "lay hold on him for he had worn armor." In part, this is a reference to the armor worn by Primal Man when he descended into the Darkness to battle the evil archons. It is a portion of the Father's Light and, as such, represents his Word or will.

"Armor" also signifies the prayer, or rather, the mantra the old man (or disciple) is chanting. Geshe Kelsang tells us that mantra means "mind protection"[3] and he mentions certain mantras, some of which are called "Armor Deities,"[4] which, if recited unceasingly for long periods of time, can insulate the mind from fearful thoughts that arise from the impure earth.

FAUST BOOK	GOSPEL OF TRUTH	TRIPARTITE TRACTATE
"I, Doctor Johann Faustus, Do declare in this mine own hand and blood;	This is the perfection in the thought of the Father, and these are the words of his meditation. Each one of his words is the work of his one will in the revelation of his Word. . . . (37:1–6)	A single one alone is appointed to give life. . . . Therefore it began to give the honors which were proclaimed by Jesus . . .
"Whereas I have truly and strictly observed my first instrumentum and pact for these nineteen years, in defiance of God and all mankind;	And the will is what the Father rests in and is pleased with.	whom we have served in his revelation and union.
"And whereas, pledging body and soul, I therein did empower the mighty God Lucifer with full authority over me so soon as five more years be past;	Nothing happens without him nor does anything happen without the will of the Father. . . . (37:19–25)	Now the promise possessed the instruction and the return to what they are from the first . . . so as to return to him,
"And whereas he hath further promised me to increase my days in death, thereby shortening my days in Hell, also not to allow me to suffer any pain;	For he knows the beginning of all of them and their end. . . . Now the end is receiving knowledge about the one who is hidden, and this is the Father. . . . (37:39)	which is that which is "the redemption."

FAUST BOOK	TRIPARTITE TRACTATE
"Now therefore, I do further promise him that I will nevermore heed the admonitions, teachings, scolding, instruction, or threats of mankind, neither concerning the word of God	
nor in any temporal or spiritual matters whatsoever, but particularly do I promise to heed no man of the cloth nor to follow his teachings."	And it is the release from the captivity and the acceptance of freedom.
Now just as soon as Faustus had executed his godless, damned pact, he began to hate the good old man so intensely that he sought some means to kill him,	In its places the captivity of those who were slaves of ignorance holds sway.
but the old man's Christian prayers and Christian ways did such great offense to the Evil Fiend that he could not even approach him.	The freedom is the knowledge of the truth which existed before the ignorance was ruling . . . and a release from the servile nature in which they have suffered.
	Those who have been brought forth from in a lowly thought of vanity (117:7–37) . . . these have received the possession which is freedom, from the abundance of the grace which looked upon the children.
Two days after the events just recounted, when the old man was retiring, he heard a mighty rumbling in his house, the like of which he was never wont to hear. It came right into his chamber, grunting like a sow and continuing for a long time.	It was, however, a disturbance of the passion
Lying abed, the old man began to mock the spirit,	and a destruction of those things which he cast off from himself
Saying: "Ah, what a fine bawdy music! What a beautiful hymn sung by a ghoul! Really a pretty anthem sung by a beautiful angel—who could not tarry in Paradise for two full days. This wretched fellow must now go a-visiting in other folks' houses, for he is banished from	when the Logos separated them from himself.

FAUST BOOK	TRIPARTITE TRACTATE
his own home." With such mockery he drove the spirit away.	
	The Logos who was the cause of their being destined for destruction,
When Doctor Faustus asked him how he had fared with the old man, Mephistopheles answered that he had not been able to lay hold on him, for he had worn armor (referring to the prayers of the old man who had mocked him besides). Now the spirits and devils cannot suffer a good humor, particularly when they are reminded of their fall.	though he kept them and allowed them to exist
Thus doth God protect all good Christians who seek in him succor against the evil one.	because even they were useful for the things which were ordained. (118:2–14)

Julius Evola quotes the seventeenth-century mystic Georg Gichtel, who speaks of the Herculean effort that is required to control the raging force of aroused life energy:

> The soul seeks to *withdraw its will* from the outer constellation in order to *turn to God* at its center: abandoning all senses and passing through the eighth form of Fire . . . which requires a relentless effort, the sweating of blood because *the soul must now struggle against God* (in order to maintain itself and not be dissolved in the light) *and it must struggle at the same time against man* (in order to overcome the human condition).[5] [author's italics]

Faustus's pact is like an inversion of the mystic's description. He draws (not withdraws) his "will" and turns to the Devil (not God) at the center. Then, even as Gichtel's soul "must struggle against God" and "at the same time against man," Faustus declares that he has served the Devil "in defiance of God and all mankind."

PART FOUR

Doctor Faustus

His Last Tricks and What He Did in the Final Years of His Contract

At the end of part three, the pious old man delivered a sermon to Faustus urging him to change his evil ways. This proved to be futile since Faustus reaffirmed his allegiance to the Devil by signing a second pact. Beneath the surface, however, the old man and his sermon were facilitating Faustus's final hypnogogic descent. Representing Faustus's enlightened ego, he kept watch as Faustus contacted the dangerous Saturnian force in order to overcome whatever remaining emotional knots or imperfections might prevent his breakthrough to universal awareness.

An analog in the tantric process of this telluric force is the Kundalini that awakens and rises through the chakras, burning out residual impurities. Now the time arrives for the disciple to engage in the act of sacred intercourse for which he has been preparing. The passion aroused in this union will augment the bliss the Kundalini brings, providing thrust for the Kundalini to pierce the cranial vault. With the opposites united and dualistic thought obliterated, the yogin will be transformed into a god.

In the alchemist's vessel, a dramatic chemical exchange reduces Sulphur and Mercury to their purest essences and they unite in a final conjunction. The Mystical Marriage turns the metal a glorious red and it takes on the aspect of the Sun. This is signified in the Faust Book by a reunion that takes place in the sunny garden Faustus conjures in the middle of winter—one filled with joy and a profusion of blooming roses.

The Red Stone's virtue must be augmented and multiplied, however, so it undergoes another series of circulations. The multiplication is dramatized in the Faust Book by the phantom armies Faustus conjures that proliferate exponentially and surround and transform a doubting knight. The Stone's final perfection is represented in the Faust Book by a union between Faustus and Helen, which produces an omniscient child.

In the surface story, Faustus's pact with the Devil leads to his tragic dismemberment, but not before he passes his powers on to his son and his spirit rises from his body. As it does, the underlying narrative ends and the final chapters "cast off" their textual "bodies" and are "liberated" along with Faustus's spirit.

In the concluding chapter, as Faustus is about to die, he shares a final meal with his students in a scene that evokes the New Testament last supper or a Manichaean ritual meal. As he bids them farewell, a spiritual light seems to flicker about him and, for a fleeting moment, the sinner disappears and the ancient Gnostic Christ or Pilgrim Savior is revealed.

34
How Doctor Faustus Brought About the Marriage of Two Lovers

In the Faust Book, a noble lady's sudden attraction to a suitor dramatizes an event in the alchemist's vessel: a sulphurous quintessence has been drawn from the Body and returns to it like a "thunderbolt" to destroy what remains of its impurity. This is followed by a powerful chemical exchange that produces the metal's final and lasting fixation. A summary of various alchemical writings compiled by Evola describes these transformations. According to J. M. Ragon, "There is an essential menstruum which washes the Earth and is raised to a quintessence in which the sulphurous thunderbolt in one instant penetrates the bodies and destroys the excrementa."

The gold that rises from the Body releases a power that," Eliphas Levi says, "is comparable to lightening that, at first, is a dry, terrestrial exhalation united with the humid vapor, but then, when exalted, takes on a fiery quality and acts on the humidity inherent to it, attracting and agitating it in its own nature, until it precipitates dizzyingly to Earth, where a fixed nature similar to its own . . . attracts it."

"With the 'descent,'" says Synesias, "the airy substance begins to coagulate, whereupon the Fire Devourer appears" and destroys the humidity, causing "the ultimate calcination and fixation."[1] The marriage that Faustus brings about in this chapter represents this alchemical union, and their respective details correspond in the following ways.

A nobleman named Reckauer, in love with an "equally noble" but unresponsive lady, falls ill while pining for her and asks Faustus for help. In his weakened condition he represents the "dry exhalation" that rises from the imperfect Earth, which, Evola says, is associated with "debility and insufficiency, the incurable disease of privation." Before the fiery Spirit is exalted it cannot attract the humid vapor, and neither can the debilitated Reckauer attract the lady.

She represents the humid component of the risen Sulphur, the feminine power, which gives form to Earth. As a last vestige of materiality, it must be evaporated by the fiery, masculine, sulphuric Spirit in order for the marriage of the etherealized substances to take place. Reckauer's desire to gain the lady's hand in marriage signifies the fiery Spirit's effort to "devour" the humid vapor. He must first be cleansed of his debility, however, and so, as the Earth is washed in "essential menstruum," he is washed in distilled water by Faustus and made handsome.

Then, at Faustus's instruction, he dances with the lady and touches her with his ring, a circle that symbolizes wholeness or unity. This is the "lightning that proceeds from the gold," the "sulphurous thunderbolt" that catalyses the chemical reaction. It "attracts" and "agitates" the lady who cannot sleep for thinking of Reckauer, and the next morning, like the humid vapor, she "precipitates dizzyingly to Earth" and begs him to marry her. A "fixed nature similar to [her] own" has attracted her, and this is, of course, Reckauer, who is "equally noble" as the lady and who has been "fixed" by Faustus, or forbidden to propose to her. When he accepts her offer and the marriage takes place, the humidity is devoured by the fiery Spirit and the metal is "calcined and fixed."

That this is a marriage of intrapsychic polarities is indicated by the dance and by Reckauer's facial transformation, or "mask." According to the *Dictionary of Symbols,* dances performed by people with locked arms symbolize "cosmic matrimony or the union of Heaven and Earth," and masks are associated with such dances are spiritual instruments: "Every dance is a pantomime of metamorphosis (and so calls for a mask to facilitate and conceal the transformation), which seeks to change the dancer into a god or demon or some other chosen form of existence."[2]

Under certain circumstances, the dance may go beyond pantomime, "with its rhythmic body movements . . . (it) may result in an altered state of consciousness or trance state, especially," adds the *Dictionary,* "when performed in a ritual setting." As the following chapter will demonstrate, the garden where the metamorphosis takes place is a ritual setting, and certainly Reckauer's movements at the dance, so strictly prescribed by Faustus, suggest a ritual performance. Indeed, the undeviating nature of ritual seems to be emblematic of the control required to integrate body and soul.

In the Pistis Sophia another wedding takes place as Jesus's Light-stream mingles with Sophia's purified Light and they form a final bond. The Gospel of Truth speaks of a divine attraction, which the text comparison equates with Reckauer's newfound irresistibility. It is a fragrance, "a psychic force," which calls divided souls to God. It "hardens and grows cold where there is disunity" says the Gospel, but "if faith warms it with the warm pleroma of love" then (like the noble lady in the Faust Book), "it gets hot."

FAUST BOOK	PISTIS SOPHIA
	And Jesus continued: "It came to pass, then, when the emanations of Self-Willed had noticed that Pistis Sophia was led forth into the higher regions of the chaos, that they also sped after her upwards, desiring to bring her again into the lower regions of the chaos. . . .
A student in Wittemberg, a gallant gentleman of the nobility named N. Reckauer, was with heart and eyes far gone in love with an equally noble and exceedingly beautiful gentlewoman.	"It came to pass, then, when the emanations of Self-Willed pursued Sophia
	that she again sang praises unto me, saying: 'I will sing praises unto thee, O Light.'"
	"'Thou hast led me to the higher regions of the chaos.

FAUST BOOK

Of the many suitors (among them even a young knight) whom she turned down

this Reckauer was privileged to occupy the least place of all.

But he was a good friend of Doctor Faustus having often sat with him at meat and drink,

so that when the acute affect of his love for the gentlewoman caused him to pine away and fall ill,

Faustus soon learned of it. He asked his spirit, Mephistopheles, about the cause of this serious condition and being told that it was the love affair, soon paid a visit to the nobleman, who was greatly astonished to learn the true nature of his illness.

Doctor Faustus bade him be of good cheer and not to despair so, for he intended to help him win the affections of his lady so completely that she should never love another.

And so it did, indeed, come to pass,

for Doctor Faustus so disturbed the heart of the maiden with his sorcery that she would look upon no other man, nor heed any other suitor

PISTIS SOPHIA

"'May the emanations of Self-Willed which pursue me sink down into the lower regions of the chaos . . . and let them not come to the higher regions to see me.

"'And may great darkness cover them and darker gloom come over them.'"

And Salome came forward and said: "My power constraineth me to speak the solution of the words which Pistis Sophia hath uttered. Thy power hath prophesied aforetime through Solomon, saying:

"'I will give thanks unto thee, O Lord, for thou art my God.'

"'Let them who pursue me fall down and let them not see me.'

"'May their resolution be impotent.

"'They are vanquished although they be mighty.

"'My hope is in the Lord, and I shall not be afraid, for thou art my God, my savior.'" (Ch. 58:114)

GOSPEL OF TRUTH

For the Father is sweet and in his will is what is good. (33:25)

He has taken cognizance of the things that are yours.

For by the fruits does one take cognizance of the things that are yours . . .

FAUST BOOK	GOSPEL OF TRUTH	PISTIS SOPHIA
although many gallant, wealthy noblemen were courting her.	because the children of the Father are his fragrance, for they are from the grace of his countenance. For this reason the Father loves his fragrance and manifests it in every place,	
		Jesus continued: "It came to pass when Pistis Sophia had uttered the thirteenth repentance—in that hour was fulfilled the commandment of all the tribulations which were decreed for Pistis Sophia . . .
	and if it mixes unto matter	
Soon after his conversation with Reckauer, Faustus commanded the young man to clothe himself sumptuously	he gives his fragrance to the Light . . . and causes it to surpass every form and every sound.	
	For it is not the ears that smell the fragrance but it is the breath that has the sense of smell and attracts the fragrance to itself . . .	
and prepare to accompany him to the maiden's house, for she was now in her garden	so that he thus shelters it and takes it to the place where it came from. (34:30)	and the time had come to save her out of the chaos and out of the Darknesses
with many other guests who were about to begin a dance, and there Reckauer was to dance with her. Doctor Faustus gave him a ring, telling him to wear it on his finger during the dance with this lady, for just as soon as he might touch her with his ring finger she would fall in love with him and no other.		and the First Mystery sent me a great Light-power out of the Height that I might help Pistis Sophia

FAUST BOOK	GOSPEL OF TRUTH	PISTIS SOPHIA
Faustus forbade Reckauer to ask her hand in marriage, explaining that she would have to entreat him.		
Now he took some distilled water and washed Reckauer with it, so that his face presently became exceeding handsome.	It is something in a psychic form, being like cold water . . . which has frozen, which is on earth that is not solid, of which those who see it think it is earth; afterwards it dissolves again	(and) another Light-power went out of me that it too might help Pistis Sophia . . . and they met together and became a great stream of Light." (Ch. 60:118)
Reckauer followed Faustus's instructions carefully, danced with the lady and, while dancing, touched her with his ring finger.		"It came to pass, then, . . . when (my Light-power) surrounded the pure Light in Sophia . . .
Instantly, her whole heart and love were his, for the good maiden was pierced through with cupid's arrow.	when a breath draws it, it gets hot. The fragrances . . . that are cold are from the division. For this reason faith came.	
That night in her bed she found no rest, so often did her thoughts turn to Reckauer.	It dissolved the division and it brought the warm pleroma of love	and her pure Light did not depart from the wreath of the power of the Light-flame . . .
Early the next morning she sent for him, laid her heart and her love before him		"When, then, this befell her, the pure Light in Sophia began to sing praises, saying:
and begged him to wed her.	in order that the cold should not come again but there should be the unity of perfect thought.	"'The Light hath become a wreath round my head; and I shall not depart from it . . .'" (Ch. 59:115)
He gave his consent for he loved her ardently. Their wedding was celebrated anon and Doctor Faustus received a handsome honorarium.	This is the word of the gospel of the discovery of the pleroma for those who await the salvation which is coming from on high. (34:35)	"'For the Light is with me, and I myself am with the Light.'" (Ch. 59:116)

35
Concerning Divers Flora in Doctor Faustus's Garden on Christmas Day

A Manichaean verse from the Coptic hymns sings of the soul's liberation and expresses the mood of this chapter.

Lo, all trees and plants have become new again.
Lo, roses have spread their beauty abroad, for the bond has been severed that does harm to their leaves. Do thou sever the chains and the bonds of our sins.
The whole air is luminous, the sphere of heaven is resplendent today, the earth puts forth blossom, also the waves of the sea are still, for the gloomy winter has past that is full of trouble.
Let us escape from the iniquity of the soul.[1]

Faustus's magic has produced a similar sense of well being along with a garden full of fruits and blossoms, including red, white and pink roses. The rose garden is a Hermetic symbol for the Mystical Marriage, or the blossoming of awareness and profound inner knowledge. The disciple's heroic effort to transcend the bonds of flesh has also "borne fruit."

In the alchemical wedding, the spiritualized Earth and fiery Spirit have been united and they lie together at the bottom of the vessel, a glorious, impalpable, scarlet ash. As in the last chapter where the bride and groom were "equally noble" this marriage is between opposite but essentially similar substances. Alchemists call these unions "incestuous" and sometimes refer to them as the "union of brother and sister." Thus, in this chapter, brothers and sisters (as well as cousins) enter the garden with red and white roses, symbolizing the mystical union. The snow they walk through on the way to the "wedding" represents the congealing, fixing, or "freezing" of the Stone.

The scarlet ash has miraculous penetrating and multiplying powers, but it must be augmented in quality and given new form before its power can be fully realized. As in the conjunction, substances that are similar are thrown together[2] and, when they are circulated, they produce a variety of colors that signify additional layers of subtlety and refinement. These colors are associated with corresponding stages of enlightenment. They are implied by the "many blossoms" and "other sweet-smelling flowers" in Faustus's garden; their lack of definition suggests that the proliferating virtues they represent are spiritual and not to be grasped. The vines in Faustus's garden "all hung with divers sorts of grapes" are a reference to Mercury, the transforming agent that will be added to the ash.

Meanwhile, the Pistis Sophia celebrates the Mystical Marriage. The disciples continue to interpret the meaning of the Light-streams Jesus and the First Mystery sent down that mingled with Sophia's Light and saved her from the chaos. In the text comparison, the mingling of these Lights is equated with the reunion of the brothers and sisters in the Faust Book. The sense of well being inspired by Faustus's garden is a metaphor for the truth and righteousness of the redeeming Lights themselves.

FAUST BOOK

PISTIS SOPHIA

Mary started forward again and said: "My Lord, I understand what thou sayest concerning the solution of this word thy Light-power hath prophesied aforetime through David in the eighty-fourth Psalm, saying:

FAUST BOOK

In the midst of winter at Christmas season, several gentlewomen came to Wittemberg to visit their brothers and cousins, all young gentlemen students who were well-acquainted with Doctor Faustus. He had been invited to their table on more than one occasion, and, desirous now of repaying such social debts, he did invite these lords to bring their ladies to his domicile for an evening draught of wine.

To come to his house, they had to trudge through a deep snow which lay over the town, but Doctor Faustus had used his particular sorcery to prepare a splendid marvel in his garden for them, and when they arrived there they beheld no snow at all, but a lovely summer day with all manner of flora. The grass was covered all over with many blossoms. Beautiful vines were growing there, all hung with divers sorts of grapes. There were roses, too, white, red, and pink, as well as many other sweet smelling flowers, and it was all a great delight to behold.

PISTIS SOPHIA

"'Grace and truth met together and righteousness and peace kissed each other.

"'Truth sprouted forth out of the earth, and righteousness looked down from heaven. (Ch. 60:118)

"'Righteousness . . . is the spirit in the height who hath brought all the mysteries of the height and given them to the race of men: and they have become righteous and good and have inherited the Light-Kingdom.'"

36
Concerning an Army Raised Against Lord Hardeck

Now Faustus journeys on horseback and encounters the knight on whose head he charmed a set of horns in chapter 24. We took this knight to represent the alchemist's imperfect Earth, or the "lifeless" Adam who was subsequently awakened by the Ennoia's spiritual Light. Faustus pursues the knight and surrounds him with a host of phantom armies, which are matched in the comparison with the Light-streams sent down by Jesus and the First Mystery in the Pistis Sophia. These are the spiritual "waters" that surrounded Sophia and mingled with her Light to destroy her "evil matters." Sophia sings her gratitude to Jesus and celebrates the mingling, or "marriage," of their Lights, and the disciples take turns interpreting the meaning of this event. As their interpretations increase in number, so do Faustus's phantom armies, and both invite a comparison to the multiplication taking place in the alchemist's vessel.

The awakened knight represents the Red Stone, and the events that befall him indicate that it is being augmented in virtue and multiplied in quantity. Faustus conjures a phantom army of one hundred men, then another and another until there are five altogether. Taking turns, they pursue the knight, then corner him with "a charge from every direction." He can "nowhere escape," and his immobility suggests that the Stone is being fixed. This takes place during the augmentation, in which the Red Elixir, mixed with its Red Water, is dissolved and then coagulated. The virtues of the Stone increase exponentially by repetition of this process even as Faustus's phantom armies multiply.

> According to Antoine-Joseph Pernety, "from this first operation, the Medicine acquires ten times more virtue than it possessed. If this process is repeated a second time, the Medicine will be augmented an hundredfold, a third time a thousandfold and so on, always by ten."[1]

The elixir sheds all vestiges of gross matter, becoming ever more refined, even as the knight is divested of his ignorant cohorts and their horses by Faustus and his armies.

Pernety is referring here to the multiplication of the Elixir in quality, but the alchemist's final goal is to augment it in quantity; here the number of armies Faustus sends forth—five—becomes significant. Pernety tells us that "an ounce of this new Elixir projected onto a hundred ounces of common purified Mercury" produces gold, but he warns that, unlike the multiplication in quality, this process should not be repeated too often.

> One cannot carry this reiteration beyond the fourth or fifth time because the Medicine would be so active and so igneous that the operation would become instantaneous . . . [and] moreover, its virtue is great enough at the fourth or fifth time to satisfy the desires of the Artist, since at the first one grain can convert one hundred grains of Mercury into Gold, at the second a thousand, at the third ten thousand, at the fourth one hundred thousand, etc.[2]

After the fifth army was "projected" onto the knight, his virtue was augmented sufficiently to satisfy Faustus's desires, for he finally acknowledged Faustus's spiritual authority. The multiplication continues in the following chapter and will soon produce the ultimate Elixir.

FAUST BOOK	TRIPARTITE TRACTATE	PISTIS SOPHIA
		It came to pass that the First Mystery continued again in the discourse and said to the disciples:
Doctor Faustus being on a journey to Eisleben and about halfway there		"I took Pistis Sophia and led her up to a region which is below the thirteenth aeon. . . .
		"It came to pass then, when I had removed her to that region that she again uttered this song thus:
did see seven horses riding in the distance. He recognized their leader, for it was that Lord Hardeck upon whose forehead (as we have reported) he had charmed a set of hart's horns while at the Emperor's court. The Lord, who knew Faustus quite as well as Faustus knew him, called his men to a halt,		"'In faith have I had faith in the Light; and it remembered me and hearkened to my song.
and when Faustus noticed this action, he immediately retired toward a little hill. The knight ordered a lively charge to intercept him, and also commanded the firing of a musket volley, but although they spurred their mounts hard to overtake Faustus, he achieved the higher ground first,	The redemption is . . . an ascent to the degrees which are in the pleroma . . .	"'It hath led my power up out of the chaos and the nether Darkness of the whole matter and it hath led me up. It hath removed me to a higher and surer aeon, lofty and firm.
and by the time the horses had topped the rise, he had vanished from their sight.		"'And it hath given unto me a new mystery, which is not that of my aeon,

FAUST BOOK	TRIPARTITE TRACTATE	PISTIS SOPHIA
Here the knight called a halt. They were looking about, trying to catch sight of Faustus again, when they heard in the copse below a loud noise of horns, trumpets, and military drums, all tooting and beating.	and it is an entrance into what is silent,	and given unto me a song of the Light.'" (Ch. 74:165)
		[Mary continues her interpretation of the Light-streams sent forth by Jesus and the First Mystery, powers she had referred to as "Grace," "Truth," "Righteousness," and "Peace."]
Some hundred horses came charging in upon them, and the knight with his men took to their heels.		"'Grace' then is the Light-power which hath come down through the First Mystery. . . .
They at first sought to slip around the side of the hill home, but they encountered a second great-armed band all ready for the charge and barring their way.		"'Truth' on the other hand is the power which hath gone forth out of thee . . . in order to save her from the chaos.
They turned about to dash away and beheld a third troop of horsemen.		"And 'Righteousness' again is the power which hath come forth through the First Mystery which will guide Pistis Sophia.
They tried still another route, but again found themselves faced with men ready for battle.		"And 'Peace' again is the power which hath gone forth out of thee . . .'" (Ch. 60:119)
		[Five of the disciples offer their interpretations, and here John, the fifth, offers his:]

FAUST BOOK	TRIPARTITE TRACTATE	PISTIS SOPHIA
The same thing happened five times, just as often as they turned in a fresh direction.		"'Righteousness' . . . is thou the First Mystery which looketh down without, as thou didst come out of the spaces of the Height with the mysteries of the Light kingdom." (Ch. 63:128)
When the knight saw that he could nowhere escape but was threatened with a charge from every direction		And Jesus continued: "It came to pass, then, when the Light-stream had surrounded Pistis Sophia
he rode alone right into the main host, ignoring the danger to himself,		that she took great courage . . . and she was no longer in fear of the emanations of Self-Willed which are in the chaos. . . .
and asked what might be the cause for his being surrounded and menaced on all quarters.		"And moreover, by commandment of myself, the First Mystery which looketh without, the Light-stream . . . surrounded Pistis Sophia on all her sides (and she) abode in the midst of the Light,
None would speak to him or say a word	where there is no need for voice, nor for knowing nor for forming a concept nor for illumination. . . . (124:15–24)	
until at last Doctor Faustus came riding up to the knight (who was now restrained on all sides) and proposed that he surrender himself as a prisoner or taste the edge of the sword.		a great Light being on her left and on her right, and on all her sides.
		"It came to pass, when I had led Pistis Sophia out of the chaos that she cried out again and said:

FAUST BOOK	TRIPARTITE TRACTATE	PISTIS SOPHIA
The knight was convinced that he had encountered a natural army prepared for battle, and when Faustus now demanded their muskets and swords, then took their horses as well,		"'And thou hast covered me with the Light of my stream and purged from me all my evil matters; and I shall be relieved of all my matters because of thy Light.'" (Ch. 68:148)
		James came forward and said: "My Lord, concerning the solution of the words which thou said, thus hath thy Light-power prophesied aforetime through David in the 84th Psalm:
it did not occur to him that it might be naught but sorcery.		"'He will shade thee with his breast, and thou shalt have trust beneath his wings;
Presently Doctor Faustus brought the men fresh, enchanted horses, and new muskets and swords,	(The Father) gives himself so that they might receive knowledge of the abundant thought about his great glory . . . he who reveals himself eternally	his truth shall surround thee as a shield.
saying to the knight (who no longer knew him to be Faustus)	who is unknown in his nature,	
"My Lord, the commander of this army hath bid me let you go this time—		"'Harm will not come nigh unto thee; scourge will not come nigh thy dwelling.
but upon a condition and probation; Will ye confess that ye did pursue a man who hath sought and received and is henceforth shielded by our commander's protection?"		"'For he will give commandment to his angels on thy behalf that they guard thee on all thy ways. . . .'" (Ch. 67:142)

FAUST BOOK	TRIPARTITE TRACTATE	PISTIS SOPHIA
The knight had to accept this condition.		"'Whoso then dwelleth under the help of the Most High, will abide under the shadow of the God of Heaven.'" (Ch. 67:143)
		The First Mystery . . . said unto Thomas: "I give thee commandment to set forth the solution of the song which Pistis Sophia sang unto me." Thomas answered and said:
When they came back to his castle again, his men rode the horses out to drink, but once in the water, the horses disappeared, and they had to ride back home afoot.		"Thou hast covered me with the Light of the stream. . . . I was relieved of the coats of skin. . . . And they have purified me of all my evil matters and I raised myself above them in thy Light.'" (Ch. 69:154)
		Andrew came forward and said:
When the knight beheld his men coming in all muddy and wet		"He hath led up my soul out of the pit of misery and out of the filthy mire;
and when he learned the cause of it all, he knew right away that it was Doctor Faustus's sorcery, even of the same sort as had been used to shame and mock him before.	so that they might receive knowledge of him, through his desire that they should come to experience the ignorance and its pains. (126:15)	
But since he had this time given Faustus his pledge, he would not break it.		"He hath set my foot on a rock and made straight my steps.

FAUST BOOK

As for Faustus, he hitched the horses together, sold them and got some money in his pockets again.

Thus did he heap coals upon the wrath of his enemy.

PISTIS SOPHIA

"He hath put in my mouth a new song, a song of praise for our God." (Ch. 74:165)

37

Concerning the Beautiful Helen from Greece, How She Lived for a Time with Doctor Faustus

Faustus conjures the beautiful Helen again. She becomes his bedfellow and together they produce a miraculous child. There is no apparent underlying text here, but a passage from an anonymous seventeenth-century alchemical treatise sums up the events in this chapter: "After the wedding of Sol the 'red man' and Luna the 'white woman,' she will come to him again and lie with him on bed and then she shall conceive and bear a Son . . . for this man and this woman getteth our Stone."[1]

Here is how the Faust Book tells it.

FAUST BOOK

Doctor Faustus would fain omit or neglect naught pleasant and good unto the flesh. One midnight towards the end of the twenty-second year of his pact, while lying awake, he took thought again of Helen of Greece, whom he had awakened for the students on Whitsunday in Shrovetide (which we reported). Therefore, when morning came, he informed his spirit that he must present Helen to him, so that she might be his concubine.

This was done, and Helen was of the following description (Doctor Faustus had a portrait made of her): Her body was fine and erect, well-proportioned, tall, snow white, and crystalline. She had a complexion, which seemed tinted with rose, a laughing demeanor, gold-yellow hair which reached almost to the calves of her legs, and brilliant laughing eyes with a sweet, loving gaze. Her nose was somewhat long, her teeth white as alabaster. *In summa,* there was not a single flaw about her body. Doctor Faustus beheld her and she captured his heart. He fell to frolicking with her, she became his bedfellow, and he came to love her so well that he could scarcely bear a moment apart from her.

While fond Faustus was living with Helen, she swelled up as were she with child. Doctor Faustus was rapturously happy, for, in the twenty-third year of his pact, she bare him a son whom he called Justus Faustus. This child told him many things out of the future history of numerous lands. Later, when Faustus lost his life, there was none who knew whither wife and child were gone.

The birth of the miraculously knowledgeable Justus Faustus—alchemy's Philosophical Child who is sometimes called Sophia or Wisdom—represents Faustus's breakthrough to a superconscious state. His students had a similar, but lesser, revelation when Helen's numinous figure appeared before them in chapter 29. This time it is Faustus who is moved by Helen's beauty, as his ecstatic transport attests.

The students had copies made from a portrait of her form that was given to them by Faustus, and now he commissions another portrait of Helen who is, herself, a copy, or a reflection of the goddess's glory. Her portrait, then, is a "reflection of a reflection," a term we encountered in a passage from Zostrianos (see chapter 14), in which the ignorant god created the world from "a reflection of a reflection" he saw in the darkness. Adam was copied from an image of the Mother/Father who mirrors the primal Light, and he, too, was a "reflection of a reflection." In the Apochryphon of John, all men are copies of the mold that produced Adam, and Zostrianos tells us in another passage that mortals are in this painful world because their souls are produced by copies.

All agree, then, that the human being is a copy of one form of aeonic prototype or another. As the portrait Faustus commissions is a copy of Helen, or the goddess Sophia, we suspect that the reference being made here is to a human being rather than a painting, and, specifically, to a woman who is modeled on a goddess's form. Faustus acquires the portrait just as Helen's conjured figure appears and he is about to consummate a union with her. The timing of its introduction into the "bridal chamber" conforms to the tantric practice of sacred intercourse in which a human consort joins the yogin to facilitate his inner union. We suggest, then, that Helen's "portrait" represents such a consort and that she will be Faustus's real sexual partner when he takes the phantom Helen to bed. This is the act that consummates the tantrist's spiritual quest, an act whose passion augments the bliss of spiritual union and transforms him into a god. We are indebted to several writers for the following summary of this sacred act, which was taken from their writings about Shaktic yoga.

As the yogin prepares for Maituna, or sacramental union, if he is not married or his wife lacks competence, his guru chooses a qualified woman to be his partner.[2] Preferably, she should be devout,[3] "of good nature and loving kindness,[4] and is considered the reflection of the Sakti . . . the divine woman who epitomizes the entire nature of femaleness."[5] Mookerjee and Khanna add: "She must bear certain auspicious signs in appearance and physical condition, among which are lotus eyes, full breasts, soft skin, slender waist 'swelled into jeweled hips,'"[6] some of which features belong to the goddess herself. According to Garrison, "In the *Lalaitavistara* it is written that she it is 'whose slender waist, bending beneath the burden of her breasts' ripe fruit, swells into jeweled hips, heavy with the promise of infinite maternities.'"[7] Other writers, however, report that a plain, even unattractive woman is preferred so the disciple not be distracted by desire for her and lose his focus on the goddess.

Before they engage in intercourse, the yogin visualizes his partner as a goddess and himself as a god. Then they perform the highly ritualized act of sacred intercourse in which they merge or identify with each other completely. "By the process of ritual projection, the adepts are imbued with divinity until both the male and female, who represent the dialectical principles, achieve an existential awareness of unity similar to the symbol of the circle."[8] With this experience of bi-unity, they become godlike and omniscient.

Faustus, of course, represents the yogin in this chapter and Helen is the goddess he has envisioned. Mephistopheles procures Helen (and, by extension, her portrait) for Faustus in imitation of the guru who chooses the yogin's sexual partner. The parenthetical mention of the portrait in the context of Helen's description virtually surrounds it with her attributes, in the same way the yogin's partner is surrounded or adorned with the visualized goddess's form.

Helen's "laughing demeanor and sweet loving gaze" clearly reflect the required "good nature and loving kindness" of the yogin's partner, while Faustus's union with Helen transforms him just as the bonding of the "dialectical principles" transforms the yogin and makes him omniscient. Indeed, Faustus's attachment to Helen reflects that bonding—"he came to love her so well he could scarcely part from her."

The goal of tantric practice is to acquire a godlike body as well as clarity of vision. The disciple begins by visualizing himself as the deity he wishes to become. In order to keep focused on the task the yogin adopts the practice of ringing a bell at intervals (just as Faustus required the spirit to do in chapter 5). With time and practice, the illusory image, like Mephistopheles' various guises, acquires a nascent individual form.

Practitioners of the Vajrayama Path use a goddess image to stimulate their senses and encourage attachment. By simultaneously meditating on emptiness, however, they overcome attachment to the delusions of the subtle body, which Geshe Kelsang says are "obstructions to omniscience" and the attainment of the Body of Light.[9] The yogin practices by visualizing a goddess and imagining, for example, "holding her hand, seeing her smile, touching, embracing, even having intercourse with her"[10]—all of which we recognize in Faustus's various encounters with dream figures and goddesses in previous chapters. The yogin overcomes attachment to his bliss by meditating on emptiness; Faustus has overcome attachment to his "bliss" involving wine and women by studying astrology and contemplating the heavens.

Gradually the disciple begins to practice with a partner, imagining the various interactions with her that he envisioned with the goddess, and all the while meditating on emptiness. Faustus's students may have been engaging in this practice when Helen appeared to them previously. After visualizing her image they had "copies" painted of her portrait—

again, "reflections of a reflection" suggesting human partners—but they seemed to have maintained chaste relationships with them since they "controlled their passion without difficulty." As neophytes, they were not prepared then, as Faustus is now, to engage in actual intercourse.

"When we can transform the bliss of embracing a 'visualized consort,'" says Geshe Kelsang, "we can try to transform the bliss of actual sexual intercourse into the quick path to Buddhahood."[11] Garrison describes a numinous visualization with which a yogin transforms his consort's body in preparation for the sacred act.

> The shakti now disrobes . . . and seats herself upright on the bed or couch. The sadhaka stands before her. The violet lamp is lighted and placed in such a position that its light falls upon the nude body of the shakti. Viewing her now as an incarnation of the Sapphire Devi, the sadhaka gazes upon her with admiration and awe as one pondering the mystery of creation and the unfathomable secret of being. For she is extremely subtle; the awakener of pure knowledge, the embodiment of all bliss . . . (he) contemplates her as the unsullied treasure house of beauty, shining protoplast, the begetter of all that is, that inscrutably becomes, dies and is born again.[12]

Like the sadhaka's dream goddess, the beautiful Helen whom Faustus has conjured is flawless. Snow white and crystalline, tinted with rose and gold—hers are the colors of the pure White Stone and the Rupravajra Goddess "who is born from an omniscient wisdom that is indivisible from the emptiness of form."[13] Faustus must have beheld his partner's body, adorned with Helen's flawless form, in the same way the sadhaka gazed at his shakti—with eyes that envisioned detail. The description of Helen attests to that. Faustus's visualization gives his consort a rather complex spiritual as well as human appearance, much as the sadhaka's creative gaze enhances his shakti's body with a nuanced metaphysical form. This is in contrast to Helen's previous appearance when her figure was largely undefined. Now, however, she is crystalline, fine, tall, and erect, suggesting the remote quality and elevated status of a goddess, while her "brilliant laughing eyes" and "loving gaze" make her seem human and accessible. From her alabaster teeth to her long, golden hair she is described with the care and admiration the sadhaka lavishes on the consecrated body of his shakti.

Complex visualization such as this requires steady practice, as Omar Garrison demonstrates in a description of a young disciple who is attempting to summon his goddess. After a series of ritual preparations the yogin closes his eyes and visualizes "a dimly lighted cavern filled with clouds of red mist. It is midnight (the hour Faustus "takes thought" of Helen) and the time at which the seventh discipline or visualization of the dream-goddess should take place. "Gradually the swirling vapor clouds part and a figure clothed in bright golden light emerges."[14] He calls to her, "Reveal, reveal thyself to me," but she dissolves in the mist and he must wait for the next night to visualize her again. When he perfects his concentration, says Garrison, she will always be with him (just as Helen comes to live with Faustus) and he can summon her image at will. The figure the yogin summons is an image of the Kundalini, the "sleeping goddess" who abides within him. He has learned to make her rise and fall according to his desire; now, as he embarks upon the sacred act, the internal fire produced by sexual intercourse heightens his experience of bliss and brings a total transformation of consciousness.

"The stronger this bliss becomes," says Geshe Kelsang, "the more subtle our mind becomes" and the appearance of duality begins to fade and be replaced by "the clear light of bliss." When this blissful light "concentrates on emptiness," he says, "it realizes emptiness directly and the two things become one, they form an immutable bond."[15]

Geshe adds that this experience transfers the locus of the sadhaka's identity away from his gross body to the illusory body of the deity he had been visualizing, which now acquires the shape and definition that it lacked. As Faustus "bonds" with Helen in rapturous bliss he sheds his old, imperfect form; with the birth of Justus Faustus, he assumes the diamond body and omniscience of a god.

38
Concerning One Whose Wife Married While He Was Captive in Egypt and How Doctor Faustus Informed and Aided Him

Faustus has become enlightened and, by his act, the "world of oblivion" that is based on ignorance of the Father has been dissolved. In the text comparison the Gospel of Truth proclaims this universal transformation in a formulation which Hans Jonas calls "the grand pneumatic equation of Valentinian thought." Since the deficiency came into being because the Father was not known, therefore, when the Father is known, from that moment on the deficiency will no longer exist. "The human-individual event of pneumatic knowledge," says Jonas, "is the inverse equivalent of the pre-cosmic universal event of divine ignorance, and in its redeeming effect of the same ontological order. *The actualization of knowledge in the person is at the same time an act in the general ground of being.*"[1] [author's italics]

The process by which Mind, or a particular state of mind, created the phenomenal world has been reversed by Faustus's liberation, and as he sheds his gross body the forms produced by ignorance vanish.

In this chapter an unlucky young nobleman is one of these forms whom the Gospel of Truth says was not "named" by the Father, and is therefore "a creature of oblivion" who "will vanish along with it." The wife of a missing lord, mistakenly thinking he is dead, marries this fellow. On their wedding night Faustus renders him impotent, and his non-performing "tool," as the Faust Book puts it, is equated in the comparison with the deficient forms that ignorance produces.

The sexual prowess of the real husband "who had rightly known how to tousle" the lady is associated with a "treasure" that is mentioned in the Tripartite Tractate. This treasure is a "revelation of the Father and a restoration of Unity"—a unity that is restored in the Faust Book when the first husband suddenly returns and the second one flees or, as the Gospel of Truth says, "vanishes in the fusion of Unity." There is much grasping, wiggling, and squeezing in this account, the sexual references perhaps referring to the internal heat in the alchemist's metal which is most intense during the multiplication.*

The Gospel of Truth formula, which holds that Mind is the creator and destroyer of the phenomenal world, is further suggested in the Faust Book by two predictions concerning Faustus's death. The previous chapter noted that, later on, "when Faustus lost his life, there was none who knew whither wife and child were gone," and in a following chapter, Faustus informs his famulus that Mephistopheles will "vanish forever" when he is dead. These vanishing characters have appeared at important moments in Faustus's spiritual development and may be considered images projected by his awakening psyche. But as the Gospel of Truth suggests, they are also forms produced by ignorance. When Faustus dies—that is, becomes enlightened—it would follow that they should vanish with the ignorance that gave them existence.

A fourth-century Christian bishop, Nemeius, who entertained a variety of beliefs, speaks of the mind as the creative center of all being, which sees itself when placed "in a rapport with visible objects, which are nothing more than itself, seeing that the mind embraces everything, and that all that exists is nothing but the mind, which contains bodies of all kinds."[3]

*John Lyly's Gallathea has two brothers gossiping about a certain alchemist's active sex life: "'I sawe a prettie wench come to his shoppe,' says one, 'where with puffing, blowing and sweating, he so plyed her, that hee multiplyed her.'"[2] (5.1.18–21)

Faustus sees nothing more than himself as well, and the Faust Book is a world of oblivion, an illusional place where devils and drunken saviors, goddesses and flying dragons, act and interact but lack true existence, for all are projections of his dreaming and evolving mind.

FAUST BOOK	TRIPARTITE TRACTATE	GOSPEL OF TRUTH
A fine gentleman of the nobility, Johann Werner of Reutpueffel from Bennlingen, who had gone to school with Faustus and was a learned man,	The Father had foreknowledge of (the Son) since he was in his thought before anything came into being. . . .	Those whose name (the Father) knew in advance were called at the end,
had been married to an extremely beautiful woman named Sabina of Kettheim		so that one who has knowledge of the Father is the one whose name the Father has uttered.
when he was one evening through guile and drink brought to take an oath: to go along to the Holy Land. He kept his pledge and promise, saw many things, endured much, and had been gone almost five years	He set the deficiency on the one who remains for certain periods and times . . .	
when there came to his wife a report that he was dead.	since the fact that he is unknown	
The lady mourned for three years, during which time she had many suitors, among them an excellent person of the nobility whose name we dare not mention,		For he whose name has not been called is ignorant. Indeed, how is one to hear if his name has not been mentioned?
but whom she now accepted.	is a cause of his production. . . . (125:25–35)	

FAUST BOOK	TRIPARTITE TRACTATE	GOSPEL OF TRUTH
		For he who is ignorant until the end is a creature of oblivion and he will vanish along with it. . . .
When the time was approaching for their marriage celebration, Doctor Faustus discovered it		Therefore, if one has knowledge he is from above.
and he asked his Mephistopheles whether this Lord Reutpueffel were still alive, the spirit answered "Yes,"	He who gave them knowledge of (the Father) was one of his powers,	If he is called, he hears, he answers. . . .
he be alive and in Egypt and in the city of Lylopolts		Each one's name comes to him.
where he lay captive having attempted to visit the city of al-Cairo.		He who is to have knowledge in this manner knows where he comes from and where he is going.
This grieved Doctor Faustus for he loved his friend and had not been pleased that the lady was remarrying so soon. He knew her husband had loved her well. The time for the marriage consummation and the subsequent ceremony being at hand, Doctor Faustus gazed into a mirror where he could see all things and by means of which he was able to inform the Lord of Reutpeuffel that his wife was about to be wed, at which the latter was much astonished.		He knows as one who having become drunk turns away from his drunkenness, and having returned to himself, has set right what are his own. . . . (22:1–20)

FAUST BOOK	TRIPARTITE TRACTATE	GOSPEL OF TRUTH
		The form of it is the world, that in which he served.
The hour of consummation arrived. The nobleman disrobed and went out to cast his water. It was then that Mephistopheles did use his art, for when the man came in and leapt into Sabina's bed to enjoy the fruits of love, when they had hoisted their shirts and squeezed close together, it was all to no avail.		Having filled the deficiency he abolished the form—
The good lady, seeing that he did not want on and was hesitating, did reach out herself for the tool, wishing to help him, but she could achieve naught, and the night wore on in mere grasping, wiggling, and squeezing.	for enabling them to grasp that knowledge in the deepest sense	For the place where there is envy and strife is deficient,
This did cause the lady to grieve and to think on her previous husband whom she thought to be dead,	is called "the knowledge of all that is thought of"	
for he had rightly known how to tousle her.	and "the treasure"	
On the very same night, Faustus had freed the nobleman and had brought him asleep back to his castle. Now when the good lady beheld her young lord she fell at his feet and begged his forgiveness, indicating at the same time that the other had been able to accomplish naught.	and "the revelation of those things which were known at first"	

FAUST BOOK	TRIPARTITE TRACTATE	GOSPEL OF TRUTH
My Lord of Reutpueffel, noting that the account corresponded with what Doctor Faustus had reported, did accept her back again.	and "the path toward harmony"	but the place where there is unity is perfect.
The other good fellow, who finally recovered his potency,	which is the increase of those who have abandoned the greatness which was theirs. . . . (127:10–25)	Since the deficiency came into being because the Father was not known, therefore, when the Father is known, from that moment on the deficiency will no longer exist,
rode hastily away, not wishing to be seen again because of what had happened to him.		as in the case of the ignorance of a person, when he comes to have knowledge, his ignorance vanishes of itself, as the Darkness vanishes when Light appears. (24:20–35)
Later he lost his life in a war.		So also the deficiency vanishes in the perfection. So from that moment on the form is not apparent but will vanish in the fusion of Unity,
The husband, however, is still jealous, and the good lady must hear from him, even though he did not witness it, how she did after all lie with another, who felt her and grasped her and had he been able to cover her, would have done that too.		for now their works lie scattered. In time, Unity will perfect the spaces. It is within Unity that each one will attain himself; within knowledge he will purify himself from multiplicity into Unity, consuming matter within himself like fire, and Darkness by Light, death by life. (24–25)

39
Concerning the Testament: What Doctor Faustus Bequeathed to His Servant Christof Wagner

Faustus's shiftless famulus, Christof Wagner, is about to inherit all that Faustus possesses, including the silver Faustus stole from the pope. This silver, we recall, represents the circulating Spirits that arise from the "dead" or corrupted metal and which return to purify it. Their emergence from the dark Body corresponds to a revelation, and now, as Faustus prepares to die, he makes Wagner his son and passes on to him his revelation and his "name."

In the previous chapter we read in the Gospel of Truth that the name is the "mysterious something," which according to G. R. S. Mead "decides the nature and class and being of every creature."[1] For humans the name is a divine dispensation—a pneumatic quality that sets them apart from all other beings. The material powers fear and oppose it and, as the Gospel asserts, only those whose name the Father has known "from the beginning"—those who have the highest calling—may triumph over those powers and receive his Word. The Father's Word is the Son, and here the Gospel of Truth informs us that he inherits all that the Father possesses; while the Word (or name) itself is invisible, the Son, as its manifestation, reveals the nature of the Godhead.

Faustus's itinerant lifestyle—"he had not lived much at home, but at inns and with students in gluttony and drunkenness"—described at the end of the chapter, identifies him as the dissolute Hero Savior in the Hymn of the Pearl and the "sleeping" or "drunken" Primal Man. Both came into the world on soul-saving missions and both succumbed to the flesh's temptations and forgot their heavenly origin. They are thus identified with the "sleeping" souls they came to save, or, like the besotted Faustus who has saved the loutish Wagner, they are "cut from the same piece of cloth."

The Savior sent down from above is a stranger in the world, and Hans Jonas describes his wandering and eternal isolation. "The savior does not come just once into the world but . . . from the beginning of time he wanders in different forms through history, himself exiled in the world . . . the constant form of his presence is precisely the other-worldly call resounding through the world and representing the alien in its midst, and between his manifestations he walks invisible through time."[2]

"'I wandered through worlds and generations,' says the alien man, 'until I came to the gate of Jerusalem.'"[3] This heavenly gate and the ghostly impalpability of the alien man are represented in the Faust Book by the Iron Gate and Faustus's haunted house. Faustus's spirit has left his "house," or body, and soon he will pass through the "Iron Gate" that separates this world from the next—his "other-worldly Call" being echoed by his son who is also an alien in the world.

FAUST BOOK	GOSPEL OF TRUTH
Now during this whole time, right into the twenty-fourth year of his pact, Doctor Faustus had been keeping a young apprentice, who studied there at the university of Wittemberg and who became acquainted with all the tricks, sorcery, and arts of his master.	Now the name of the Father is the Son. It is he who first gave a name to the one who first came forth from him,
The two were cut from the same piece of cloth.	who was himself,

FAUST BOOK

Wagner was a wicked, dissipated knave who had gone about begging in Wittemberg but had found no kindness with anyone until he had met Doctor Faustus who took the stripling in as his famulus and even called him his son.

When his twenty-four years were all but run out, Faustus called unto himself a notary together with several magisters who were his friends. In their presence he bequeathed his famulus his house and garden, which were located on the Ring-Wall in Scherr Alley, not far from the Iron Gate and indeed right beside the houses of Ganser and of Veitt Rottinger (since that time, it has been rebuilt, for it was so uncanny that none could dwell therein). He also left him 1600 guilders lent out on usury, a farm worth 800 guilders, 600 guilders in ready money, a gold chain

worth 300 crowns, some silver plate given him by a man named Kraffter, as well as such other things as he had taken away from various courts—those of the Pope and the Turk, for example. All these items together were worth many hundred guilders.

There was not really much household stuff on hand, for he had not lived much at home but in inns and with students, in gluttony and drunkenness.

GOSPEL OF TRUTH

and begot him as a son.

He is the one to whom belongs all that exists around him, the Father. (38:6–14)

40
The Discourse Which Doctor Faustus Held with His Son Concerning His Last Will and Testament

Faustus has shed his gross body and now he dwells in spirit beyond the material plane. As if reflecting his liberation, these last five chapters of the Faust Book have cast off the underlying texts and exist as disembodied analogs of certain features of the themes we have been following. In this chapter Faustus grants a request and gives a final instruction to his son.

FAUST BOOK

The testament being drawn up, Faustus summoned his famulus, explained to him how he had made that person beneficiary of his estate who had been a trusty servant throughout his life and had never revealed any of his secrets, and how he would, in addition, like to grant this person one other request, if he would but name it. Wagner asked for Faustus's cunning, but this fine father reminded his pretty son (who should have been named Christ*less* Wagner) that he would after all inherit all his books, and that he must diligently guard them, not letting them become common knowledge, but taking his own profit from them by studying them well (this route to Hell).

"As to my cunning" (spake Faustus), "thou canst win it if thou wilt but love my books, heed no man else, and follow in my footsteps. Hast thou none other request?—That thou be served by my spirit? This cannot be, for Mephistopheles oweth me no further debt, nor doth he bear affinity to any other man. But if thou art fain to have a spirit as servant I will help thee to another."

Three days later, Faustus again called his famulus unto him, asking whether he were still of a mind to possess a spirit, and, if so, in what form he would have him.

"My Lord and Father," answered Wagner, "in the form of an ape let him appear, for even in such a manner and form would I have him."

A spirit immediately came bounding into the parlor in the figure of an ape, and Doctor Faustus said:

"Lo, now seest thou him, but he will not obey thee until I be dead. At that time my Mephistopheles will vanish forever, and thou shalt never see him more. Then, if thou wilt perform what is necessary—this being thine own decision—then canst thou summon thy spirit unto thee by calling upon Urian, for that is his name. In return, I do beg of thee not to publish my deeds, arts, and adventures before the time of my death, but then to write all these matters down, organizing and transferring them into a *Historia* and compelling Urian to help thee by recalling unto thee whatever thou canst not remember, for men will expect these things of thee."

Faustus's instruction to Wagner to write down his "deeds, arts and adventures" and to "publish" them in a book is a reference to the concluding passages in a number of Gnostic and Hermetic writings. Some of them appeared earlier in the text comparisons, as in the Apochryphon of John, for instance, where the Holy Spirit gives this instruction to the disciple: "And I have completed everything for you in your hearing. And I have said everything to you that you might write them down and give them secretly to your fellow spirits. . . . And the savior presented these things to him that he might write them down and keep them secure." (31:30)

In Allogenes, the disciple, Messos, is given the same assignment with some additional details. "Write down the things that I shall tell you and of which I shall remind you for the sake of those who will be worthy after you. And you will leave this book upon a mountain and you will adjure the guardian: 'Come, Dreadful One.'" (68:10)

The recipients of this secret knowledge are called the "living elect" in Zostrianos (68:1–24) and, in the Apocalypse of Adam, a revelation by Adam to his son in the Nag Hammadi collection, they are called the "seed," or "those who know the eternal knowledge" (65:10, 85:27). They descend from Adam through his son, Seth, to whom he imparted a divine revelation. Seth wrote it in a book and placed it on a high mountain from where it was handed down through generations of Seth's descendants and revealed occasionally to those who were not "incorporeal," or not "begotten by God." In the "Discourse on the Eighth and Ninth," another Nag Hammadi text, a spiritual guide offers hope that exposure to this book, or Word of God, will help the unbegotten slowly join the ranks of the enlightened (63:1–14).

On the mortal plane, the secret transmission from master to disciple amounts to a symbolic sacrifice as the former "gives birth to a new, immortal self out of the old" and the disciple becomes "as important as his master."[1] Wagner seems to be well aware of his importance, not hesitating to ask for Faustus's cunning and for his servant, Mephistopheles. His request takes us back to the beginning of this cycle when the Father's reflection in the Apochryphon of John first appeared and made a similar request of the Father, asking for "a fellow worker, which is the Mind." Mephistopheles is Faustus's "fellow worker" and the transforming power of his mind. When Wagner learns that Mephistopheles bears no "affinity to any other man" and will "vanish forever" when Faustus dies, he requests a servant or "fellow worker" of his own and it appears in the form of an ape called Urian.

Since Urian wears Mephistopheles' mantle, we assume that the sounding of his name will have the same transforming power over Wagner as the sounding of Mephistopheles' name had on Faustus. The lowly ape represents the aspect of Wagner's mind that the "Discourse on the Eighth and Ninth" says "by stages, will advance" him and lead him "into the way of immortality" (63:10).*

According to Mani, in different epochs and cycles of time Messengers have come to bring the living book to humankind. The daily rounds of sacrifice by Jesus patibilis, the physician who brings enlightenment in Mani's myth, exemplifies this cycle, and it is he above all who is represented when the dying Doctor Faustus hands his mission over to his son and the cycle begins anew.

---

*The ape also signifies Wagner's acquisition of the alchemical power to transform nature. According to Frances Yates: "The monkey is Man, or rather Man's art by which he imitates nature with simian mimicry. Man here seems to have lost some of his dignity, but he has gained in power. He has become the clever ape of nature who has found out the way that nature works and, by imitating it, will obtain her powers."[2]

41
What Doctor Faustus Did in the Final Month of His Pact

This is a gloomy chapter. Faustus has retreated to his chamber and lies in his bed, "depressed and deeply melancholic." While the darkness of his mood logically anticipates his coming death in the surface story, it is the precise opposite of the "radiant light" that marks the final stage of a disciple's illumination as Mookerjee and Khanna describe it: "It is an inner radiance of intensely bright pure light in which the yogi has the sense of being immersed into a blaze of dazzling flame."[1]

Faustus's melancholy is to this radiant light as the shadow is to the Sun—it defines it and gives it meaning. Michael Maier points this out in an emblem, which appears near the end of his *Atalanta Fugien,* a collection of emblems, epigrams and verses based on 50 of his fugues. It depicts the Sun with its shadow cast behind the earth and bears the epigram "The Sun and its shadow complete the Work."[2]

The shadow-reflection is associated with the Philosopher's Stone, a symbol of illumination, for the Stone itself is thought to be a shadow or "a perfect reflection . . . of the macrocosm." The Moon is identified with it as well, for it reflects the light of the Sun and "evokes the final cosmic wedding of . . . masculine and feminine polarities."[3] The gloom that engulfs Faustus in his role as the failed psychic soul in the surface story is nothing less than an affirmation of the disciple's illumination and a confirmation that his struggle for transformation has been won.

FAUST BOOK

His days ran out like sand in an hourglass, and when only one month remained of the twenty-four years which he had contracted with the Devil (as ye have read) Doctor Faustus became fainthearted, depressed, deeply melancholic, like unto an imprisoned murderer and highwayman over whose head the sentence hath been pronounced and who now in the dungeon awaiteth punishment and death. Filled with fear, he sobbed and held conversations with himself, accompanying such speeches with many gestures of his hands. He did moan and sigh and fall away from flesh. He kept himself close and could not abide to have the spirit about him.

42
Doctor Faustus: His Lamentation, That He Must Die at a Young and Lusty Age

Faustus continues to lament, and as he sets his grief in words he expresses the plight of the divided and failed psychic soul. He bemoans his inner conflicts, his lusts, his recklessness, and even his free will. Each of his laments or groups of laments is preceded by "Alas," and on three occasions by two "Alases," making sixteen in all. This is one more than the number of sections in the Turkish *Kuastuanift,* a Manichaean confession prayer that lists a few of the lapses that Faustus mentions. One must assume that the number sixteen was not chosen arbitrarily by the Faust Book author and may refer to some other confessional prayer or signify completion in some other context, but the similarities to the *Kuastuanift* are worth noting, as is one important difference.

The first part of the prayer refers to failures of religious observance or faith, while the second half addresses questions of right conduct. It includes some of Faustus's sins of thought and deed, such as giving way to wanton pleasures, cleaving to love of the body, and foolish attachment to things of the world. Francis Legge suggests that prohibitions against lying, greed, adultery, and theft, which are enumerated in the

Fihrist version of the Manichaean confession, might be added to this list and they reflect more of Faustus's stated regrets.[1] The notable difference between Faustus's laments and the prayer is one of mood and involves a typical Faust Book reversal of meaning.

Each section of the prayer ends with the supplication "If we have been found lacking and unprofitable, and have day by day and month by month committed trespasses . . . to cleanse ourselves from sin, so pray we now: 'Our sins remit!'"[2]

The hope expressed in the supplication is turned to grief by Faustus. He ends his first group of laments with "Alas, of what help is this complaint?" and concludes the last one with a heart "so troubled that he could speak no more." In the surface story he goes to his death unreconstructed, a hopelessly divided soul.

FAUST BOOK

Sorrow moved Doctor Faustus to set his grief in words, lest he forget it. Here followeth one such written complaint:

Alas, thou reckless, worthless heart! Thou hast seduced the flesh round about thee, and my fate is fire. The blessedness, which once thou didst know is lost.

Alas, Reason and Free Will! What a heavy charge ye do level at these limbs, which may expect naught else than rape of their life!

Alas ye limbs, and thou yet whole body! It was ye let Reason indict Soul, for I might have chosen succor for my soul by sacrificing thee, my body.

Alas, Love and Hate! Why abide ye both at once in my breast? Your company hath occasioned all mine anguish.

Alas, Mercy and Vengeance! Ye have caused me to strive after glory and rewarded me with infamy.

Alas, Malice and Compassion! Was I created a man that I might suffer those torments which now I see before me?

Alas, alas, is there aught in the wide world that doth not conspire against this wretch?

Alas, of what help is this complaint?

43
Doctor Faustus Lamenteth Yet Further

FAUST BOOK

Alas, alas, wretched man, o thou poor accursed Faustus, now in the number of the damned! I must wait the inestimable pains of a death far more miserable than any tortured creature hath yet endured.

Alas, alas, Reason, Willfulness, Recklessness, Free Will! O what a cursed and inconstant life hast thou led! How unseeing, how careless wast thou! Now become thy parts, soul and body, unseeing and ever more unseen.

Alas, Worldly Pleasure! Into what wretchedness hast thou led me, darkening and blinding mine eyes!

Alas, my timid heart! Where were thine eyes?

And thou my poor soul! Where was thy knowledge?

All ye senses! Where were ye hid?

O miserable travail! O sorrow and desperation forgotten of God!

Alas, grief over grief, and torment upon woe and affliction! Who will release me? Where am I to hide? Whither must I creep? Whither flee? Wherever I may be, there am I a prisoner.

The heart of Doctor Faustus was so troubled that he could speak no more.

44
Doctor Faustus: His Hideous End and Spectaculum

As Faustus's allotted time runs out, he has a last supper with his students. After sharing a final cup with them, he reveals his connection to a greater power (in this case his pact with the Devil), informs them that he is about to die, and then suffers a horrible death. This account, so reminiscent of Jesus's last hours in the Gospel of John, also has some of its spiritual grace. But this seems to be a Christian overlay on a Manichaean ritual involving the consumption of food as it relates to the death of Jesus patibilis and the freeing of the Light.

The Manichaeans, as we learned, believed that particles of the Father's Light were scattered throughout creation and imprisoned in the plants and animals. Consequently, they were enjoined to eat circumspectly and to fast with regularity in order to spare the sacred Light. The elect among them were exceptions, they believed, for their purity enabled them to absorb the Light in the food they ate, thus freeing it or preventing it from recombining with the Darkness in new material forms. For this reason, the lay members of the community made offerings of food to the pneumatics, which they themselves could not eat. Faustus's last supper suggests a ritual such as this, which celebrates the freeing of the Light.

The effectiveness of this practice had its limits, however, and it was acknowledged that some of the tiny particles were released through a holy man's excrement to recombine with material forms. St. Augustine scoffed at their belief, and in a debate with a Manichaean priest, he called it "a foolish notion to make your disciples bring you food, that your teeth and stomach may be the means of relieving Christ who is bound up in it."[1]

The concept of Christ as food that is chewed, digested, and released in excrement is expressed in myth by the fate of Jesus patibilis, of whom the *Kephalia* says, "What has been called the 'slaughtered, killed, oppressed, murdered soul' is the life force of the fruits, the cucumbers and seeds which are beaten, plucked, torn to pieces, and give nourishment to the worlds of flesh."[2]

The "hideous spectaculum" of Faustus's bloody, dismembered body cast away on a heap of dung represents the ritual sacrifice of Jesus patibilis, who is born from a dung hill in each of his cycles of death and renewal. While Jesus patibilis's Light-soul persists in the "fruits and seeds," Faustus's spirit lives on in his famulus who now inhabits his "uncanny house." Indeed, it is said that he "himself walked about at night making revelations to Wagner as regardeth many secret matters," and people passing by after his death reported "seeing his face peering out at the windows." His mysterious return to the house near the Iron Gate represents the "resurrection" the Naassene treatise speaks of, and his house is "the House of God where the Good God dwells alone."[3] No "impure man shall enter there," it warns, "no psychic, no fleshly man but it is kept under watch for the spiritual alone."[4] Only Wagner can enter there for he is Faustus's son and has inherited his gold. Faustus has "cast away his garments" and "like the Virgin with child," has conceived and brought forth a son, "which is neither psychic, animal, nor fleshly, but a blessed aeon of aeons."[5]

FAUST BOOK

His twenty-four years were run out. As he lay awake in the night, his spirit came unto him to deliver up his writ, or contract, thus giving him due notice that the Devil would fetch his body in the following night, and allowing him to make any necessary preparations for that event. This occasioned such a renewed moaning and sobbing into the night that the spirit returned, consoling him and saying:

My Fauste, be not so faint of heart. Thou dost indeed lose thy body, but thy time of judgment is yet far distant. Why surely thou must die—even shouldst thou live for many hundreds of years. The Jews and the Turks must also die expecting the same perdition as thou—even emperors die thus, if they be not Christian. After all, thou knowest not yet what it be that awaiteth thee. Take courage, and despair not so utterly. Dost not remember how the Devil did promise thee a body and soul all of steel, insensitive to the pain which the others will feel in Hell?

This and such like comfort and consolation he gave him, but it was false and not in accord with the Holy Scriptures. Doctor Faustus, having none other expectation but that he must absolve his debt and contract with his skin, did on this same day (in which the spirit had announced that the Devil was about to fetch him) betake himself unto the trusted friends with whom he had spent many an hour, the magisters, baccalaureates, and other students, entreating them now to go out to the little village of Rimlich with him, about a half mile removed from the town of Wittemberg, there to take a repast with him. They would not turn him away, but went along and ate a morning meal with many costly courses both of meat and drink, served by the host at an inn.

Doctor Faustus joined in their merriment, but he was not merry in his heart. Afterward, he requested all his guests to do him the great kindness of remaining to eat supper with him, too, and to stay the night here as well, for he had something important to tell them. Again they agreed, and they took the evening meal with him also.

It was finished, and a last cup had been passed. Doctor Faustus paid the host, and addressed the students, saying that he wished to inform them of some things. They gave him their attention, and Doctor Faustus said unto them:

My dear, trusted, and very gracious Lords: I have called you unto me for this good and sufficient cause. For many years now, ye have known what manner of man I be, the arts and sorcery I have used. All these things come from none other than from the Devil. I fell into such devilish desires through none other cause than these: bad company, mine own worthless flesh and blood, my stiff-necked, godless will, and all the soaring, devilish thoughts I allowed in my head. I gave myself up unto the Devil and contracted with him for a term of twenty-four years, setting my body and soul in forfeit. Now are these twenty-four years run out. I have only this night left. An hourglass standeth before mine eyes, and I watch for it to finish.

I know that the Devil will have his due. As I have consigned my body and soul unto him with my blood in return for certain other costly considerations, I have no doubt that he will this night fetch me. This is why, dear and well-beloved, gracious Lords, I have summoned you here just before the end to take one last cup with me, not concealing from you the manner of my departure. I entreat you now, my dear gracious Brothers and Lords, to bring my cordial and brotherly greetings to my friends and to those who do honor my memory, to bear no ill will toward me but, if ever I have offended you, to forgive me in your hearts. As regardeth my *Historia* and what I have wrought in those twenty-four years, all these things have been written down for you.

Now let my hideous end be an example unto you so long as ye may live, and a remembrance to love God and entreat Him to protect you from the guile and deceit of the Devil, praying that the Dear Lord will not lead you into temptation. Cling ye unto Him, falling not away from him as I damned godless mortal have done, despising and denying Baptism (Christ's own Sacrament), God, all the Heavenly Host and mankind—such a sweet God, who desireth not that one shall be lost. Shun bad company, which would lead you astray as it hath me, go earnestly and often to church, war and strive constantly against the Devil with a steadfast faith in Christ and always walking a godly path.

Finally, my last request is that ye go to bed and let nothing trouble you, but sleep on and take your rest even if a crashing and tumult be heard in the house. Be not afraid. No injury shall befall you. Arise not out of your beds. Should ye find my corpse, convey it unto the earth, for I die both as a bad and as a good Christian. Contrition is in my heart, and my mind doth constantly beg for Grace and for the salvation of my soul. O I know that the Devil will have this body—and welcome he is to it, would he but leave my soul in peace. Now I entreat you: betake yourselves to bed. A good night to you—unto me, an evil, wretched, and a frightful one.

Faustus needed great resolve and courage to make this confession and to tell his tale without weakening and becoming fearful and faint. As for the students, they were cast into great wonderment that a man could be so reckless as thus to imperil body and soul for no more profit than knavery, knowledge, and sorcery. But, as they loved him well, they sought to console him thus:

"Alas dear Fauste, how have ye imperiled yourself! Why remained ye so long silent, revealing none of these things to us? Why, we should have brought learned *theologi* who would have torn you out of the Devil's nets and saved you. But now it is too late and surely injurious to body and soul."

Doctor Faustus answered saying: "Such was not permitted me. Often was I amind to seek counsel and succor of god-fearing men. Indeed, once an old man did charge me to follow his teachings, leave my sorcery and be converted. Then came the Devil, ready to put an end to me (even as he will this night do), saying that in the moment of my conversion—nay, even in the instant of such an intent on my part—all would be over with me."

Upon hearing these words, and understanding that the Devil would surely dispatch

Faustus this night, the students urged him to call upon God, begging Him for forgiveness for Jesus Christ's sake, saying:

"O God, be merciful unto me poor sinner, and enter not into judgment with me, for I cannot stand before Thee. Although I must forfeit my body unto the Devil, wilt Thou preserve my soul!"

Faustus agreed to do this. He tried to pray, but he could not. As it was with Cain, who said his sins were greater than could be forgiven him, so was it with Faustus also, who was convinced that in making his written contract with the Devil he had gone too far. But the students and good lords prayed and wept for Faustus. They embraced one another and, leaving Faustus in his chambers, retired to bed, where none could rightly sleep, for they lay there awake, waiting the end.

And it came to pass between twelve and one o'clock in the night that a great blast of wind stormed against the house, blustering on all sides as if the inn and indeed the entire neighborhood would be torn down. The students fell into a great fear, got out of their beds and came together to comfort one another, but they did not stir out of their chamber. The innkeeper went running out of the house, however, and he found that there was no disturbance at all in any other place than his own. The students were lodged in a chamber close by those of Doctor Faustus, and over the raging of the wind they heard a hideous music, as if snakes, adders, and other serpents were in the house. Doctor Faustus's door creaked open. There then arose a crying out of "Murther!" and "Help!" but the voice was weak and hollow, soon dying out entirely.

When it was day the students, who had not slept this entire night, went into the chamber where Doctor Faustus had lain, but they found no Faustus there. The parlor was full of blood. Brain clave unto the walls where the Fiend had dashed him from one to the other. Here lay his eyes, here a few teeth. O it was a hideous *spectaculum*. Then began the students to bewail and beweep him, seeking him in many places. When they came out to the dung heap, here they found his corpse. It was monstrous to behold, for head and limbs were still twitching.

These students and magisters who were present at Faustus's death gained permission afterwards to bury him in the village. Subsequently, they retired to his domicile where they found the famulus Wagner already mourning his master. This little book, *Doctor Faustus: His Historia,* was already written out. Now, as to what the famulus wrote, that will be a different, new book. On this same day the enchanted Helen and her son Justus Faustus were also gone. So uncanny did it become in Faustus's house that none could dwell there. Doctor Faustus himself walked about at night, making revelations unto Wagner as regardeth many secret matters. Passers-by reported seeing his face peering out at the windows.

Now this is the end of his quite veritable deeds, tale, *Historia,* and sorcery. From it the students and clerks in particular should learn to fear God, to flee sorcery, conjuration of spirits, and other works of the Devil; not to invite the Devil into their houses, nor to yield unto him in any other way, as Doctor Faustus did, for we have before us here the frightful and horrible example of his pact and death to help us shun such acts and pray to God alone in all matters, love Him with all our heart and with all our soul and with all our strength, defying the Devil with all his following, that we may through Christ be eternally blessed. These things we ask in the name of Jesus Christ our only Lord and Savior, Amen, Amen.

And so Faustus dies, "both as a bad and as a good Christian"—as the failed psychic soul in the surface story and the resurrected man in the underlying texts. His story survives, however, along with his spirit, having passed down the centuries from artist to artist as the secret transmission is passed from Seth to his descendants or guru to disciple in a mystical chain. Faustus's longing for transcendence is still compelling, whether understood in terms of Gnostic myth or alchemical or yogic transformation, and its mystery continues to stir human imaginings. Perhaps, even now, in some quiet study turned sorcerer's den, another author or composer has been captured by its magic and is conjuring up another great Faustian work of art.

Notes

INTRODUCTION: SETTING THE STAGE

1. Philip M. Palmer and Robert P. Moore, *Sources of the Faust Tradition: From Simon Magus to Lessing* (New York: Haskell House, 1977).
2. Hans Jonas, *The Gnostic Religion* (Boston: Beacon Press, 1963), 111.
3. Eliza Marian Butler, *The Myth of the Magus* (Cambridge, U.K.: University Press, 1979), 143.
4. Carl G. Jung, *The Portable Jung* (New York: The Viking Press, 1971), 342.
5. Jonas, *The Gnostic Religion,* 112–29.
6. Frances A. Yates, *The Occult Philosophy in the Elizabethan Age* (London: Ark Paperbacks, 1983), 116.
7. Edward Fanton, ed., *The Diaries of John Dee* (Oxfordshire, U.K.: Day Books, 1983), 215.
8. Frances A. Yates, *Giordano Bruno* (Chicago and London: University of Chicago Press, 1964), 278.
9. Geshe Kelsang Gytso, *Tantric Grounds and Paths* (London: Tharpa Publications, 1995), 142–44.
10. David Gordon White, *The Alchemical Body* (Chicago and London: University of Chicago Press, 1996), 220.
11. Omar Garrison, *Tantra: The Yoga of Sex* (New York: Causeway Books, 1964), 187–88.
12. Guy Beck, *Sonic Theology* (Delhi: Motilal Banarsidass Publisher, 1995), 124.
13. This is not the view of the Manichaeans, for whom a strife-filled, dualistic universe was a terrifying reality.

14. White observes that "the rhythms of yoga are all bipolar systems in which two opposing principles interact, constructively and destructively; after the fashion of the up or down motion of a firing rod, piston, or camshaft, to produce a cycle characterized by alternations." White, *The Alchemical Body,* 28.
15. Lynn Picknett and Clive Prince, *The Templar Revelation* (New York: Simon and Schuster, 1998).
16. Mead, *Fragments of a Faith Forgotten,* 168. In the Simonian literature, the Simon/Helen coupling seems to represent sidereal symbolism. According to Mead, Simon (the Logos) and Helen (his Thought or World Soul) were symbolized as the sun (Simon) and moon (Selene or Helen). In microcosmic terms, she was the human soul fallen into matter and he was the Mind or her redeemer.
17. Manly Hall, *The Secret Teachings of All Ages* (San Francisco: H. S. Crocker, 1928), clxxvii. According to Hall, "The key to the Grail mysteries will be apparent if in the sacred spear is recognized the pineal gland with its peculiar point like projection and in the Holy Grail the pituitary body containing the mysterious Water of Life."
18. David Frawley, *Tantric Yoga* (Twin Lakes, Wis.: Lotus Press, 2003), 115.
19. Picknett and Prince, *The Templar Revelations,* 78–83. See also Ean Begg's exhaustive survey of Black Madonna sites in Europe.
20. Hippolytus quotes from the Naasene Sermon: "'if ye return into Egypt,' that is, into earthly intercourse, '. . . You shall die.' For mortal existence . . . is the generation below, born of water only, but the immortal is that which is above, born of spirit. . . . This is the great Jordan, which flowing on below, prevented the children of Israel from departing out of Egypt, in other words, keeping them in terrestrial intercourse. For Egypt is . . . the body. But Jesus drove it [the Jordan] back and made it flow upwards." *The Refutation of All Heresies,* book 5, ch. 2:39–40, in Mark H. Gaffney, *Gnostic Secrets of the Naassenes* (Rochester, Vt.: Inner Traditions, 2004), 223.
21. Antoine-Joseph Pernety, *The Great Art,* edited by Edouard Blitz (New York: Samuel Weiser, 1976), 158.
22. Indra Sinha, *Tantra: The Cult of Ecstacy* (London: Hamlyn, 2000), 116.
23. Garrison, *Tantra: The Yoga of Sex,* 73.
24. This burning desire to communicate knowledge of the "higher symbolic planes" was also reflected in the emblems of various artists. According to R. J. W. Evans, they "were the visual representations of abstract thought and could

be interpreted at various levels: literal, figurative, allegorical, analogical," but were so abstruse they required explanation. Evans mentions an artist named Jacopo Zuccchi whose obscure fresco cycle adorned the Palazzo Rucellai in Rome. He thought it so important for others to understand it "that he wrote a commentary on it which, however, only a learned fellow initiate could understand." R. J. W. Evans, *Rudolf II and His World* (London: Thames and Hudson, 1997), 270.

25. Yates, *The Occult Philosophy,* 170.
26. Nicholas H. Clulee, "John Dee and the Paracelsians" in *Reading the Book of Nature,* edited by Allen Debus and Michael T. Walton (Kirksville, Mo.: Sixteenth Journal Publishers and Truman State University, 1998), 131.
27. J. W. Hamilton-Jones, trans., *The Hieroglyphic Monad of John Dee* (Kila, Mont.: Kessinger Publishing, 1946).

INTRODUCTION TO THE FAUST BOOK

1. H. G. Heile, trans., *The History of Doctor Johann Faustus* (Urbana: University of Illinois Press, 1965).
2. This and all of the Nag Hammadi texts are from *The Nag Hammadi Library in English,* vol. 3, edited by James M. Robinson (San Francisco: Harper and Row, 1988).

CHAPTER 1. OF HIS PARENTAGE AND YOUTH

1. Ajit Mookerjee and Madhu Khanna, *The Tantric Way* (New York: Thames and Hudson, 1989), 192.
2. Robinson, *The Nag Hammadi Library in English.*

CHAPTER 2. HOW DOCTOR FAUSTUS DID ACHIEVE AND ACQUIRE SORCERY

1. Johann Valentin Andreae, *The Chymical Wedding of Christian Rosenkreutz,* 1690. Translated by Edward Foxcroft (Edmonds, Wash.: The Alchemical Press, 1991), 1.
2. Roland Edighoffer, "Hermeticism in Early Rosicrucianism," *Gnosis and Hermeticism,* edited by Roelof van den Broek and Wouter Hanegraaf (Albany: State University of New York, 1998), 198.

3. John Dee's Monas also introduces *The Chymical Wedding*, just as its variation introduces this chapter. Christian Rosenkreutz receives a letter upon which a seal depicting the Monas is affixed. It is accompanied by the inscription, "In this sign you will be victorious." The meaning of this message is suggested by Nicholas Clulee, who discusses the rewards of contemplating the Monas: "the natural philosopher, by mastering this language, is given access to the innermost secrets of the cosmos, raising the philosopher to the level of 'adeptship.' Adeptship grants the philosopher command of a cabalistic magic that includes mastery of the 'magic of the elements' (alchemy) but also a spiritual magic that opens the way to the 'horizon aeternitatis.'" Clulee, "John Dee and the Paracelsians," 125.
4. G. R. S. Mead, trans., *Pistis Sophia: A Gnostic Gospel* (Blauvelt, N.Y.: Spiritual Science Library, 1984).
5. Mead, *Fragments of a Faith Forgotten,* 331.
6. Jonas, *The Gnostic Religion,* 59. This text from a Mandaean prayer book is speaking about the descent into matter of the Messenger, a Manichaean logos. Their cosmology, like that of the Manichaeans, rests on an uncompromising dualism and their extensive writings concerning the alienation of the Light Soul trapped in Darkness are among the most beautiful and anguished in Gnostic literature. While they condemned the "stinking body" they were not ascetic and reproduced sufficiently to maintain themselves (Christian heresy hunters notwithstanding) so that some of their followers still exist in Iraq and Iran.
7. Mead, *Fragments of a Faith Forgotten,* 323.
8. Jonas, *The Gnostic Religion, 56.*
9. Morton Smith, *Jesus The Magician* (New York: Harper and Row, 1978), 112.
10. Mookerjee and Khanna, *The Tantric Way,* 192.
11. Herbert V. Guenther and Chogyam Trungpa, *The Dawn of Tantra* (Berkeley and London: Shambhala Publications, 1975), 41.
12. Mookerjee and Khanna, *The Tantric Way,* 15.
13. Ibid., 144.
14. Ibid., 192–93.
15. Garrison, *Tantra: The Yoga of Sex,* 163.
16. Ibid., 75.
17. Mookerjee and Khanna, *The Tantric Way,* 193.
18. J. E. Cirlot, *A Dictionary of Symbols* (New York: Philosophical Library, 1962), see "Sword."

CHAPTER 3. HERE FOLLOWETH THE DISPUTATIO HELD BY FAUSTUS AND THE SPIRIT

1. This and all subsequent quotes from On the Origin of the World are from *The Nag Hammadi Library in English,* vol. 3, edited by James M. Robinson (San Francisco: Harper and Row, 1988).
2. The Tripartite Tractate omits the appearance of a female reflection and describes instead the emanation of the Son. The Faust Book uses the Apochryphon version of the myth here not for doctrinal reasons, it seems, but because Barbelo's requests were a ready metaphor for Faustus's bargaining with the Devil.
3. The interaction of Sulphur and Mercury is at times a vicious process. According to the prominent fifteenth-century alchemist Nicholas Flamel: "After both have been placed in the 'vessel' of the grave [that is to say, the inward, 'hermetically sealed' vessel], they begin to bite one another savagely, and, on account of their great poison and raging fury, do not let go of each other—unless the cold should deter them—until both, as a result of their dripping poison and deadly wounding, are drenched in blood . . ." Flamel, *On the Hieroglyphic Figures.*

INTRODUCTION TO CHAPTERS 4–7

1. Irenaeus, *Adversus Haereses,* edited by W. W. Harvey (Cambridge, England: n.p., 1857), 1.17.2.
2. Arthur Avalon, *The Serpent Power* (New York: Dover Publications, 1974), 235–6.
3. White, *The Alchemical Body,* 316.

CHAPTER 4. THE SECOND DISPUTATIO WITH THE SPIRIT

1. Titus Burckhardt, *Alchemy: Science of the Cosmos Science of the Soul* (Baltimore: Penguin Books, 1967), 143.
2. Evola, *The Hermetic Tradition,* 131.
3. Stanislas Klossowski de Rola, *Alchemy: The Secret Art* (London: Thames and Hudson, 1973), 23.
4. Antoine-Joseph Pernety, *The Great Art* (New York: Samuel Weiser, 1976), 193.

CHAPTER 5. DOCTOR FAUSTUS'S THIRD COLLOQUIUM WITH THE SPIRIT

1. This and all subsequent quotes from Allogenes are from the *Nag Hammadi Library in English,* vol. 3, edited by James M. Robinson (San Francisco: Harper and Row, 1988).
2. This and all subsequent quotes from Gospel of the Egyptians are from the *Nag Hammadi Library in English,* vol. 3, edited by James M. Robinson (San Francisco: Harper and Row, 1988).
3. Mookerjee and Khanna, *The Tantric Way,* 132.
4. Gyatso, *Tantric Grounds and Paths,* 58–59.
5. Ibid.
6. Garrison, *The Yoga of Sex,* 74.
7. Ibid., 187.
8. Lyndy Abraham, *Dictionary of Alchemical Imagery* (Cambridge, U.K.: Cambridge University Press, 1998), see "Opus Contra Naturam."

CHAPTER 6. DOCTOR FAUSTUS'S INSTRUMENTUM OR DEVILISH AND GODLESS WRIT OBLIGATIO

1. Sir George Ripley, "The Compound of Alchemy," in Elias Ashmole, *Theatrum Chemicum Brittannicum* (Kila, Mont.: Kessinger Publishing, 1991), 144–45.
2. White, *The Alchemical Body,* 312.

CHAPTER 7. CONCERNING THE SERVICES THAT MEPHISTOPHELES USED TOWARD FAUSTUS

1. This and all other quotes from Zostrianos are from the *Nag Hammadi Library in English,* vol. 3, edited by James M. Robinson (San Francisco: Harper and Row, 1988.
2. Ripley, "Compound of Alchemy," 145–46.

CHAPTER 8. CONCERNING DOCTOR FAUSTUS'S INTENDED MARRIAGE

1. This and all other quotes from the Testimony of Truth are from the *Nag Hammadi Library in English,* vol. 3, edited by James M. Robinson (San Francisco: Harper and Row, 1988).
2. Ripley, "Compound of Alchemy," 149.
3. Mookerjee and Khanna, *The Tantric Way,* 130.
4. Ibid., 9.
5. Ibid., 193.
6. Garrison, *Tantra: The Yoga of Sex,* 94.
7. Ibid., 61.
8. Ibid., 95.
9. Ibid., 159.

CHAPTER 9. DOCTOR FAUSTUS'S QUAESTIO OF HIS SPIRIT MEPHISTOPHELES

1. Ripley, "The Compound of Alchemy," 148.

CHAPTER 10. A DISPUTATIO CONCERNING BANISHED ANGELS

1. Jonas, *The Gnostic Religion,* 188.

CHAPTER 11. A DISPUTATIO CONCERNING HELL

1. Cant. V of Huyadagaman, a Parthian Manichaean hymn cycle in Hans-Joachim Klimkeit, *Gnosis and the Silk Road* (New York: HarperCollins, 1993) 103.
2. Guenther and Trungpa, *The Dawn of Tantra,* 43.
3. Ripley, "The Compound of Alchemy," 149.

CHAPTER 12. HIS ALMANACS AND HOROSCOPES

1. Ripley, "The Compound of Alchemy," 150.
2. Mookerjee and Khanna, *The Tantric Way,* 192.

3. Some members of the Valentinian school had a different notion concerning baptism and its effect on astrological prediction. Astrologers' accuracy, they held, depended on the spiritual state of their subjects rather than their own. Francis Legge quotes Theodotus: "Until baptism they say the destiny (he is talking of that which is foretold by the stars) holds good: but thereafter the astrologers' predictions are no longer unerring. For the baptismal font not only sets us free, but it is also the Gnosis which teaches us what we are, why we have come into being, where we are, whither we have been cast up, whither we are hastening, from what we have been redeemed, why there is birth and why rebirth." Francis Legge, *Forerunners and Rivals of Christianity,* vol. 2 (New York: University Books, 1965), 115.

CHAPTER 13. A DISPUTATIO OR INQUIRY CONCERNING ASTRONOMIA, OR ASTROLOGIA

1. White, *The Alchemical Body,* 291. Elsewhere White says, "the cremation ground . . . was long the preferred haunt of tantrikas who, in their drug—or austerity—induced trances, saw and danced with the wild and fulminating Kali and Bhairava. The infernal dance of this divine pair is purificatory, serving as it does to burn away the decaying matter of a dying cosmos—both within themselves, in the bodies consumed there, and in the universal conflagration for which the burning ground is a microcosm—for it is only when an ash-smeared Siva incinerates the universe with his ecstatic dance that universal liberation becomes possible" (286).
2. Mookerjee and Khanna, *The Tantric Way,* 161.

CHAPTER 15. HOW DOCTOR FAUSTUS TRAVELED DOWN TO HELL

1. This and all other quotes from the Paraphrase of Shem are from the *Nag Hammadi Library in English,* vol. 3, edited by James M. Robinson (San Francisco: Harper and Row, 1988).
2. Mookerjee and Khanna, *The Tantric Way,* 188–90.
3. Avalon, *The Serpent Power,* 481–590.
4. Ibid., 495.
5. Ibid., 490.

6. Mookerjee and Khanna, *The Tantric Way,* 172.
7. Avalon, *The Serpent Power,* 221.
8. White, *The Alchemical Body,* 276.
9. Cirlot, *The Dictionary of Symbols,* 272.
10. White, *The Alchemical Body,* 229.
11. Avalon, *The Serpent Power,* 488.
12. White, *The Alchemical Body,* 234.
13. Ibid., 231.
14. Ibid., 233.
15. Avalon, *The Serpent Power,* 495.
16. Indra Sinha reminds us that Siva and Sakti cannot be separated. "Although we may speak of a triangle being Sakti or a point being Siva, and of static and active energies, in fact, these energies are aspects of one another. . . . For devotees of the 'samaya' tradition, their highest spiritual aim is by meditation to experience the blissful unity of Siva and Sakti in the thousand petalled lotus of the 'Sahasrara Cakra' in the crown of the head." Sinha, *Tantra: The Cult of Ecstasy,* 98.
17. Avalon, *The Serpent Power,* 497.
18. Ibid., 499.
19. Ibid., 243.
20. Mead, *Fragments of a Faith Forgotten,* 200–203.
21. This and all other quotes from "An Exposition Upon Sir George Ripley's Vision" by Aeyrenaeus Philalethes are in *Alchemy: The Secret Art,* Stanislas de Rola, 23–30.
22. Ripley, *The Compound of Alchemy,* 152.
23. Mead, *Fragments of a Faith Forgotten,* 201.

CHAPTER 16. HOW DOCTOR FAUSTUS JOURNEYED UP TO THE STARS

1. John D. Chambers, trans., *The Divine Pymander* (New York: Samuel Weiser, 1975), 1.
2. Jonas, *The Gnostic Religion,* 221. The story of Primal Man's awakening is from a compilation by Jonas of accounts by Theodore bar Konai, Hegemonius, and En-Nadim.
3. Mani said the following about the dialogue between the Living Spirit and Primal Man: "The Living Spirit sent [the summons] to the First Man. It

is a peace letter and greeting . . . in which all the tidings are written down, together with everything it will bring about." The call and answer are a sharing of knowledge about what has happened and "is ordained to happen," and according to Aian Gardner in his commentary on "Concerning the Letter" in chapter 75 of the *Kephalaia,* the "two are the essence of redemption." Aian Gardner, ed. and trans., *The Kephalaia of the Teacher* (Leiden: E. J. Brill, 1995), 182.1–20.

4. Evola, *The Hermetic Tradition,* 153.

CHAPTER 17. NOW I WILL TELL YOU WHAT I DID SEE

1. Chambers, trans., *The Divine Pymander,* 1.
2. Jonas, *The Gnostic Religion,* a compilation by Jonas of accounts by Sharastant, Hegemonius, and En-Nadim, 233.
3. Ibid., 234.
4. Chambers, trans., *The Divine Pymander,* 13.
5. Mead, G. R. S., *Thrice Greatest Hermes,* vol. 2 (Detroit: Hermes Press, 1978), 244.
6. Ibid., 241.
7. Chambers, trans., *The Divine Pymander,* 39.
8. Garrison, *Tantra: The Yoga of Sex,* 189.
9. Ibid., 170.
10. Gyatso, *Tantric Grounds and Paths,* 41.
11. Mead, *Thrice Greatest Hermes,* vol. 2, 242.
12. Marcel Oscar Hinz, *Tantra Vidya* (Delhi, Motilal Banarsidass Publications, 1989), 107.
13. Mead, *Thrice Greatest Hermes,* 98.
14. Hinz, *Tantra Vidya,* 107.
15. Ibid., 108.

CHAPTER 18. DOCTOR FAUSTUS'S THIRD JOURNEY

1. Jonas, *The Gnostic Religion,* quote compiled by Jonas from Bar Konai and Augustine, 225.
2. White, *The Alchemical Body,* 138–39.

CHAPTER 19. CONCERNING THE STARS

1. Cirlot, *A Dictionary of Symbols,* see "Stars."
2. Ripley, "Compound of Alchemy," 166.
3. Mookerjee and Khanna, *The Tantric Way,* 193.
4. Guenther and Trungpa, *The Dawn of Tantra,* 44.

CHAPTER 21. THE SECOND QUESTION

1. Ripley, "Compound of Alchemy," 168.

CHAPTER 22. THE THIRD QUESTION

1. de Rola, *Alchemy: The Secret Art,* 11.

CHAPTER 23. A HISTORY OF THE EMPEROR CHARLES V AND DOCTOR FAUSTUS

1. Ripley, "The Compound of Alchemy," 169.

CHAPTER 25. CONCERNING THREE LORDS WHO WERE RAPIDLY TRANSPORTED

1. Sophia is called Ennoia in her enlightened state and Prunikos when she is fallen.
2. Abraham, *Dictionary of Alchemical Imagery,* see "Prison."
3. Ripley, "The Compound of Alchemy," 173.

CHAPTER 26. CONCERNING AN ADVENTURE WITH A JEW

1. "The Alchemic Figures of Abraham the Jew" in *Picture Museum of Sorcery, Magic and Alchemy* by Emile Grillot de Givry; translated by Courtenay J. Locke (New Hyde Park: University Books, 1963), 353.

CHAPTER 27. AN ADVENTURE AT THE COURT OF COUNT ANHALT

1. Abraham, *Dictionary of Alchemical Imagery,* see "Snow."
2. Evola, *The Hermetic Tradition,* 155.

3. Abraham, *Dictionary of Alchemical Imagery,* see "Fruit."
4. Ibid., see "Green."
5. Ripley, "Compound of Alchemy," 174.
6. Burckhardt, *Alchemy: Science of the Cosmos,* 133.
7. White, *The Alchemical Body,* 291.

CHAPTER 28. THE MANNER IN WHICH DOCTOR FAUSTUS KEPT SHROVETIDE

1. Burckhardt, *Alchemy: Science of the Cosmos,* 89.
2. Mead, *Fragments of a Faith Forgotten,* 597.
3. MS Latin 3236A of the Bibliothèque Nationale in Paris.
4. *The Kephalaia of the Teacher,* translated by A. Bohlig and H. J. Polotsky (New York: E. J. Brill, 1995), 72.15–30.

CHAPTER 29. CONCERNING HELEN CHARMED OUT OF GREECE

1. *The Gnostic Religion,* 107, from a compilation by Jonas of passages from Hippolytus, "Refutation of All Heresies," 6:19; Irenaeus, "Against Heresies," 1:23.2; and Tertullian, "De Anima," Ch. 34.
2. This and all other quotes from the Gospel of Philip are from the *Nag Hammadi Library in English,* edited by James M. Robinson (San Francisco: Harper and Row, 1988), 67:10–17.
3. Nicholaus Cusanus, "De Visione Faciale" in *Visione Dei IV.*
4. Edgar Wind, *Pagan Mysteries in the Renaissance* (New York: W. W. Norton, 1968), 139.
5. Garrison, *Tantra: The Yoga of Sex,* 188.
6. Mookerjee and Khanna, *The Tantric Way,* 87.

CHAPTER 30. CONCERNING A GESTICULATION INVOLVING FOUR WHEELS

1. Burckhardt, *Alchemy: Science of the Cosmos,* 86.
2. Evola, *The Hermetic Tradition,* 166.
3. Ripley, "Compound of Alchemy," 137.

4. Ibid., 137.
5. Burckhardt, *Alchemy: Science of the Cosmos,* 110.
6. Like Faustus, the tantric adept, in his anonymity, resembles the Manichaean Jesus and, in a striking sense, the Rosicrucian who wanders unobserved and serves mankind. Indra Sinha quotes the Kularnarva-tantra, "The Kaula adept may be anyone, may live anywhere, may go under any disguise, may be at any stage of life . . . and not a soul recognizes him. Masters of the Kaula-yoga wander the earth under many guises, working for the good of others, but nobody recognizes them. They do not squander their precious knowledge . . . but live as if they, too, were dumb, drunken idiots, in the midst of humanity." Sinha, *Tantra: The Cult of Ecstasy,* 132.
7. "We Would Fulfill," (Parthian), verse from Mani's psalm to Jesus the Splendor, in *Gnosis and the Silk Road,* edited by Hans Klimkeit, 64.

CHAPTER 31. CONCERNING FOUR SOCERERS WHO CUT OFF ONE ANOTHER'S HEADS

1. Abraham, *Dictionary of Alchemical Imagery,* see "Mercury."
2. Ibid., see "Head."
3. Ibid., see "Soul."
4. Evola, *The Hermetic Tradition,* 171.
5. Petrus Bonus, "Zoroaster's Cave," in *Eglinus, An Easie Introduction,* 1667. 85–86. Quoted in Abraham, *Dictionary of Alchemical Imagery*, 85–86.
6. Ibid., 85–86.
7. Gardner, *The Kephalaia of the Teacher,* ch. 31, 84:20–25.
8. Ibid., 62.
9. White, *The Alchemical Body,* 293.

CHAPTER 32. CONCERNING AN OLD MAN WHO WOULD HAVE CONVERTED DOCTOR FAUSTUS

1. Mani, "Concerning His Impure Doctrine," translated by Kurt Schubert in *The Other Bible,* edited by Willis Barnstone (San Francisco: HarperSanFrancisco), 48. The church father introduced his summary of Mani's words as follows: "In this volume we must present some of the senseless doctrine and blasphemous views of the godless Mani, to the shame of the Manichaeans."

2. Evola, *The Hermetic Tradition,* 164.
3. Ibid., 170–71.
4. Guy Beck, *Sonic Theology,* 132–33.
5. Ibid.
6. Gyatso, *Tantric Grounds and Paths,* 158.
7. Garrison, *Tantra: The Yoga of Sex,* 70.

CHAPTER 33. PACT

1. Evola, *The Hermetic Tradition,* 170.
2. Compare the Old Man's actions and Faustus's response to an account from the Mani myth concerning Primal Man's resistance to the invasion of the powers of Darkness—an invasion which, according to a *Chinese Manichaean Treatise,* is symbolic of the "entrance of evil into the human soul," JA. 1911, p. 546. "He [Mani] says that the Father of Greatness evoked the Mother of Life; and the Mother of Life evoked the Primal Man; and the Primal Man evoked his Five Sons, just as a man who puts on armor for war. . . . Thereupon the Primal Man gave himself and his Five Sons as food to the Five Sons of Darkness, just as a man who has an enemy mixes deadly poison in a cake and gives it to him. And . . . when [they] had eaten . . . the intelligence of the Five Luminous Gods was taken from them, and by reason of the venom of the Sons of Darkness, they became like unto a man who is bitten by a mad dog or snake." "Bar Khoni on Mani" in A. W. Jackson, *Researches in Manichaeism* (New York: AMS Press, 1965), 224.
3. Gyatso, *Tantric Grounds and Paths,* 157.
4. Ibid., 155.
5. Evola, *The Hermetic Tradition,* 126.

CHAPTER 34. HOW DOCTOR FAUSTUS BROUGHT ABOUT THE MARRIAGE

1. J. M. Ragon, "Initiation Hermetique," 45; Eliphas Levi, "Dogma and Ritual," 395; "Livre de Synesius," BPC. 2:185; in Evola, *The Hermetic Tradition,* 171.
2. O. Drury, *Dictionary of Symbols* (New York: Harper and Row, 1985), see "Ring" and "Dance."

CHAPTER 35. CONCERNING DIVERS FLORA IN DOCTOR FAUSTUS'S GARDEN

1. "Psalm Book II," Psalm 222, Chester Beatty Collection and Berlin Academy.
2. Pernety, *The Great Art,* 196. Pernety gives a warning: "Color your white elixir with the Moon, and the Red with the Sun . . . be careful not to be mistaken in the mixture of the ferments, and do not take one for the other, or you would lose all."

CHAPTER 36. CONCERNING AN ARMY RAISED AGAINST LORD HARDECK

1. Pernety, *The Great Art,* 197.
2. Ibid.

CHAPTER 37. CONCERNING THE BEAUTIFUL HELEN FROM GREECE

1. Abraham, *Dictionary of Alchemical Imagery,* see "Philosophical Child."
2. Garrison, *Tantra: The Yoga of Sex,* 102.
3. Mookerjee and Khanna, *The Tantric Way,* 165.
4. Gyatso, *Tantric Grounds and Paths,* 73.
5. Mookerjee and Khanna, *The Tantric Way,* 165.
6. Ibid.
7. Garrison, *Tantra: The Yoga of Sex,* 112.
8. Mookerjee and Khana, *The Tantric Way,* 175.
9. Gyatso, *Tantric Grounds and Paths,* 43.
10. Ibid., 21.
11. Ibid., 22.
12. Garrison, *Tantra: The Yoga of Sex,* 112.
13. Gyatso, *Tantric Grounds and Paths,* 143.
14. Garrison, *Tantra: The Yoga of Sex,* 230.
15. Gyatso, *Tantric Grounds and Paths,* 113–18.

CHAPTER 38. CONCERNING ONE WHOSE WIFE MARRIED WHILE HE WAS CAPTIVE

1. Jonas, *The Gnostic Religion,* 176.
2. R. Warwick Bond, ed., *The Complete Works of John Lyly* (Oxford: Clarendon Press, 1967).
3. Nemesia, the Bishop of Emesa, "The Nature of Man," in de Rola, *Alchemy: The Secret Art,* 18.

CHAPTER 39. CONCERNING THE TESTAMENT: WHAT DOCTOR FAUSTUS BEQUEATHED TO HIS SERVANT

1. Mead, *Fragments of a Faith Forgotten,* 300.
2. Jonas, *The Gnostic Religion,* 79.
3. Ibid.

CHAPTER 40. THE DISCOURSE WHICH DOCTOR FAUSTUS HELD WITH HIS SON

1. Mookerjee and Khanna, *The Tantric Way,* 271.
2. Frances Yates, *Giordano Bruno,* 144.

CHAPTER 41. WHAT DOCTOR FAUSTUS DID IN THE FINAL MONTH OF HIS PACT

1. Mookerjee and Khanna, *The Tantric Way,* 194.
2. Michael Maier, *Atalanta Fugiens,* translated and edited by Joscelyn Godwin (Grand Rapids, Mich.: Phanes Press, 1989).
3. Abraham, *Dictionary of Alchemical Imagery,* see "Sun" and "Shadow."

CHAPTER 42. DOCTOR FAUSTUS: HIS LAMENTATION

1. Legge, *Forerunners and Rivals of Christianity,* 342.
2. Ibid., 335.

CHAPTER 44. DOCTOR FAUSTUS: HIS HIDEOUS END AND SPECTACULUM

1. Augustine, "Contra Faustus," book 2, ch. 5. in Legge, *Forerunners and Rivals of Christianity,* 346.
2. Gardner, *The Kephalaia of the Teacher,* 23.175 5 ff.
3. Mead, *Fragments of a Faith Forgotten,* 203.
4. Ibid.
5. Ibid.

Bibliography

Abraham, Lyndy. *A Dictionary of Alchemical Imagery*. Cambridge, U.K.: Cambridge University Press, 1998.

al-Nadim, Ibn. *The Fihrist*. Edited and translated by Bayard Dodge. New York: Columbia University Press, 1998.

Andreae, Johann Valentin. *The Chymical Wedding of Christian Rosenkreutz, 1690*. Translated by Edward Foxcroft. Edmonds, Wash.: The Alchemical Press, 1991.

Angus, S. *The Mystery Religions*. New York: Dover Publications, 1975.

Ashmole, Elias. *Theatrum Chemicum Britannicum*. Kila, Mont.: Kessinger Publishing, 1991.

Avalon, Arthur. *The Serpent Power*. New York: Dover Publications, 1974.

Baigent, Michael, Richard Leigh, and Henry Lincoln. *Holy Blood, Holy Grail*. New York: Dell Publishing, 1983.

Bamford, Christopher, ed. *Homage to Pythagoras*. Hudson, N.Y.: Lindisfarne Press, 1980.

Barnstone, Willis, ed. *The Other Bible*. San Francisco: HarperCollins, 1984.

Beck, Guy. *Sonic Theology*. Delhi: Motilal Banarsidass Publishers, 1995.

Begg, Ean. *The Cult of the Black Virgin*. New York: Penguin Books, 1996.

Burckhardt, Titus. *Alchemy: Science of the Cosmos, Science of the Soul*. Baltimore: Penguin Books, 1967.

Burland, G. A. *The Arts of the Alchemists*. New York: The Macmillan Co., 1968.

Butler, Eliza Marian. *The Myth of the Magus*. Cambridge, U.K.: University Press, 1979.

Chambers, John D., trans. *The Divine Pymander.* New York: Samuel Weiser, 1975.

Cirlot, J. E. *A Dictionary of Symbols.* New York: Philosophical Library, 1962.

Clulee, Nicholas H. "John Dee and the Paracelsians." In *Reading the Book of Nature,* edited by Allen A. Debus and Michael T. Walton. St. Louis, Mo.: Sixteenth Century Journal Publishers and Truman State University, 1998.

Cusanus, Nicolaus. "De Visione Faciale." In *De Visione Dei IV.* N.p., n.d.

de Rola, Stanislas Klossowski. *Alchemy: The Secret Art.* London: Thames and Hudson, Ltd., 1973.

de Rougemont, Denis. *Love in the Western World.* New York: Harper and Row, 1956.

Delafarge, Gaetan. *The Templar Tradition in the Age of Aquarius.* Putney, Vt.: Threshold Books, 1987.

Doresse, Jean. *The Secret Books of the Egyptian Gnostics.* Rochester, Vt.: Inner Traditions, 1986.

Eamon, William. *Science and the Secrets of Nature.* Princeton: Princeton University Press, 1994.

Evans, R. J. W. *Rudolf II and His World.* London: Thames and Hudson, 1997.

Fanton, Edward, ed. *The Diaries of John Dee.* Oxfordshire, U.K.: Day Books, 1998.

Eliade, Mircea. *The Forge and the Crucible.* Chicago: University of Chicago Press, 1962.

Evola, Julius. *Eros and the Mysteries of Love.* Rochester, Vt.: Inner Traditions, 1991.

———. *The Hermetic Tradition.* Rochester, Vt.: Inner Traditions, 1995.

———. *The Mystery of the Grail.* Rochester, Vt.: Inner Traditions, 1997.

Faivre, Antoine. *The Golden Fleece and Alchemy.* Albany: State University of New York Press, 1993.

Flaherty, Gloria. *Shamanism and the Eighteenth Century.* Princeton: Princeton University Press, 1992.

Flamel, Nicholas. *On the Hieroglyphic Figures.* N.p., n.d.

Frater Albertus. *Alchemist's Handbook.* New York: Samuel Weiser, 1976.

Frawley, David. *Tantric Yoga and the Wisdom Goddesses.* Twin Lakes, Wisc.: Lotus Press, 2003.

Gardner, Iain, trans. *Kephalaia of the Teacher.* New York: E. J. Brill, 1995.

Garrison, Omar. *Tantra: The Yoga of Sex.* New York: Causeway Books, 1964.

Gettings, Fred. *Secret Symbolism in Occult Art.* New York: Harmony Books, 1987.

Gilchrist, Cherry. *Alchemy.* Longmead, England: Element Books, 1991.

Goodrick-Clarke, Nicholas, trans. *Paracelsus.* Northamptonshire, England: Crucible, 1980.

Grillot de Givry, Emile. *Picture Museum of Sorcery, Magic and Alchemy.* Translated by J. Courtenay Locke. New Hyde Park, N.Y.: University Books, 1963.

Guénon, René. *Fundamental Symbols.* Cambridge, U.K.: Quinta Essentia, 1995.

Guenther, Herbert V. *The Tantric View of Life.* Berkeley and London: Shambhala Publications, 1972.

Guenther, Herbert V., and Chogyam Trungpa. *The Dawn of Tantra.* Berkeley and London: Shambhala Publications, 1975.

Gyatso, Geshe Kelsang. *Tantric Grounds and Paths.* London: Tharpa Publications, 1995.

Hall, Manly. *The Secret Teachings of All Ages.* San Francisco: H. S. Crocker, 1928.

Hamilton Jones, J. D., trans. *The Hieroglyphic Monad of John Dee.* Kila, Mont.: Kessinger Press, 1946.

Heile, H.G., trans. *The History of Doctor Johann Faustus.* Urbana, Ill.: University of Illinois Press, 1965.

Hinze, Oscar Marcel. *Tantra Vidya.* Delhi: Motilal Banarsidass Publications, 1989.

Hopkins, Jeffrey. *Emptiness Yoga.* Edited by Joe B. Wilson. Ithaca, New York: Snow Lion Publications, 1987.

Irenaeus, *Adversus Haereses.* Edited by W. W. Harvey. Cambridge, England, 1857.

Jackson, A. V. *Researches in Manichaeism.* New York: Columbia University, 1965.

Jonas, Hans. *The Gnostic Religion.* Boston: Beacon Press, 1963.

Jung, Carl G. *The Portable Jung.* New York: The Viking Press, 1971.

Keith, Thomas. *Religion and the Decline of Magic.* London: Weidenfeld and Nicholson, 1971.

Kelsey, Morton, and Barbara Kelsey. *Sacrament of Sexuality.* Rockport, Mass.: Element Books, 1991.

King, Francis. *Sexuality, Magic and Perversion.* London: Neville Spearman, 2002.

King, Karen L. *The Gospel of Mary of Magdala.* Santa Rosa, Calif.: Polebridge Press, 2003.

———. *What Is Gnosticism?* Cambridge: Cambridge University Press, 2003.

Klimkeit, Hans Joachim. *Gnosis on the Silk Road*. New York: HarperCollins, 1993.

Knight, Gareth. *The Rose Cross and the Goddess*. New York: Destiny Books, 1985.

Lawlor, Robert. *Sacred Geometry*. London: Thames and Hudson, 1998.

Leadbeater, C. W. *The Chakras*. Wheaton, Ill.: The Theosophical Publishing House, 1985.

Legge, Francis. *Forerunners and Rivals of Christianity*. New Hyde Park, N.Y.: University Books, 1965.

Lincoln, Henry. *Key to the Sacred Pattern*. Gloucestershire, England: The Windrush Press, 1997.

Maier, Michael. *Atalanta Fugiens*. Translated and edited by Joscelyn Godwin. Grand Rapids, Mich.: Phanes Press, 1989.

Matthews, John. *The Grail Tradition*. Rockport, Mass.: Element Books, 1992.

Mayer, Marvin, and Richard Smith, eds. *Ancient Christian Magic*. San Francisco: HarperSanFrancisco, 1994.

McLean, Adam. *The Alchemical Mandela*. Grand Rapids, Mich.: Phanes Press, 1989.

McLean, Adam, trans. *The Magical Calendar*. Grand Rapids, Mich.: Phanes Press, 1994.

Mead, G. R. S. *Fragments of a Faith Forgotten*. New Hyde Park, N.Y.: University Books, 1960.

Mead, G. R. S., trans. and ed. *Thrice Greatest Hermes,* vol. 2. Detroit: Hermes Press, 1978.

Mead, G. R. S., trans. *Pistis Sophia: A Gnostic Gospel*. Blauvelt, N.Y.: Spiritual Science Library, 1984.

Merkur, Dan. *Gnosis: An Esoteric Tradition of Mystical Visions and Unions*. Albany: State University of New York Press, 1993.

Miller, Richard, and Iona Miller. *The Modern Alchemist*. Grand Rapids, Mich.: Phanes Press, 1994.

Mookerjee, Ajit, and Madhu Khanna. *The Tantric Way*. New York: Thames and Hudson, 1989.

Needleman, Jacob, ed. *The Sword of Gnosis*. Baltimore, Md.: Penguin Books, 1974.

Odier, Daniel. *Tantric Quest: An Encounter with Absolute Love*. Rochester, Vt.: Inner Traditions, 1997.

Pagels, Elaine. *The Gnostic Gospels.* New York: Vintage Books, 1989.

Palmer, Philip M., and Robert P. Moore. *Sources of the Faust Tradition: From Simon Magus to Lessing.* New York: Haskell House, 1977.

Pater, Walter. *The Renaissance.* New York: The Modern Library, 1976.

Pernety, Antoine-Joseph. *The Great Art.* Edited by Edouard Blitz, M.D. New York: Samuel Weiser, 1976.

Philalethes, Aeyrenaeus. *An Exposition Upon Sir George Ripley's Vision.* N.p., 1677.

Picknett, Lynn, and Clyde Prince. *The Templar Revelation.* New York: Simon and Schuster, 1998.

Regardie, Israel. *The Philosopher's Stone.* Saint Paul, Minn.: Llewellyn Publications, 1978.

Ripley, Sir George. "The Compoind of Alchemy," in Elias Ashmole, *Theatrum Chemicum Brittannicum.* Kila, Mont.: Kessinger Publishing, 1991.

Robinson, James M., ed. *The Nag Hammadi Library in English,* 3rd edition. San Francisco: Harper and Row, 1988.

Rudolph, Kurt. *Gnosis.* Translated by Robert McLachlan Wilson. San Francisco: Harper and Row, 1983.

Sannella, Lee. *The Kundalini Experience.* Lower Lake, Calif.: Integral Publishing, 1987.

Schneider, Michael S. *A Beginner's Guide to Constructing the Universe.* New York: Harper Perennial, 1995.

Shaw, Miranda. *Passionate Enlightenment: Women in Tantric Buddhism.* Princeton: Princeton University Press, 1994.

Sherman, William H. *John Dee: The Politics of Reading and Writing in the English Renaissance.* Amherst: The University of Massachusetts Press, 1995.

Silberer, Herbert. *Hidden Symbolism of Alchemy and the Occult Arts.* New York: Dover Publications, 1971.

Sinha, Indra. *Tantra: The Cult of Ecstasy.* London: Hamlyn, 2000.

Smith, Morton. *Jesus the Magician.* New York: Harper and Row, 1978.

Starbird, Margaret. *Magdalene's Lost Legacy.* Rochester, Vt.: Bear and Co., 2003.

Stone, Brian, trans. *Sir Gawain and the Green Knight.* Middlesex, U.K.: Penguin Books, 1959.

Trismosin, Solomon. *Splendor Solis.* London: Kegan Paul, Trench, Trubner and Co., n.d.

Vanden Broek, Roelof, and Wouter Hanegraaf, eds. *Gnosis and Hermeticism.* Albany: State University of New York Press, 1998.

Waite, A. E. *A Short Lexicon of Alchemy.* Edmonds, Wash.: The Alchemical Press, 1990.

Waite, A. E., trans. *The New Pearl of Great Price.* London: Vincent Stuart, 1963.

Walker, Benjamin. *Sex and the Supernatural.* Baltimore, Md.: Ottenheimer Publishers, 1973.

Weeks, Andrew. *Paracelsus.* Albany: State University of New York Press, 1997.

Weyer, Johann. *Witches, Devils and Doctors in the Renaissance.* Tempe, Ariz.: Medieval and Renaissance Texts and Studies, 1998.

White, David Gordon. *The Alchemical Body.* Chicago and London: University of Chicago Press, 1966.

Wind, Edgar. *Pagan Mysteries in the Renaissance.* New York: W. W. Norton and Company, 1968.

Yamauchi, Edwin. *Pre-Christian Gnosticism.* London: Tyndale Press, 1973.

Yates, Frances A. *Giordano Bruno.* Chicago and London: University Press, 1964.

———. *The Occult Philosophy in the Elizabethan Age.* London: Ark Paperbacks, 1983.

———. *The Rosicrucian Enlightenment.* London: Ark Paperbacks, 1986.

INDEX

BOOKS OF RELATED INTEREST

Gnostic Philosophy
From Ancient Persia to Modern Times
by Tobias Churton

Lords of Light
The Path of Initiation in the Western Mysteries
by W. E. Butler

Shakespeare and the Ideal of Love
by Jill Line

Meditations on the Soul
Selected Letters of Marsilio Ficino
Edited by Clement Salaman

The Way of Hermes
New Translations of *The Corpus Hermeticum* and *The Definitions of Hermes Trismegistus to Asclepius*
Translated by Clement Salaman, Dorine van Oyen, William D. Wharton, and Jean-Pierre Mahé

The Hermetic Tradition
Symbols and Teachings of the Royal Art
by Julius Evola

Eros and the Mysteries of Love
The Metaphysics of Sex
by Julius Evola

Mysteries of the Bridechamber
The Initiation of Jesus and the Temple of Solomon
by Victoria LePage

Inner Traditions • Bear & Company
P.O. Box 388
Rochester, VT 05767
1-800-246-8648
www.InnerTraditions.com

Or contact your local bookseller